Environmental Politics and Governance in the Anthropocene

The term Anthropocene denotes a new geological epoch characterized by the unprecedented impact of human activities on the Earth's ecosystems. While the natural sciences have advanced their understanding of the drivers and processes of global change considerably over the last two decades, the social sciences lag behind in addressing the fundamental challenge of governance and politics in the Anthropocene.

This book attempts to close this crucial research gap, in particular with regards to the following three overarching research themes: 1) the meaning, sense-making and contestations emerging around the concept of the Anthropocene related to the social sciences; 2) the role and relevance of institutions, both formal and informal as well as international and transnational, for governing in the Anthropocene; and 3) the role and relevance of accountability and other democratic principles for governing in the Anthropocene. Drawing together a range of key thinkers in the field, this volume provides one of the first authoritative assessments of global environmental politics and governance in the Anthropocene, reflecting on how the planetary-scale crisis changes the ways in which humans respond to the challenge.

This volume will be of great interest to students and scholars of global environmental politics and governance, and sustainable development.

Philipp Pattberg is Professor of Transnational Environmental Governance at the Institute for Environmental Studies (IVM), Vrije Universiteit Amsterdam, the Netherlands.

Fariborz Zelli is an Associate Professor at the Department of Political Science at Lund University, Sweden.

Routledge Research in Global Environmental Governance

Series Editors

Philipp Pattberg
Vrije Universiteit Amsterdam and the Amsterdam Global Change Institute (AGCI) the Netherlands

Agni Kalfagianni
Utrecht University, the Netherlands

Global environmental governance has been a prime concern of policymakers since the United Nations Conference on the Human Environment in 1972. Yet, despite more than 900 multilateral environmental treaties coming into force over the past 40 years and numerous public–private and private initiatives to mitigate global change, human-induced environmental degradation is reaching alarming levels. Scientists see compelling evidence that the entire Earth system now operates well outside safe boundaries and at rates that accelerate. The urgent challenge from a social science perspective is how to organize the co-evolution of societies and their surrounding environment; in other words, how to develop effective and equitable governance solutions for today's global problems.

Against this background, the Routledge Research in Global Environmental Governance series delivers cutting-edge research on the most vibrant and relevant themes within the academic field of global environmental governance.

Environmental Politics and Governance in the Anthropocene

Institutions and legitimacy in a complex world

Edited by
Philipp Pattberg and Fariborz Zelli

Routledge
Taylor & Francis Group

LONDON AND NEW YORK

First published 2016
by Routledge
2 Park Square, Milton Park, Abingdon, Oxon OX14 4RN

and by Routledge
711 Third Avenue, New York, NY 10017

First issued in paperback 2017

Routledge is an imprint of the Taylor & Francis Group, an informa business

British Library Cataloguing-in-Publication Data
A catalogue record for this book is available from the British Library

Library of Congress Cataloging-in-Publication Data
Names: Pattberg, Philipp H., 1975- editor. | Zelli, Fariborz, editor.
Title: Environmental politics and governance in the anthropocene : institutions and legitimacy in a complex world / edited by Philipp Pattberg and Fariborz Zelli.
Description: New York, NY : Routledge, 2016. | Series: Routledge research in global environmental governance | Includes bibliographical references and index.
Identifiers: LCCN 2015031329 | ISBN 9781138902398 (hb : alk. paper) | ISBN 9781315697468 (e-book)
Subjects: LCSH: Global environmental change. | Nature--Effect of human beings on. | Human ecology. | Philosophical anthrophology.
Classification: LCC GE149 .E595 2016 | DDC 304.2--dc23
LC record available at http://lccn.loc.gov/2015031329

ISBN 13: 978-1-138-50698-5 (pbk)
ISBN 13: 978-1-138-90239-8 (hbk)

Typeset in Goudy
by Saxon Graphics Ltd, Derby

Contents

Figures

Tables

Acknowledgements

We would like to acknowledge support from the Netherlands Organization for Scientific Research (CONNECT project on 'Assessing and Reforming the Current Architecture of Global Environmental Governance') and the Swedish Research Council Formas (NAVIGOV project on 'Navigating Institutional Complexity in Global Climate Governance').

Notes on contributors

Manuel Arias-Maldonado is Associate Professor in Political Science at the University of Málaga. His latest book is *Environment and Society: Socionatural Relations in the Anthropocene* (Springer, 2015).

Walter F. Baber is Senior Scientist at the US Center of the Stockholm Environment Institute. His research focus is on sustainability, resource use and environmental change in the developing world. He explores these issues principally, though not exclusively, in the context of energy.

Robert Bailis is Associate Professor at the Yale School of Forestry and Environmental Studies, Yale University. His research focus is on sustainability, resource use and environmental change in the developing world. He explores these issues principally, though not exclusively, in the context of energy.

Robert V. Bartlett is Gund Professor of the Liberal Arts at the University of Vermont. With Baber he is co-author of many articles and three books, including most recently *Consensus and Global Environmental Governance: Deliberative Democracy in Nature's Regime* (2015).

Simon Hailwood is Senior Lecturer in Philosophy at the University of Liverpool where he teaches moral, political and environmental philosophy. He has published widely in environmental and political philosophy and is the managing editor of the journal *Environmental Values*. His latest book is *Alienation and Nature in Environmental Philosophy* (Cambridge University Press, 2015).

Marija Isailovic is a researcher and PhD candidate at the Institute for Environmental Studies (IVM) at the Vrije Universiteit Amsterdam where she works on fragmentation in global environmental governance. She is a core member of the CONNECT-project team and Earth System Governance Project research fellow.

Martina Kühner is a PhD candidate at the Faculty of Arts and Social Sciences at Maastricht University in the Netherlands. As part of the NWO-funded project 'No carrots, no sticks: How do peer reviews among states acquire authority in global governance?' she investigates the role of global monitoring mechanisms and peer reviews in fostering sustainable development.

Simon Meisch is head of the 'Ethics of Science in the Research for Sustainable Development' Junior Research Group at the International Centre for Ethics in the Sciences and Humanities of the University of Tübingen. His research interests are water ethics and the ethics of science in the water sciences and governance. He has published on conceptual issues of ethics and the theory of sustainable development.

Christine Moser is a PhD candidate at the Faculty of Sustainability, Leuphana Universität Lüneburg, Germany.

Philipp Pattberg is Professor for Transnational Environmental Governance and the head of the Department of Environmental Policy Analysis (EPA), Institute for Environmental Studies (IVM), Vrije Universiteit Amsterdam. His most recent book is the *Encyclopedia of Global Environmental Governance and Politics* (co-edited with Fariborz Zelli).

Christine Prokopf is a researcher at the Chair of International Relations and Sustainable Development at the University of Münster, Germany.

Judith van Leeuwen is Assistant Professor at the Environmental Policy Group of Wageningen University, the Netherlands. Her research focus lies on the changing role of public and private actors (especially industry actors) given the increased fragmented and polycentric nature of environmental and marine governance.

Linda Wallbott is a researcher at the Institute for Political Science at the Westfälische Wilhelms-Universität Münster and PhD candidate at Goethe University Frankfurt in Germany.

Oscar Widerberg is a PhD candidate at the Institute for Environmental Studies (IVM) at the Vrije Universiteit Amsterdam working on fragmentation in global climate governance. He is a core member of the CONNECT-project team, an Earth System Governance Project research fellow, and affiliated with Trinomics.

Marcel Wissenburg is Professor of Political Theory and Head of the Department of Public Administration and Political Science at the Radboud University Nijmegen, the Netherlands.

Fariborz Zelli is Associate Professor at the Department of Political Science at Lund University. He is vice-chair of the Environmental Studies Section of the International Studies Association. His publications include a special issue of *Global Environmental Politics* on institutional fragmentation (as guest editor with Harro van Asselt, 2013) and, most recently, the *Encyclopedia of Global Environmental Governance and Politics* (co-edited with Philipp Pattberg, 2015).

1 Global environmental governance in the Anthropocene

An introduction

Philipp Pattberg and Fariborz Zelli

The meaning of the Anthropocene is contested. No agreement exists concerning a number of important issues, including the exact start date and appropriate stratigraphic markers, its normative implications and political consequences. In the social sciences, various disciplines have started to explore what the Anthropocene means for studying interactions between society and the environment. Broadly speaking, there have been two reactions to proposing the Anthropocene as a new epoch in planetary history. First, a positive reception of the concept, using it as an argument to call for more and better governance of the environment. And second, a critical notion that questions the rationales and interest-configurations underlying the Anthropocene hypothesis and further scrutinizes the resulting politics of the Anthropocene and its theoretical and normative implications.

These disagreements notwithstanding, the scale and scope of environmental challenges has significantly broadened as we are collectively entering the Anthropocene as an epoch of planetary-scale changes that threaten the very processes – from a stable climate to biodiversity – on which human development is ultimately based. In addition, the causes and consequences of global environmental change are increasingly acknowledged to be highly complex, constituting a class of wicked problems (Roberts 2000).

What does this mean for global environmental governance research? Global environmental governance, both as an empirical object and as a field of study, is likely to be transformed by the Anthropocene hypothesis. We see two alternative reactions. First, the Anthropocene hypothesis is greeted with much enthusiasm as it provides a strong argument for the relevance of environmental governance research. However, rather than critically engaging with what the Anthropocene means for global governance, research practice remains largely unaltered. Second, global environmental governance research is fruitfully challenged by the Anthropocene hypothesis, leading to a reorientation of theory and practice. In other words, is the Anthropocene hypothesis a constructive, reinvigorating challenge to the study of environmental politics, or rather just an ingenious framing that gives more weight to environmental concerns? We put forward three arguments why the Anthropocene is a substantial challenge but also an opportunity for the social sciences in general and environmental governance research in particular to reorient itself in light of fundamental transformations.

First, the Anthropocene hypothesis calls into question long-held assumptions about the human-nature dualism and has therefore been associated with the end-of-nature discourse (see Wapner 2014). At the heart of most environmental activism of the last five decades lies the conviction that nature exists independent of human agency and that (supposedly) 'natural' states of our planet, such as a stable climate system, should be protected. However, if the nature-human dualism is questioned by the advent of the Anthropocene, what does this mean for popular conceptions of conservation, wilderness and sustainability and for environmental politics more generally?

One important realization is that the terms 'human' and 'nature' are both social constructions. If humans have developed (as all other current and historic species) through a natural process of evolution to become the dominant species on earth, then we must conclude that anthropogenic global change is a result of natural processes (by which we mean generic and stable patterns of cause and effect). Is not then human domination of nature 'natural'? However, how can nature, and what is natural, be appreciated other than through human norms and values? In Wapner's words (2014, p. 39): 'Nature, then, is not a separate realm, as many environmentalists assume but, because it is always interpreted through cultural lenses, is part and parcel of human affairs.' The challenge for global environmental governance scholarship is to scrutinize human agency as part of a broader 'earth-system' perspective.

Second, the notion of the Anthropocene, and the related idea of a unified human force that exerts unprecedented influence on the earth system, challenges political science scholarship in two ways. First, it urges scholars to take a more system-theoretical perspective in order to identify the system-wide drivers of anthropogenic global change. For example, social science knowledge is indispensable in analysing how historic and current human impacts (think of the Neolithic revolution, the European expansion of the fifteenth and sixteenth century AD and the advent of the nuclear age) have been triggered by a combination of technological progress and changes in political and economic organization and governance. And second, the social sciences, and political science and governance scholarship in particular, are urgently needed as a corrective to accounts of the Anthropocene that neglect the fact that human agency is not uniform across the planet, and that contributions to the problem and the distribution of risks and opportunities are highly uneven.

Third, the Anthropocene discourse places governance research in the centre of attention, as the central question becomes: how can we steer towards socio-natural co-evolution and a resulting safe operating space (in most interpretations: for human development)? As a result, this centrality opens up opportunities for genuine inter-disciplinarity, in which the social sciences are not just a 'junior partner' of the sciences, but contribute fundamental insights into drivers, solutions and complex feedbacks between agency, unintended consequences and reactions to these.

In this introduction, we discuss the key issues and guiding questions that will structure the entire volume. First, we introduce three defining characteristics that are reflected in different theoretical, conceptual and empirical discussions of the Anthropocene: urgency, responsibility and complexity. As a second step, we introduce the three broad areas of inquiry that are covered in this volume: 1) the meaning, sense-making and contestations emerging around the concept of the Anthropocene related to governance research; 2) the role and relevance of institutions, both formal and informal as well as international and transnational, and the implications of increasing institutional complexity for governing in the Anthropocene; and 3) the role and relevance of accountability and other democratic principles for governing in the Anthropocene.

The Anthropocene hypothesis

The term Anthropocene denotes a new epoch in planetary history, one that is characterized by the unprecedented impact of human activities on the earth's ecosystems:

> Human activity is now global and is the dominant cause of most contemporary environmental change. The impacts of human activity will probably be observable in the geological stratigraphic record for millions of years into the future, which suggests that a new epoch has begun.
>
> (Lewis and Maslin 2015, p. 171)

When this new epoch in planetary history began is a matter of intense debate and is, as of 2015, also under formal review with the Anthropocene Working Group of the International Commission on Stratigraphy (ICS), the international body that defines earth's geological timescale. Geologists of the future might well remember 16 July 1945 as the start of the Anthropocene, the day the first atomic bomb was exploded at the White Sands Proving Ground, New Mexico, under the code name 'Trinity'. Debris from more than 500 above-ground nuclear tests conducted between 1945 and 1963 (when the Limited Test Ban Treaty took effect) has created a detectable layer of radioactive elements in sediments all around the planet. However, other potential start dates have been put forward. In their original proposal of the Anthropocene, Crutzen and Stoermer (2000) suggest the beginning of the Industrial Revolution as an appropriate start date. In their own words:

> To assign a more specific date to the onset of the Anthropocene seems somewhat arbitrary, but we propose the latter part of the 18th century, although we are aware that alternative proposals can be made ...
>
> (Crutzen and Stoermer 2000, p. 17)

Other researchers (e.g. Ruddiman 2013) have suggested earlier start dates, highlighting the continuous influence of the human species on a planetary scale since at least 3000 BC, when agriculture and livestock cultivation intensified and the first centralized political authorities emerged. An intermediate position between the early anthropogenic hypothesis and the nuclear hypothesis is taken by Lewis and Maslin (2015) who propose the noticeable decline in atmospheric CO_2 concentrations between 1570 and 1620 as a good marker for the start of the Anthropocene. On this account, the European expansion into the Americas resulted in the death of some 50 million indigenous people, triggering a re-growth of abandoned agricultural lands, causing a measurable decrease in CO_2 concentrations. The 'Orbis hypothesis' is interesting from a social sciences perspective, as the observed atmospheric changes coincide with the emergence of the capitalist world system (Wallerstein 1974). The meeting of European and American cultures and the related dip in atmospheric CO_2 concentrations illustrate the complex and unpredictable nature of human-nature interactions. While humans are a force of nature, this force is neither directional nor necessary.

Irrespective of ongoing debates among geologists and stratigraphers, the Anthropocene hypothesis has gained political ground as a symbolic representation of complex transformations within the earth system. As one observer notes, 'What you see here is, it's become a political statement. That's what so many people want' (cited in Monastersky 2015, p. 147). On this account, the Anthropocene hypothesis has become a rallying call for action in the light of scientific evidence that warns against global environmental change. For example, in 2001, the four international global change research programmes – the International Geosphere-Biosphere Programme (IGBP), the International Human Dimensions Programme on Global Environmental Change (IHDP), the World Climate Research Programme (WCRP) and the international biodiversity programme DIVERSITAS – jointly issued the Amsterdam Declaration on Global Change, warning that:

> Human activities are significantly influencing Earth's environment in many ways in addition to greenhouse gas emissions and climate change. Anthropogenic changes to Earth's land surface, oceans, coasts and atmosphere and to biological diversity, the water cycle and biogeochemical cycles are clearly identifiable beyond natural variability. They are equal to some of the great forces of nature in their extent and impact. Many are accelerating. Global change is real and is happening now.
>
> (Pronk 2002, p. 208)

There is in fact robust evidence that a number of 'planetary boundaries' (Rockström et al. 2009; Steffen et al. 2015) have already been crossed and urgent action in terms of governance and policy is required. Scientists have consequently argued for societal transformations that would steer away from paths that might lead to rapid and irreversible change, while ensuring sustainable livelihoods for all (Biermann et al. 2012). Suggestions reach from reforming and upgrading the environmental agencies of the United Nations to strengthening considerations of equity and fairness in global environmental governance.

Governance challenges in the Anthropocene

The Anthropocene blurs all possible boundaries and puts human action in an ever closer connection to nature. Not only are there no spatial boundaries, also the temporal boundaries are open. Time has to tell to what extent we can change our behaviour to ever allow again for spaces untouched by human action. Possibly these days are numbered. This places an even bigger demand on governance, as the intentional and collective aspect of human action. To what extent are we to blame and could we have done better? And to what extent can we really induce change – of our societies and of the way that we affect the environment?

We see three characteristics as central in the governance discussion in the Anthropocene. None of them is new, but in their combination and intensity they set an unprecedented challenge. All contributors to this volume tried to address these challenges in their work – and could hardly avoid this, even if they had wanted to.

Urgency. The Anthropocene is marked by an unprecedented urgency to act. Its defining feature of the earth system comprehensively impacted by human actions implies that we need to be more vigilant than ever about irreversible impacts that should be avoided. This avoidance may, in many cases, imply immediate changes of course. To be clear, urgency does not consider hard targets like avoiding dangerous climate change or species loss altogether. In a system affected by human behaviour, species have been lost and extreme weather events indicate an increasing effect of climate change. The Anthropocene rather means to act as quickly as possible to achieve relative goals: mitigating climate change, losing less species, reducing the ozone depletion of the ozone layer. In addition, the notion of urgency also raises questions about irreversibility. In how far can the process that led to the Anthropocene be slowed down, stopped or even reversed?

Responsibility. Anthropocene also means a shift in responsibility. With mankind as a whole impacting nature as a whole it is more difficult than ever to assign clear-cut responsibilities for environmental damages and losses. This does not mean that such an assignment is impossible. But we need a more dynamic view of responsibility. Fault lines might run through societies and social groups and they might quickly change over time. These changes have to be mapped and assessed since they entail crucial questions of governance and social behaviour: Why do certain groups have a particular responsibility to act? Through which processes is responsibility shifted in the Anthropocene? Which actors gain responsibility, which actors lose out?

Complexity. Finally, the Anthropocene is marked by an ever-increasing material complexity. The human impact on nature goes back to an intricate sequence of intended and unintended causations and consequences, overlapping subjects and goals and the co-existence and mutual intrusion of different social and natural systems. This material complexity is partly mirrored in our efforts to govern the Anthropocene with complex networks of institutions and processes that may be synergistic or conflictive.

Many disciplines have reacted to the Anthropocene hypothesis by re-examining their core assumptions, research objectives and normative under-pinnings, including organizational studies (Hoffman and Devereaux Jennings 2015), geography (Johnson and Morehouse 2014), theology (Simmons 2014) and Asian studies (Philip 2014), to name a few examples. This volume aims to provide a similar critical reflection from the perspective of environmental governance research.

Structure of the book

The book is structured in three parts, each engaging with a different broad question about global environmental governance and the Anthropocene, and each addressing the cross-cutting challenges identified above.

Part I critically engages with the origins and conceptual issues surrounding the Anthropocene hypothesis. While it has received support from many natural scientists as a plausible descriptor of our current geological time, the reception from the social sciences has been mixed. Contributions to Part I enquire into the various interpretations of the Anthropocene concept, from celebratory and affirmative to critical and concerned, the relation between conceptual notions and political practices as well as into the concrete interests involved in arguing for the Anthropocene as a genuine characteristic of our current epoch.

Part II analyses the changing governance landscape in the Anthropocene by scrutinizing the increase and changing role of institutions, both intergovernmental and transnational, in governing the global and worldwide problems associated with the Anthropocene diagnosis. In more detail, global environmental governance research has highlighted the extent to which our responses to environmental problems have been broadened significantly to reach beyond the confines of formal, legally binding multilateral environmental agreements (MEAs). Consequently, global environmental governance in the Anthropocene poses new and challenging questions to the analyst.

Since the emergence of global environmentalism as a political topic and social movement in the 1960s and 1970s, there has been a proliferation of cross-border environmental governance arrangements. The 1990s witnessed a 'golden age' in international norm-setting where the number and type of intergovernmental environmental regimes increased substantially and states adopted well-known MEAs such as the UN Framework Convention on Climate Change and the Convention on Biological Diversity. Today, more than 1100 MEAs and an estimated 1500 bilateral agreements govern inter-governmental relations across different environmental domains forming a dense web of international public environmental law. From 2000 onwards, however, fewer MEAs have been adopted and a general 'stagnation' in international law-making has been observed (Pauwelyn et al. 2012). Instead, the new millennium saw the birth of a broad range of private and transnational institutions, public–private partnerships, private norms and global public policy networks addressing environmental issues (Pattberg 2007). As a result, we observe the emergence of a patchwork of governance arrangements at all levels of the world political system (Biermann et al. 2009; Zelli 2011; Zelli and van Asselt 2013).

In other words, the structure of global environmental governance has changed dramatically. However, the implications of this governance transformation, both in terms of effectiveness to address the overarching challenge of sustainability and the resulting (re)configuration of political power are not well understood. Consequently, this part analyses relevance and implications of increased institutional complexity in the Anthropocene.

In Part III, authors study the principles, old and new, that can help us address these challenges, placing particular focus on the relevance of legitimacy and accountability. Recent scholarship in global environmental governance has highlighted the legitimacy challenges resulting from hyper-globalization and neo-liberal environmental policies, including the intensifying integration of non-state actors (in particular multinational corporations) in transnational rule-making. For example, Biermann and Gupta (2011) identify the process of globalization as a major driving force in the search for accountable and legitimate governance, strengthening the need for new rule-making institutions at all levels of the political system. In their words:

> the complexities of globalization have also given rise to a stronger political role for actors beyond the nation-state, from multinational corporations and transnational advocacy groups to science networks and global coalitions of municipalities.
>
> (Biermann and Gupta 2011, p. 1856)

On this account, the Anthropocene presents a unique challenge for democratic, legitimate and accountable global governance, as both drivers and solutions to global environmental change have become complex and disaggregated.

Following this broad overview, we briefly introduce the individual contributions to this volume.

In Chapter 2, Marcel Wissenburg critically engages with the problematic prescriptive notion of the Anthropocene by arguing for a comprehensive normative theory to embed the Anthropocene debate in current notions of politics. In more detail Wissenburg argues that the term 'Anthropocene' is different from other geological periods, as it denotes an artificial break in geological and climate history. Criteria for the definition of other geological periods are ethically and politically more or less neutral and give rise to few conflicts – at worst polite debates among academics. Defining the Anthropocene on the other hand, characterizing it, locating its beginning in time (see above) are all cause for heavily politicized controversies. The chapter therefore contends that a prescriptive use of the notion of an Anthropocene can only be justified, if at all, using comprehensive political theories, which would have to evolve from theories of the body politic into theories of the body ecologic.

In Chapter 3, Manuel Arias-Maldonado scrutinizes whether the Anthropocene concept denotes the end of nature. The philosophical answer to that question may determine the political answer to the phenomenon that is described by this geological-cum-historical notion. On this account, the notion of the Anthropocene might indeed confirm that nature has ended in a particular yet important way, but that such ending does not preclude further reflection about the human relation with the environment. In fact, such recognition makes possible another understanding of the task that lies ahead: a reflective re-organization of socionatural relations and a reconceptualization of sustainability that might open up potential avenues for fair and just governance in the Anthropocene.

Chapter 4 by Simon Hailwood identifies three interpretations and responses to the Anthropocene hypothesis: the first argues that the Anthropocene in fact signifies the 'end of nature' in the sense that the ubiquity and depth of human impact makes it no longer intelligible to raise concerns about human impacts on nonhuman nature. Although it is easy to see how the end of nature discourse can dovetail with the Anthropocene discourse, the chapter argues that this is a delusional reading of the situation. The second reaction is one of celebration, taking it as a sign that (aside from some significant malfunctions of the programme such as climate change) human mastery of nature for the sake of anthropocentric ends is proceeding apace and can be expected to increase indefinitely. The third interpretation is a critical one and takes the Anthropocene as a sign that we should be deeply concerned about the implications both for human interests and for nonhuman nature, and consider ways to lessen anthropogenic impacts on the latter.

Concluding the critical self-reflections on the Anthropocene concept, Chapter 5 by Simon Meisch discusses questions of distributive justice to provide an ethical foundation to the concept. Building on a normative understanding of sustainable development, the chapter asks which norms ought to steer political action and ethically inform governance within the Anthropocene. In more detail, the chapter first asks: what do we owe other contemporary and future human beings in a sustainable world? In answering this question, the paper employs two ethical approaches that base human rights on human dignity and aim to give a substantial account of human rights: Martha Nussbaum's *Capability Approach* and Alan Gewirth's *Principle of Generic Consistency*. And second, the chapter consequently engages with the question of to whom we have moral and political obligations and how these insights translate into political rules. While both might look like mere theoretical questions, they have practical impact on governing the Anthropocene.

Chapter 6 opens Part II on institutions with Oscar Widerberg's discussion of institutional complexity and fragmentation through a network perspective. The chapter starts from the assumption that the traditional manner of addressing global problems, by negotiating multilateral environmental agreements between states under the auspices of the United Nations, has been complemented by a surge in governance initiatives driven by smaller groups of countries, cities, regions, international organizations, companies, non-governmental organizations and philanthropists. The chapter then moves on to explore how to best address this emerging heterogeneity and diversity methodologically. It suggests a network-based approach to map and measure the degree of fragmentation of global governance architectures. The approach is illustrated by a case study on global climate governance with a focus on networks involving public actors, including governments, municipalities and sub-national regions.

Chapter 7 by Christine Moser and Robert Bailis employs a polycentric perspective on institutional complexity in the Anthropocene, taking the field of sustainable biofuels governance in Europe as the empirical illustration. In more detail, the chapter starts from the assumption that little is known about the measurable effectiveness of novel modes of governance that may be more flexible to address some of the challenges in the Anthropocene. In its sustainable production of biofuels, the EU relies on hybrid governance, which can be considered such a novel governance approach: the 2009 Renewable Energy Directive provides an environmental meta-standard for sustainable biofuels production under which it accepts private certification systems as 'quasi-implementing agencies', including in non-EU countries of production. Synergies resulting from mixing public and private modes of governance are obviously assumed by policymakers. The question then arises how constructive interplay across levels is facilitated. The chapter thus interrogates the institutional design of biofuels governance as an illustration of institutional complexity in the Anthropocene.

Chapter 8 by Judith van Leeuwen explores the implications of increased accessibility of the Arctic due to climate change and the subsequent growth of maritime activities in the region, also from a polycentric governance perspective. Shipping routes become available which are economically attractive as they shorten the voyage between continents. The concern with regard to increased Arctic shipping relates both to operational pollution as well as possible accidents which would result in spillage of oil and/or cargo. In short, this chapter analyses how corporate environmental performance is influenced by both industry-specific characteristics as well as the polycentric nature of Arctic shipping governance. The chapter also examines which governance solutions, private or state-led, are ultimately preferred by actors and why this is the case.

In Chapter 9, Christine Prokopf analyses international river governance through the example of the Rhine river basin. The economic and social uses of rivers by humanity conflict with claims to protect and restore nature, i.e. the rivers' ecosystems. Institutions like international river basin organizations are founded to address the resulting governance problems. This chapter assesses the relevance of contextual factors for the development of comprehensive institutional governance strategies that include economic, social and ecological considerations. In other words, what induces institutional change in the Anthropocene? The author illustrates how, ultimately, extreme events and their perceptions trigger this change. She thereby links large-scale global change to institutional innovation. To substantiate this argument, the chapter examines the case of the International Commission for the Protection of the Rhine (ICPR).

Part III on accountability and legitimacy in the Anthropocene starts with Chapter 10 by Robert Bartlett and Walter Baber proposing a deliberative model of transnational democratic accountability to overcome the democratic deficit of governance in the Anthropocene. The primary mechanism for holding administrative agencies accountable in democratic states has been the practice of legislative oversight. Yet, humankind's ability to disturb the ecosystem in fundamental ways creates the need for effective governance responses, which will unavoidably rely on strong administrative capacities. What is more, two of the forces of globalization that combine to create this ecological challenge (the internationalization of capital and weakening of the Westphalian nation state) also conspire to make legislative oversight of administrative action unlikely, if not impossible. Drawing primarily on an analysis of the emerging administrative practices of the European Union, the chapter describes a model of democratic accountability that does not rely on legislative oversight.

Chapter 11 by Martina Kühner analyses the role of global monitoring mechanisms as an increasingly used tool of 'holding and being accountable'. The chapter contributes to the investigation of the significance of 'soft' instruments for improving accountability for and, ultimately, compliance with environmental actions agreed upon in the context of the complex, multi-actor environment of the Anthropocene. As a case study, the chapter puts the main focus on the parties of the Kyoto Protocol (KP) within the framework of the United Nations Framework Convention on Climate Change (UNFCCC). Finally, lessons learned from this case are translated into recommendations on how to set up a monitoring framework for climate action that exhibits both flexibility and effectiveness in times of the Anthropocene.

In Chapter 12, Marija Isailovic engages with the question of legitimacy related to the engagement of actors from the global South in governing the Anthropocene. The Anthropocene concept does not fully do justice to the specific position of the global South and its actors. Research and practice of negotiations and agenda-setting in global environmental governance have shown that differences in opinions, interests and norms as well as access to resources between the global North and global South are still considerable. Against this backdrop, this chapter offers a legitimacy-based understanding of ongoing transformations of world politics from a global South perspective. Rather than providing empirical evidence-based research, the question is how shifts in authority entail changes in legitimacy and what this implies for questions of complexity, responsibility and urgency to act.

Chapter 13 by Linda Wallbott asks critical questions about how indigenous peoples have built and exerted their agency in international negotiations on forests and genetic resources. She analyses how far the narrative of the Anthropocene provides for potentials and pitfalls for indigenous peoples' claims to more effective participation in international environmental negotiations. Which new spaces open up and which new fault lines emerge? The Anthropocene aims to capture the substantial impact of human activities on the earth system.

Yet, often it comes with a Western, anthropocentric bias – and also with some negative normative imprint, as it usually describes impacts such as biodiversity loss and climate change. On the other hand, the activities of indigenous peoples and local communities are often considered to contribute to the sustainability and stewardship of natural resources 'in harmony with nature'. However, a linkage between these two images is rarely drawn, neither in actual debates nor in scientific analyses.

In our concluding chapter (Zelli and Pattberg, this volume), we summarize this broad survey of global environmental governance and the Anthropocene along the three guiding concepts explored throughout the book. Finally we distil a number of important avenues for future research on global environmental governance in the Anthropocene.

References

Biermann, F., Abbott, K., Andresen, S., Bäckstrand, K., Bernstein, S. et al. (2012) Navigating the Anthropocene: Improving earth system governance. *Science* 335: 1306–1307.

Biermann F. and Gupta A. (2011) Accountability and legitimacy: An analytical challenge for earth system governance. *Ecological Economics* 70: 1854–1855.

Biermann, F., Pattberg, P., Van Asselt, H. and Zelli, F. (2009) The fragmentation of global governance architectures: A framework for analysis. *Global Environmental Politics* 9(4): 14–40.

Crutzen, P. J. and Stoermer, E. F. (2000) *IGBP Newsletter* 41: 17–18.

Hoffman, A. and Devereaux Jennings, P. (2015) Institutional theory and the natural environment: Research in (and on) the Anthropocene. *Organization & Environment* 28(1): 8–31.

Johnson, E. and Morehouse, H. (2014) After the Anthropocene: Politics and geographic inquiry for a new epoch. *Progress in Human Geography* 38(3): 439–456.

Lewis, S. L. and Maslin, M. A. (2015) Defining the Anthropocene. *Nature* 315: 171–180.

Monastersky, R. (2015) The human age. *Nature* 519: 147–149.

Pattberg, P. (2007) *Private Institutions and Global Governance: The New Politics of Environmental Sustainability*. Cheltenham: Edward Elgar.

Pauwelyn, J., Wessel, A. and Wouters, J. (2012) *Informal International Lawmaking*. Oxford: Oxford University Press.

Philip, K. (2014) Doing interdisciplinary Asian Studies in the age of the Anthropocene. *Journal of Asian Studies* 73(4): 975–1000.

Pronk, J. (2002) The Amsterdam Declaration on Global Change. In W. Steffen, J. Jäger, D. Carson and C. Bradshaw, *Challenges of a Changing Earth*. Berlin, Heidelberg: Springer, pp. 207–208.

Roberts, N. (2000) Wicked problems and the network approach to resolution. *International Public Management Review* 1(1): 1–19.

Rockström, J., Steffen, W., Noone, K., Persson, A., Chapin III, F. S., Lambin, E. et al. (2009) Planetary boundaries: Exploring the safe operating space for humanity. *Ecology and Society* 14(2): 32.

Ruddiman, W. F. (2013) The Anthropocene. *Annual Review of Earth and Planetary Sciences* 4: 45–68.

Simmons, E. (2014) Theology in the Anthropocene. *Dialog – A Journal of Theology* 53(4): 271–273.

Steffen, W., Richardson, K., Rockström, J., Cornell, S., Fetzer, I. et al. (2015) Planetary boundaries: Guiding human development on a changing planet. *Science* 347(6223): 736.

Wallerstein, I. (1974) *The Modern World-System I: Capitalist Agriculture and the Origins of the European World-Economy in the Sixteenth Century*. New York and London: Academic Press.

Wapner, P. (2014) The changing nature of nature. Environmental politics in the Anthropocene. *Global Environmental Politics* 14(4): 36–54.

Zelli, F. (2011) The fragmentation of the global climate governance architecture. *Wiley Interdisciplinary Reviews: Climate Change* 2(2): 255–270.

Zelli, F. and van Asselt, H. (2013) Introduction: The institutional fragmentation of global environmental governance. *Global Environmental Politics* 13(3): 1–13.

Part I

Making sense of the Anthropocene

2 The Anthropocene and the body ecologic

Marcel Wissenburg

Introduction

While the original introduction of the notion of an Anthropocene, an Age of Humankind, may have been inspired by the noblest of intentions, this chapter will argue that the prescriptive claims put forward by many advocates of the Anthropocene are morally and politically flawed. For one, they consistently rely on rule by experts, either in the form of a technocratic regime or that of quasi-democratic social engineering. For another, they fail to appreciate that political and moral diversity are ultimately irreducible, i.e. that the nature of politics is conflict not consensus, and that these conflicts are not purely 'technical' but originate in logically and often also practically incompatible theories of the good life and the good society. The narrative of the Anthropocene is, to use Weberian terms, exclusively one of goal rationality, at the expense of (self-)critical, reflective, value rationality. For the message of the Anthropocene to be taken seriously, it needs to be supported – of course – by good natural science and good social science (as discussed elsewhere in this book), but also by a political theory that embeds a just and good society characterized by politico-moral diversity in a broader perspective on 'the good environment'.

The chapter starts with an introduction to and historical contextualization of the first generation of advocates of the idea of an Anthropocene, of earth system science to develop and assess solutions and (for at least some of the original advocates) of geo-engineering as a practical response to the most urgent problem of global warming. I then proceed to discuss the major moral and political gaps in the Anthropocene narrative, one of which is the initial lack of recognition for the unique ('non-natural') complexity of society. A second generation of advocates of the Anthropocene can be thought of as the 'extended circle' of the first group. These academics are active mostly in the fields of social and political geography and public administration, and they do recognize how the complexity of society can be a hurdle to effective global action, but as I intend to show, they too tend to fall back on expert rule and goal-rational policymaking, assuming a broad background consensus on the goals of global environmental policies. I end by sketching the problems faced in the development of a theory of the body ecologic rather than one of the body politic alone – which is something most of political theory has not seriously engaged with for the past twenty centuries.

The Anthropocene narrative

Suddenly, we no longer live in the Holocene (the 'wholly new' era that started 11,700 BC), successor of the Pleistocene (the 'newest new' era that covered the preceding 2.6 million years) – we find ourselves in the Anthropocene, the Age of Humankind. Unlike other geological and biological periods, the term 'Anthropocene' denotes an *artificial* break in geological and climate history. Unlike those other periods, it is named after the (alleged) origin of the break – otherwise the Pleistocene would be known as the Ice Age and the Holocene as the Temporarily Fairly Warm Age.

There is evidently politics going on here. Criteria for the definition of other geological and biological periods are ethically and politically more or less neutral and give rise to few conflicts – at worst polite debates among academics. Defining the Anthropocene on the other hand, characterizing it, locating its beginning in time, proving it is significantly different enough to qualify as an era in its own right and, most of all, assessing its meaning in biology, geology, not to mention human affairs – these exercises all result in heavily politicized controversies (cf. e.g. Certini and Scalenghe 2015).

One area of contention concerns the question whether it is *descriptively* correct to attribute to a second of human history, a mere flicker of Earth's history, a degree of importance comparable to the comet that supposedly ended the Jurassic. In other words, is the Anthropocene a megalomaniac construct giving too much honour to a newcomer? A further source of controversy is whether it is *prescriptively* appropriate to employ the term the way it is now often employed: to *accuse* humanity of megalomania, of being the arrogant species that believes itself to have chased the gods from Olympus but has in doing so destroyed Elysium. But of course both areas of contention are far more complex: the descriptive aspect of the concept of the Anthropocene has prescriptive – ethical, moral and ultimately political – implications, and the prescriptive aspect can be reformulated into a call to recognize as fact humankind's new status as Master of the Universe.

The concept of the Anthropocene originated in a circle of biologists and climate scientists I shall refer to as the 'original advocates'. For these scientists, the urgency and complexity of (presumably human-made) global environmental changes suggested that humanity should take its responsibility, and develop and execute global solution strategies to adapt our environment: it should understand these changes as affecting 'earth system', understand them through 'earth system science', and respond with geo-engineering (for an analysis of the Anthropocene discourse as a mix of three distinct narratives, one of science history, one of earth system and one of the Anthropocene, see Uhrqvist and Linnér 2015).

Although the term Anthropocene may be relatively new, a whole history and prehistory has already been built around it, complete with founding fathers and a conceptual genealogy. But the Anthropocene is not just any concept – it is an instrument of politics, wielded by a growing and diversifying network of academics. At the core of this network we find as the most active original advocates among others Frans Berkhout, Jacques Grinevald, John McNeill, Frank Oldfield, Will Steffen, Jan Zalasiewicz and, the central source of inspiration, Dutch Nobel Prize winner Paul Crutzen. It is in particular Crutzen who, around 2000, popularized the term Anthropocene, although it dates back to the 1980s, when Eugene F. Stoermer coined it (Steffen et al. 2011, p. 843).

One of the central nodes for developing the Anthropocene narrative is the International Geosphere-Biosphere Programme (IGBP.net), which claims to coordinate 'international research on global-scale and regional-scale interactions between Earth's biological, chemical and physical processes and their interactions with human systems'. An access point to the network, to IGBP and its partner institutions, is offered by the website www.anthropocene.info. Its founder, Owen Gaffney (a writer with a degree in astronautic and aeronautic engineering and post-graduate qualifications in journalism and film production), also maintains a blog with fewer claims to scientific objectivity and more room for straightforward value judgements: The Anthropocene Journal (http://anthropocenejournal.com/). There are also indications of strong personal ties between the original advocates and the Encyclopedia of Earth (http://www.ncseonline.org/encyclopedia-earth). Several of them publish in the Elsevier journal *Anthropocene*, while some also contribute to edited volumes. The few academic monographs (which are rare in the natural sciences anyway) expounding general theories of the Anthropocene narrative's key concepts are not written by any of the original advocates.

The original advocates' core message is that 'Anthropocene' is a real, existing empirical phenomenon. Thus, for example, Steffen et al. present the case for a formal recognition of 'the Anthropocene' (starting around 1800 with the Industrial Revolution) as a 'new geological epoch or era in Earth history', since 'the human imprint on the global environment has now become so large and active that it rivals some of the great forces of Nature in its impact on the functioning of the Earth system' (Steffen et al. 2011, p. 842).

As proof of this thesis, Steffen et al. (2011) offer scores of figures on, on the one hand, dramatic changes in biology and climate since 1800, and on the other hand equally dramatic changes in human society's rising (also urban) population, rising GDP, foreign investment (globalization), damming of rivers, water use, fertilizer consumption, paper consumption, the rise of the McDonald's empire, the number of motor vehicles and telephones, increases in international tourism (for an updated set, see Steffen et al. 2015; these figures are now almost universally used as the authoritative depiction of the Anthropocene).

While the case for humanity's sudden, deep impact on the planet is strong, proponents of the Anthropocene narrative sometimes also overstate their case. Many of the figures used by Steffen et al. (2011, 2015), for instance, are redundant, and their inclusion is therefore suspicious: with a rising GDP, for example, one may automatically expect consumption in general to rise, therefore also the use of fertilizers and the consumption of paper, hamburgers, cars and miles. Moreover, the graphs all look alike: by adapting the measures used on the y-axis, every one of 40-plus graphs shows the exact same exponential increase of every natural and human phenomenon from zero to max over the same 200 years. Finally, Steffen et al. (2011, 2015) offer no data on extremes in previous ages to show that humanity's act is indeed unique, that no such sudden and extreme change has ever made an equally deep and lasting impression on the Earth's biology and geology.

The last point is acknowledged, implicitly, by Crutzen and Stoermer (2010) when they argue that it is not just 'the central role of mankind (sic, MW) in geology and ecology' during the *past* 200 years that justifies talk of a distinct era, but even more the effect of those 200 years, because thanks to man (sic, MW), for instance 'climate may depart significantly from natural behaviour over the next 50,000 years'. Of course, this hypothesis still awaits its final test.

At the core of the Anthropocene concept are its prescriptive and ultimately political implications. In the words of Crutzen and Stoermer (2010), the facts about the Anthropocene 'prove' that we need a 'world-wide accepted strategy leading to sustainability of ecosystems against human induced stresses'. There are two key components of that strategy: a new and better science (an earth science of earth system) on the one hand, and a proper understanding of humanity's place relative to that science on the other.

Starting with the latter, the original advocates of the Anthropocene concept have created a canon of authors and ideas predating and allegedly predicting the emergence of the Anthropocene and earth system science. Guillaume (2014) for example starts with Suess, who introduced the concept of a biosphere in 1875, followed by Vernadsky who popularized it, with Bergson, who was the father of vitalism, and with – among others – Teilhard de Chardin, who introduced a distinction between two co-evolving spheres, the biosphere (physical nature) and the noösphere (the sphere of human thought). Teilhard de Chardin and Vernadsky are interpreted as arguing for a bridging of the gap between biosphere and noösphere, for a deep and holistic understanding of the biosphere to help the noösphere guide, direct and perfect the biosphere. Vernadsky is particularly popular because of his enthusiasm for technological fixes (e.g. Steffen et al. 2011).

In recognition of the facts defining the Anthropocene, the new science, earth system science, should be the product of the re-interpretation and integration of our scattered disciplinary knowledge of biology, physics, meteorology etc., merged into one set of knowledge of the one indivisible earth system. It is to be more than trans- or interdisciplinary – it is to be holistic. The parallel to Teilhard's Hegelian scheme of a co-evolving and uniting biosphere (earth system) and noösphere (earth science) will be obvious.

Earth system science knows a goal for the earth system, a telos that, in the Teilhardian vernacular, it is 'pointing to'. Steffen et al. (2011) argue that there are only two options we can choose from in view of the cosmic disaster that the Anthropocene is promising to develop into. Both imply respect for the earth system's 'planetary boundaries' (cf. Rockström et al., 2009). One is to return life, including human activities, to within classic boundaries, basically a return to the ecology of the Holocene. This position – which reflects the ideas of scores of authors and decades of conservationist and ecological thought – is identified as self-contradictory and as 'cognitive dissonance' (Steffen et al. 2011, p. 861). The advocates' message is that there is no going back to times in which there was no need for earth system science, earth control and earth management.

Instead, at least some of the original advocates of the Anthropocene concept opt for what they see as the only viable alternative: global geo-engineering (or as it is called in science-fiction and in plans for Mars: terraforming). Steffen et al. (2011, pp. 856–859) for example identify as the problems to be addressed and henceforth simultaneously managed (as if they are of the same order requiring the same technocratic solution strategies) biodiversity, climate change, pollution affecting human health, threats to water support and life, and the 'failure to build effective global governance systems'. For another example, Oldfield et al. (2014) characterize the Anthropocene as a time of interrelated changes in the biosphere on the one hand, and processes of globalization and economic and industrial growth in human society on the other. What is needed is to control both 'the capacity of systemic self-organization on a global scale also enables human society, at least in principle, to use Earth System knowledge for self-governance' (ibid. p. 4). Taking such a long-term holistic view will pose tremendous 'challenges for human society'. (Note that the existence of one and only one undivided global human society is assumed.) Oldfield and colleagues do not specify which challenges these are exactly, other than that creating communication among academic disciplines is one of them. With the natural scientist's typical focus on practical (technological) solutions, they only observe that the 'key challenge for the future is to ensure that the negative changes do not outweigh the positive ones' (ibid. p. 5).

In short, global geo-engineering, the permanent adaptation of nature to human needs while keeping humanity within proper 'planetary boundaries', figures prominently as a solution to the imminent self-destruction of humanity among proponents of the Anthropocene. The necessary (social, economic and political) 'effective global governance systems' are seen as means to be designed for use by the same technocrats managing, and as part of the same set of physical processes making up, the earth system. To characterize these arguments as a classic plan for world domination by an elite of well-meaning engineers and scientists may be rhetorical – but that does not necessarily make it incorrect. It is, at this point, crucial to realize that in the political parts of the original advocates' proposals some words consistently and persistently fail to make an appearance – words like democracy, human rights, respect, autonomy, freedom, self-determination, pluralism, diversity, culture, plan of life and so on.

Omission and circumvention

The original advocates' characterization of the Anthropocene is, in all fairness, almost one-dimensional: the Anthropocene is a technically complex but theoretically simple problem with, in essence, an equally simple solution. The simple problem is that humanity (as one undivided subject) unbalances system earth, thereby threatens the existence of humanity (as one indivisible object). The simple solution is using earth science in designing an integrated, solution-oriented, technocratic model to steer the earth system.

A second dimension is added only when an alternative solution strategy is discussed: a return to a world of non-action. It is only in responding to opponents that the possibility of an alternative narrative of the Anthropocene is acknowledged – but an analysis (which follows momentarily) of the construction of that narrative and the advocates' rebuttal shows that, for them, there is only one rational and sensible conception of the Anthropocene, and therefore only one rational approach to its problems.

While the absence of (self-)critical reflection on the goals of Anthropocene policies, geo-engineering in particular, may be the most fundamental 'sin of omission' committed by the original advocates, it is by no means the only one that reveals hidden, therefore undefended, assumptions in the narrative. In the second part of this section I address another problem for advocates of geo-engineering: accusations of oversimplifying the complexity of the earth system, in particular of its human component and even more particularly politics.

First, then, the one-dimensional concept of the Anthropocene. The original advocates make no attempt to present the Anthropocene as a *mere* matter of fact – it is a value-laden fact, a negatively laden fact. So do many outside of the natural sciences use the concept, by the way: ecological philosophers, social scientists, scholars in the humanities. Note the use of the word 'fact': value-laden or not, the fact of the (existence of the) Anthropocene does not seem to be open to debate. In this respect, the term Anthropocene is used in a way quite similar to 'the ecological crisis': the choice of words suggests an objective, undeniable fact with a negative connotation, a connotation that would be universally indubitable.

Neutral positions, accepting the fact of large-scale ecological change without branding it an imminent threat to nature, are unpopular (as we shall see below, in the case of Robyn Eckersley's critique of global warming alarmism). Nor are there, to my knowledge, texts presenting the Anthropocene as a positive fact – while this may well be a quite defensible position. From a non-consequentialist point of view, living in a world that is basically a creation of rational and autonomous entities rather than a structure cast upon them, can after all be cheered as humanity's greatest achievement ever. Still, the closest some arguments come to a positive assessment is where some of them implicitly praise the proven ability to geo-engineer as a great achievement, inspired by good intentions gone wrong; arguing that it is time to take the next step and get it under control (for instance Hobbs et al. 2011; Minteer 2012). Yet this cannot be construed as a positive assessment of the Anthropocene in itself.

Yet all is not gloom. By embracing geo-engineering, earth system science and the notion of an earth system, the many advocates of the Anthropocene concept paint an undeniably positive *prescriptive* picture of the Anthropocene. The Anthropocene is not just a disaster, it is also an opportunity, an invitation, a call to arms, or better still a duty: a duty to take responsibility for system earth and humankind. And since the Anthropocene is taken as an undisputable (negative) fact, there is no further ethical argument required for the use by scientists and academics of (would-be) expert knowledge as a weapon to actively engage in politics.

Oddly enough, there are few texts *directly* praising the idea of earth system management. Most are either in praise of particular policies and technologies (e.g. alternative energy, herding the ocean, etc.) or argue indirectly for earth system management. Examples of the former can be found in Oksanen and Siipi (2014). Contributors to that volume discuss, in the context of the Anthropocene, the ethics of 'reversing extinction': may and should extinct species be recreated, with or without genetic modification, and what for? One argument presented in favour of reparation, rewilding, reinventing and replacing extinct species with alternative ones is that it can promote biodiversity – but is that enough reason to have H. Neanderthalensis return?

Indirect praise for global ecosystem engineering is also detectable in the critique of its opponents, whom the original advocates (e.g. Rockström et al. 2009, Steffen et al. 2011) depict as living in denial, displaying cognitive dissonance, and as inconsistent. They (the opposition) are seen as rejecting geo-engineering while, through non-action where action is possible, they actually engineer the natural environment just as much, only in an apparently undesirable, because allegedly unstable, direction.

One clear illustration, employing the 'end of nature' vocabulary, is given by Hobbs et al. (2011), who argue that 'restoration ecology' must develop into intervention ecology: 'There is a strong need for the development of a more effective ecology to enable the analysis and management of ecosystems in a rapidly changing world' (p. 442). Intervention ecology is goal-oriented – and while Hobbs et al. leave these goals undefined, hence give no grounds for intervention, they still, fallaciously, believe intervention is justified. For the advocates, there is no alternative: ecosystems cannot be returned to their old state, cannot be recreated – in intervention ecology, words beginning with re- are to be rejected. 'Humanity is already intervening in ecosystem function on a planetary scale' (p. 443). In fact, restoration ecology is dangerous: it encourages a 'moral hazard' attitude. The only hesitation they voice is the obligatory bow to scientific uncertainty (and explicitly *not* to human fallibility): 'Do we know enough to intervene?' (p. 448).

A similar argument is presented by Preston (2012) in a case study in geo-engineering on radiation management. He opposes 'naturalists', who would worship the 'fetish' of a nature existing independently from humanity (p. 195) and supports as an alternative the idea that 'artefacts retain something that is beyond human design' – hence the opposition of artifice and nature is 'nonsense'. A garden always has nature in it – a point Simon Hailwood, author of the next chapter, whom Preston would undoubtedly characterize as a 'naturalist', would still wholeheartedly agree with. In defence of ecological intervention, Preston argues (or from a 'naturalist's' point of view, jumps to the conclusion):

> another defining feature of the Anthropocene would be the change in our moral responsibilities … Contemplating those obligations is not for the squeamish … Rather than viewing nature in the traditional fashion as a deep source of solace and meaning, we might start to view the climate as a constant (and self-created) threat, leading to the existential anxiety Mark [Jason 2009] claims would plague us.
>
> (Preston 2012, p. 198)

Preston, too, is an interventionist whose only hesitation is an obligatory bow, in this case to superstition: 'Our mortality and fallibility are certainly traits we will want to keep in mind if we ever choose to intentionally enter the domain of the gods' (p. 199).

But who are these naturalist opponents, really? Hourdequin (2013) helps us identify them. He argues that the Anthropocene confronts us with two questions: are we 'the key drivers of biological, geological, and chemical processes on Earth? And second, if the answer to the first question is affirmative, then what should we do about it?' (p. 116). Immediately focusing on the second question, and without argument assuming 'something' has to be done, he too opposes intervention to restoration. Referring to John Stuart Mill, he maintains that there is no more nature to *follow*. 'True' nature cannot be a guiding principle. Hence restoration makes no sense – it is not the return of (or to) nature, it is outright creation. Narratives of restoration like John O'Neill's, Alan Holland's, and Andrew Light's (p. 123ff) are basically calls to fake nature – where it would be more consistent not to look backwards but forwards, to continue (perhaps complete?) an evolving history by overcoming the dichotomy of natural/ anthropogenic creation.

In addition to the use of straw man arguments, there is also a degree of circular reasoning in the critique of 'non-interventionists'. Dalby (2007) for example criticizes Robyn Eckersley's (2007) too quietist or 'Gaiaist' attitude in allowing intervention in nature only for an environmental emergency – what, he asks, counts as an emergency? Eckersley's criterion, immediate danger, is not good enough – that would preclude action against climate change, and that, Dalby feels, is ducking responsibility. Of course, it can only be ducking responsibility if we assume beforehand that the harm done by global warming must be combatted at any cost.

These critical readers of the Anthropocene narrative are not a random collection of accidentally connected authors expressing a negative judgement on all-out terraforming: O'Neill, Holland, Light and Eckersley form the almost complete canon of ecological political thought since 1980. The Anthropocene certainly has a mobilizing potential, a potential to enhance internal unity and inspire action, *both* for the advocates of geo-engineering and their opponents.

As the discussion shows, handling value-rational critique is not frequently encountered in many of the advocates' arguments. The problem returns when opponents suggest that the proponents oversimplify the complexity of the human factor in the earth system. The response is that it is either 'not really all that much of a problem', or they admit that further research is needed, i.e. that the already very multidisciplinary research community needs to embrace even more disciplines: the social sciences in addition to the natural sciences. Clearly, this response misses the point: it turns an, in essence, value-rational fundamental critique into a relatively innocent goal-rational technical problem.

Oldfield and Steffen (2014), for example, defended the validity of earth system science against Popperian accusations of immunization. Their critics, they argue, accuse them of producing junk science, a mishmash of incompatible data and untestable hypotheses. Oldfield and Steffen's defence remains weak (though sincere): they argue that they have an 'only ever imperfectly knowable past and an inconceivably complex environmental system' (p. 73) to work with – projective models are the only alternative to dealing with this mess of data, and these models evolve 'in an iterative rather than linear fashion'; they offer pathways rather than scenarios. Both the critique of earth system science and the reply echo the familiar positions defended by climate sceptics and IPCC in the debate on global warming – yet given that global warming is just one of many earth system deficiencies, i.e. given that earth system science is several degrees more complex than one already exceptionally complex environmental problem alone, the defence is several degrees less convincing.

Geo-engineering, the 'deliberate modification of the climate to achieve specific effects such as cooling' (Robock 2008, p. 14) as defended by Crutzen and others, gets an equally weak defence. Alan Robock lists what he sees as the major arguments against geo-engineering: several varieties of expected and unaccounted-for side-effects, the risk of human error and financial costs – plus, on the socio-political side, the risks of commercial control of technology, of military use of technology, and of political control of technology. All these Robock seems to see as practical problems only. Almost as an afterthought, he mentions the question of 'moral authority' (p. 17), which he operationalizes as a question of control (i.e. who has a say in the use of technologies) rather than as a question about whether geo-engineering (on principle or in specific cases) is morally right or wrong. An even more striking example of a goal-rational defence of, rather than a self-critical value-rational reflection on, geo-engineering is offered by Bunzel (2008), whose perspective remains limited to an environmental cost-benefit analysis of geo-engineering, mentioning no political, social, cultural or moral costs or benefits whatsoever.

To weaknesses other than those in scientific facts, the advocates have (until recently) only paid scant attention – yet there was and is good reason to expect that none of the prescriptions originating in the discourse on the Anthropocene, earth system science and geo-engineering stand a chance of being embraced, let alone implemented, if only nature is qualified as a complex system while the unique kind of complexity of society remains underrated. Just one illustration: Karlsson and Symons (2014) implicitly criticized the Anthropocene advocates' easy plea for global political initiatives on these grounds. Arguing on the basis of (neo-)realist assumptions as common in the field of international relations, they show that controlling (for example) carbon emissions in a world of sovereign states is impossible as long as carbon is linked to economic development. While their argument is that more research and development is needed, together with more policies aimed at technological innovation to reduce carbon dependency, it is equally clear that the advocates of the Anthropocene cannot afford to underestimate the complexities of politics. Their lack of attention to the type of problems identified by the social sciences and political philosophy has also been highlighted by the Australian Environment Institute (Sydney.edu.au/ Environment-Institute) with its alternative reading of the Anthropocene.

The second circle

In 2013, inspired by the desire to extend the reach of earth system science from the natural sciences to the social sciences and humanities, a new journal was born: *The Anthropocene Review*. According to its website (http://anr.sagepub. com/), its aim is to bring together 'peer-reviewed articles on all aspects of research pertaining to the Anthropocene, from earth and environmental sciences, social sciences, material sciences, and humanities', so as to 'communicate clearly and across a wide range of disciplines and interests, the causes, history, nature and implications of a world in which human activities are integral to the functioning of the Earth System'. It will be no surprise that many of those involved in its foundation are also involved in the International Geosphere-Biosphere Programme and related organizations, first and foremost the journal's editor, Frank Oldfield, one of the original advocates of the Anthropocene concept.

While the journal expands the research area of earth system science to society, thus finally acknowledging the complexity of society as distinct and different from that of the biological and geological parts of earth system, its mission statement is still that of a technocratic, goal-rational enterprise: the promotion of earth system science and with that, geo-engineering. That same mission shines through in many of the contributions to the journal – sometimes exceptionally clearly, as the following illustrations show.

Malm and Hornborg (2014) offer a critical theory perspective on the Anthropocene, which they say is partly a fuel crisis. Living with fossil fuel is not a human choice, they argue, but an investment decision that is in turn the consequence of current technology and current modes of production. Population growth has nothing to do with the growing use of fossil fuel, and figures prove this. Change in general is not anthropogenic but sociogenic, originating in processes at the macro level of society rather than the micro level of individuals. Climate change is no exception; it 'has arisen as a result of temporally fluid social relations as they materialize through the rest of nature', thus 'one can no longer treat humankind as merely a species-being determined by its biological evolution' (p. 66). The Anthropocene narrative is a 'useful concept and narrative for polar bears … who want to know what species is wreaking such havoc on their habitats, but alas, they lack the capacity to scrutinise and stand up to human actions' (p. 67). What lacks in the field, they argue, is a decent power analysis so as to be able to move beyond the attribution of blame. While Malm and Hornborg may be critical of the social scientific assumptions of early earth system science, it is a constructive critique – it identifies a new, under-researched area of complexity, and it does so with an eye to aiding the mission; Malm and Hornborg do not investigate the goals and objectives of the advocates of earth system science and geo-engineering itself.

Frank Biermann (2014) analysed the socio-political implications and effects of the Anthropocene from a governance perspective. Like Malm and Hornborg, he stresses that Anthropocene advocates ignored complexity – in this case, the complexities of politics as evident in reinforcing relations between societies, in their interdependence, in intergenerational dependence, and in the emergence of ever more elements of the risk society. This, he argues, calls for earth system governance (Biermann's own term and research programme), the 'societal steering of human activities with regard to the long-term stability of geobiophysical systems' (p. 59). Earth system governance requires better governance, governance that offers not merely technological changes but also involves civil society and new global institutions monitoring incremental policies at the (sub)national level. In addition, earth system governance presupposes a scientifically based, politically supported redefinition of material 'sufficiency' (as in 'sufficient for a good life'). In brief, earth system governance is to be built on evidence-based policy research supporting political reform programmes. Biermann does not mention that there may be a normative dimension to politics: his is instead the Popperian social engineer's technocratic understanding of politics as policymaking guided by predetermined political goals, immunized against critical reflection.

Biermann shows, elsewhere, that he is quite aware that he embraces a value-laden view on earth system governance and on politics in general (Biermann 2012) – he just does not see it as even potentially contentious. Earth system governance's prime task is apparently uncontroversial: 'to regulate norm-conflicts between … institutions, and to increase efficiency and effectiveness' (p. 7). Where it meets the most fundamental challenge on its way, sovereignty, 'it appears questionable whether full national sovereignty can be upheld for the most essential environmental standards that are needed to protect the planetary boundaries' (p. 8). Why sovereignty exists and persists, and what might justify it, seem irrelevant – for earth system governance it is merely a technical obstacle that 'needs' to be taken into account because 'urgent action is required' (p. 8). All in all, earth system governance would be an innocent enterprise: 'The concept of planetary boundaries does not necessarily require grand institutional designs, as they are sometimes found in op-eds and press announcements, or ideas of rational rule by scientists, reminding of Plato's philosopher kings' (p. 9). But of course, this is exactly what earth system governance is: rational rule by social engineers.

A final telling illustration: Jasper Knight (2015) argues that the major problems for use of the concept of sustainability as a standard for Anthropocene policies are uncertainty about the exact functioning of the ecosystem and inefficiency in the adaptation of 'structures and management tools used by societal actors' to changing ecological circumstances. For Knight, too, earth system science has to acknowledge the importance and uniqueness of socio-political complexity in addition to the biological and climatologic complexity of nature – but only for practical reasons. Earth system science, social science included, is management science.

Of all the Anthropocene advocates, Frans Berkhout (2014) comes closest to identifying the far more fundamental (value-rational) problem so far ignored in both natural and social science research in the service of earth system science: the irreducible plurality of morality and, consequently, political theory, i.e. theories of the good and just society. Berkhout points out that the non-natural science parts of the Anthropocene narrative were mostly backward-looking, while the narrative lacks forward-looking perspectives on (un)sustainable development and feasible futures. Side constraints for the development of such scenarios are the costs and opportunities of global sustainability problems, including those in the short run. Crucial, however, for the realization of any scenario, any 'future', is not just adequate knowledge nor the design of adequate institutions and forms of cooperation – but also justice: the fair distribution of benefits and burdens globally. Part of doing justice will have to be acknowledging the desire to create 'multiple Anthropocene Futures', which will inevitably be 'contradictory and co-existing'. Berkhout unfortunately does not take the next step, towards political theory. He observes that there 'will be' multiple perspectives on the desired future of our planet, but leaves that observation hanging in the air – he has no answer on how to deal with this moral-political pluralism.

In sum then, the Anthropocene narrative has three kinds of weaknesses. Of one, the advocates are aware: the natural science basis is uncertain to controversial. Of the second kind, awareness is increasing: the social and political science part of earth system, which turns out to be far more complicated than anticipated. To a third weakness, even the extended circle of advocates remains virtually blind: why and in which specific way should we re-terraform the Earth anyway? In other, more clearly political words, what kind of society-conjoined-with-environment can be morally justified?

The body ecologic

Among the very few to address the ethical aspects of the Anthropocene narrative, specifically in its interventionist form, are Ben Minteer and Robert McKim – and both ultimately point beyond ethics towards political theory. Minteer (2012) argues that the classic critique of technology and human intervention as voiced by icons like Thoreau, Leopold and Carson is not compelling in an era where, thanks to geo-engineering, we face change on a scale never thought of before. Geo-engineering in turn is a response to a problem that is also larger in every sense than anything humanity faced before. Both the problem and the suggested solution force us to reconsider our 'environmental responsibility' (p. 857). To fill this void, what is needed is a 'new and comprehensive ethical paradigm of human solicitude for species and ecosystems that can accommodate significant, perhaps unprecedented, human interventions in nature' (p. 858) – but it is obvious that ethics alone will not be enough. As McKim (2013) reminds us, ecological intervention touches other peoples' lives and expectations as well – it has political repercussion and therefore, in addition to a new ethics, a theory of 'good planetary citizenship' is also required. And that brings us to the role of political theory in the Anthropocene narrative.

Let us assume, in spite of the pessimism of Malm and Hornborg (2014), that anthropogenic change or at least deliberate collective change is possible, i.e. that humans and polities have a degree of freedom and a degree of control over the instruments of change, from law, customs and economy to scientific research and technology development. Against such a background, it makes sense not only to expect the emergence in empirical reality of Berkhout's co-existing and at times incompatible 'multiple Anthropocene futures', but also to expect reasonable disagreement on desirable Anthropocene futures, i.e. on the goals of ecological intervention. It is only those goals defining a good society respecting planetary boundaries, that can justify any interpretation of the Anthropocene, and consequently any form and kind of intervention or non-intervention. Self-critical value rationality logically precedes goal rationality. And – by definition – only political theories generate value-rational models of the good society.

In the past centuries political theory has, however, changed, and not all for the better. Classical Greek political philosophy – first and foremost Aristotle – understood the good life (a life 'in harmony with nature') as one lived within a healthy polis, but both that polis itself and the individual's virtues had in turn to be attuned to the local geography, biology and climate. In modern political theories, 'is does not imply ought' usually implies that the natural environment is not supposed to dictate political structures – and where it does, rather than submit to its whims, we make it a duty to overcome nature's limits through mitigation and adaptation of nature. Harmony with nature is no longer a political goal – nature is a means to an end, not part of that end.

In addition, one of the most popular images in medieval political philosophy, that of the polity as a body politic, has lost its appeal as well. A functionalist image of the good society as a system in which each cell has its predetermined role seems to be at odds (though logically it need not be) with our broadly liberal understanding of society as a mechanism to accommodate the realization of divergent and contradictory individual dreams and desires or 'plans of life'. As with nature, it is the social (political, economic, etc.) environment that is supposed to be adapted to the desires of individuals, not the other way around.

A political theory that wants to give guidance to an interventionist wielder of earth system science or offer guidance in dealing with contradictory 'Anthropocene futures' needs both these lost elements: it needs to provide a functional model of the good society, a 'body' delineating the moral limits of individual freedom, and it needs to define what a good nature, a good natural environment, for that society would be, taking account of its physical limits. In our post-postmodern times, ideologies and 'grand narratives' will revive: we need answers to Islamism and populism, but also to Anthropocene technocracy. To answer the latter challenge, and in recognition of earth system science's assumption of the existence of an earth system one and indivisible, political theories will need to evolve into theories of the good body ecologic.

Environmental political thought in general has, since its emergence in the 1980s, been focused on integrating green ideas like sustainability and stewardship in 'classic' political theories (cf. Dobson 2007) without fundamentally changing them. Only the 'naturalist' opponents mentioned earlier, the key thinkers in ecological political thought, have set an example for the Anthropocene advocates by developing 'deep green' theories of human society as part of a body ecologic, e.g. in Robyn Eckersley's *The Green State* (2004). Diverse though these ecological theories may be, they share a deep distrust of 'technofixes', a strong preference for restoration over adaptation, for non-interference over (even beneficially intended) intervention, and for reducing human ambitions and desires and their demands on nature rather than satisfying those ambitions and desires.

Other imperfections aside, the ecologists' idea of a good body ecologic is obviously not what we are looking for. First, it is incompatible with the original advocates' enthusiasm for unlimited ecological and social engineering. Second, it excludes the greater part of the material diversity of multiple Anthropocene futures that, for example, Berkhout would like to offer. Last but by no means least, the ecologists' body ecologic has far less room for the moral and political diversity, and consequently the broadly liberal freedom of lifestyle, that one would want a viable Anthropocene narrative, cleansed of authoritarian and technocratic tendencies, to embrace.

In conclusion, this chapter has illustrated how the urgent tends to crowd out the important: two generations of proponents of the idea of an Anthropocene and of earth system-wide intervention have put technocratic goal-rationality before self-critical value-rationality: little or no reflection has taken place to substantiate which exact answers to the changes defining the Anthropocene would be desirable and appropriate. Addressing that issue will add a third dimension of complexity to the narrative of the Anthropocene: in addition to the natural complexity of the planet's ecology and the psycho-social complexity of human institutions, there is the complicating factor of irreducible political and moral diversity to be taken into account. The ball now lies in the corner of political theory, rather than with the original advocates: developing a broadly liberal theory of the body ecologic lies within its exclusive area of expertise and therefore their primary responsibility. Not until such a framework becomes available can we really assess whether the technologies and policies the two preceding generations of advocates believe to be possible and sellable are also morally admissible.

References

Berkhout, F. (2014) Anthropocene futures. *The Anthropocene Review* 1(2): 154–159.
Biermann, F. (2012) Planetary boundaries and earth system governance: Exploring the links. *Ecological Economics* (81): 4–9.

Biermann, F. (2014) The Anthropocene: A governance perspective. *The Anthropocene Review* 1(1): 57–61.

Bunzl, M. (2008) An ethical assessment of geoengineering. *Bulletin of the Atomic Scientists* 64(2): 18.

Certini, G. and Scalenghe, R. (2015) Is the Anthropocene really worthy of a formal geologic definition? *The Anthropocene Review*. [Online] 17 December. DOI: 10.1177/2053019614563840 [accessed 13 February 2015].

Crutzen, P. and Stoermer, E. (2010) Have we entered the 'Anthropocene'? *International Geosphere-Biosphere Programme* [Online] 31 October. Available from: http://www.igbp.net/news/opinion/opinion/haveweenteredtheanthropocene.5.d8b4c3c12bf3be638a8000578.html [accessed 13 February 2015].

Dalby, S. (2007) Ecological intervention and Anthropocene ethics. *Ethics & International Affairs*. [Online] 21(3). Available from: http://www.ethicsandinternationalaffairs.org/2007/ecological-intervention-and-anthropocene-ethics-full-text/ [accessed 13 February 2015].

Dobson, A. (2007) *Green Political Thought*, 4th edn. London: Routledge.

Eckersley, R. (2004) *The Green State: Rethinking Democracy and Sovereignty*. Cambridge, MA: MIT Press.

Eckersley, R. (2007) Ecological intervention: Prospects and limits. *Ethics & International Affairs*. [Online] 21(3). Available from: http://www.ethicsandinternationalaffairs.org/2007/ecological-intervention-and-anthropocene-ethics-full-text/ [accessed 13 February 2015].

Guillaume, B. (2014) Vernadsky's philosophical legacy: A perspective from the Anthropocene. *The Anthropocene Review* 1(2): 137–146.

Hobbs, R. J., Hallett, L. M., Ehrlich, P. R. and Mooney H. A. (2011) Intervention ecology: Applying ecological science in the twenty-first century. *BioScience* 61(6): 442–450.

Hourdequin, M. (2013) Restoration and history in a changing world: A case study in ethics for the Anthropocene. *Ethics & the Environment* 18(2): 115–134.

Karlsson, R. and Symons J. (2014) Scalability and realist climate insights. *Weather, Climate and Society* 6: 289–292.

Knight, J. (2015) Anthropocene futures: People, resources and sustainability. *The Anthropocene Review*. [Online] DOI: 10.1177/2053019615569318 [accessed 13 February 2015].

Malm, A. and Hornborg, A. (2014) The geology of mankind? A critique of the Anthropocene narrative. *The Anthropocene Review* 1(1): 62–69.

Mark, J. (2009) Hacking the sky, *Earth Island Journal*; http://joun.leb.net/mark09182009.html

McKim, R. (2013) On comparing religions in the Anthropocene. *American Journal of Theology and Philosophy* 34(3): 248–263.

Minteer, B. A. (2012) Geoengineering and ecological ethics in the Anthropocene. *BioScience* 62(10): 857–858.

Oksanen, M. and Siipi, H. (2014) Introduction. In M. Oksanen and H. Siipi (eds.), *The Ethics of Animal Re-creation and Modification: Reviving, Rewilding, Restoring*. Basingstoke: Palgrave Macmillan.

Oldfield, F. and Steffen, W. (2014) Anthropogenic climate change and the nature of Earth System science. *The Anthropocene Review* 1(1): 70–75.

Oldfield, F., Barnosky, A. D., Dearing, J., Fischer-Kowalski, M., McNeill, J., Steffen, W. and Zalasiewicz, J. (2014) The Anthropocene Review: Its significance, implications and the rationale for a new transdisciplinary journal. *The Anthropocene Review* 1(1): 3–7.

Preston, C. J. (2012) Beyond the end of nature: SRM and two tales of artificity for the Anthropocene. *Ethics, Policy & Environment* 15(2): 188–201.

Robock, A. (2008) 20 reasons why geoengineering may be a bad idea. *Bulletin of the Atomic Scientists* 64(2): 14–18.

Rockström, J., Steffen, K., Noone, Å., Persson, F. and Stuart Chapin, III. (2009) A safe operating space for humanity. *Nature* 461: 472–475.

Steffen, W., Grinevald, J., Crutzen, P. and McNeill, J. (2011) The Anthropocene: Conceptual and historical perspectives. *Philosophical Transactions of the Royal Society A* 369: 842–867.

Steffen, W., Broadgate, W., Deutsch, L., Gaffney, O. and Ludwig, C. (2015) The trajectory of the Anthropocene: The Great Acceleration. *The Anthropocene Review*. [Online] DOI: 10.1177/2053019614564785 [accessed 13 February 2015].

Uhrqvist, O. and Linnér, B.-O. (2015) Narratives of the past for Future Earth: The historiography of global environmental change research. *The Anthropocene Review*. [Online] DOI: 10.1177/2053019614567543 [accessed 13 February 2015].

3   Nature and the Anthropocene
The sense of an ending?

Manuel Arias-Maldonado

Introduction

Since it first appeared a few years ago, the notion of the Anthropocene has been gaining ground in the field of environmental studies and now seems to be ubiquitous. Admittedly, the label is appealing, while – or because – the news it communicates is dramatic. The success, then, seems justified. However, there is something else. The Anthropocene might just be what we were waiting for, namely, a notion able to encompass and express a number of shared intuitions about the human place in the world and the state of socionatural relations. In that regard, the Anthropocene provides a framework for discussing such relations from an interdisciplinary perspective, ranging from the natural sciences to the social sciences and the humanities. To some extent, we had been discussing the Anthropocene before we had the concept, lacking, so to speak, the scientific validity that it seemingly provides to an old idea: that human beings are deeply entangled with nature and vice versa.

Yet the coming of the Anthropocene, both literally and epistemologically, does not amount to the closing of any conversation, rather it is the starting point for a new one. Because if we acknowledge that human beings and societies are a major force in nature, that we have transformative powers that have reached a formidable degree, then we have to reflect upon the meaning of this geological shift, as well as upon the normative consequences that it entails. And such is the topic of this chapter. Consequently, it tries to make sense of the Anthropocene by exploring how the latter is related to our understanding of nature and to the historical process that has led to the irreversible social entanglement that it describes. Thus we are dealing with ontological and epistemological questions, but also with crucial aspects of agency: What is the Anthropocene? How can it be approached? Which are the main actors involved in its production and how do they relate to each other?

These are by no means technical questions. They involve normative interrogations that have to do with the position of the human species within nature, both historically and contemporarily: depending on how we see the human species unfolding on Earth, our understanding of the Anthropocene will vary. Apparently pre-political questions end up having fully political consequences insofar as they influence the way in which the Anthropocene itself is framed and hence also the conversation about how to deal with it. In this sense, the meaning of the Anthropocene is provided by the wider history of socionatural relations, upon which a philosophy of the human species can be built that helps us to develop a realistic understanding of this challenging phenomenon. By doing this, an additional layer of complexity is added to the picture, as hybridization stands out as a main feature of current socionatural relations, thus complicating simple attributions of responsibility and making it harder to act urgently to stop the dangers associated with an unorderly Anthropocene.

However, as will soon be emphasized, the Anthropocene is not an unmediated fact, but rather a theoretical construction that tries to describe a complex reality in meaningful terms. Likewise, as such, it is a contested notion. Interestingly, it being originally a scientific hypothesis, the science behind the Anthropocene is not as contested as the associated sociopolitical aspects that ultimately deal with questions of agency, power, and responsibility. That is so because even though the original geological proposition might be refused, the overwhelming evidence supporting this general case – the human colonization of natural systems – is strong enough. And this is what explains the current anthropocenic turn in environmental studies. That said, this turn involve the rise of a counter-narrative, i.e. a critique of the mainstream description of the Anthropocene that I would like to call the 'Counter-Anthropocene'. According to it, the Anthropocene is either a megalomaniac construct (see Wissenburg, this volume) or, more commonly, a new trope of modernity, whose destructive effects can ultimately be attributed to hyper-capitalism.

This chapter is organized as follows. To begin with, I argue that the Anthropocene gives credit to a view of nature that focuses on hybridization and environmental recombination as the main outcomes of the human adaptation to the natural world. Second, I explore some normative implications of the Anthropocene hypothesis, pondering on how it relates to the human–nature dualism and to the claim that nature has ended (see also Hailwood, this volume). A concluding section will explore the implications that these normative questions entail for the governance of the Anthropocene.

Nature and the Anthropocene

The Anthropocene is an overarching concept that has appeared and gradually risen to prominence in the last decade, embodying scientifically the idea that the relationship between human beings and nature has shifted dramatically in the course of the last centuries. The Anthropocene tries to captures the quantitative shift in the relationship between humans and the global environment, as provoked by the massive influence of the former in the natural systems that constitute the latter. Consequently, the term Anthropocene suggests that the Earth is moving out of its current geological epoch, called the Holocene, and that human activity is largely responsible for this exit, i.e. that humankind has become a global geological force in its own right (see Steffen et al., 2011).

Yet it is worth noting that the term Anthropocene denotes two different, albeit complementary, meanings. On the one hand, it is a period of time, one that, according to an increasingly large number of natural scientists, should be recognized as a new geological epoch. This is so because of the socionatural events that take place within it. But those very events that may be summed up in the anthropogenic transformation of nature at a global scale lead us to use the term in a different way: as an epistemic tool. In other words, the Anthropocene is (i) a *chronology* that, by comprising a number of processes and phenomena whose common feature is the anthropogenic influence on the planet, ends up designing as well (ii) a given *state* of socionatural relations.

What the science behind the notion suggests is that natural and social systems are coupled and the extent of the anthropogenic influence on ecological systems and natural processes is unprecedented (Liu et al., 2007; Ellis et al., 2010; Ellis, 2011). Climate change is the most spectacular outcome of this shift, but it is far from being the only one – disappearance of pristine land, urbanization, industrial farming, transportation infrastructure, mining activities, loss of biodiversity, organism modification, technological leaps, growing hybridization are also on the list. Thus, it is a quantitative shift that constitutes also a qualitative change. Or rather it is the human *realization* of a change undergone some time ago. And even if the notion is finally not recognized by geologists or fails to capture the public imagination, the reality it describes will not fade away.

In this regard, the Anthropocene may be said to constitute the geological translation of the idea that nature has ended. Furthermore, I would like to suggest that the Anthropocene has *confirmed* the plausibility of a particular view of nature and the corresponding relations between the social and the natural.

But which is this view? Which is the understanding of nature and socionatural relations involved in the Anthropocene hypothesis or that the latter can support? If we put it briefly, the Anthropocene confirms that society and nature are not two separate entities influencing each other, but rather that there exists a socionatural entanglement – that is, an irreversible, complex and increasingly hybrid socionatural system. Yet, paradoxically, this does not mean that there remains no *separation* between human beings and nature. Ironically, it is because we have separated ourselves from nature in a certain way throughout history that this deep entanglement has been produced. In fact, that very separation allows us to be aware of this entanglement and offers us the chance to rearrange socionatural relations in a new, in some regards more refined ways. Or at least the chance to try it.

To further reflect on this point, let us take a reasonable starting point for isolating what nature is: nature is that what is not artificial. Thus we can understand it, following the oft-quoted definition by John Stuart Mill, as 'all the powers existing in either the outer or the inner world and everything which takes place by means of those powers' (Mill, 1998, p. 8). Therefore, the concept of nature would cover all those entities and processes that come into being or exist without any human intervention. Nature can then be characterized as a self-generating and self-sustaining entity defined by its *telos*, i.e. by its ability to maintain its organization in the presence of external forces and to exert its own force on its environment while trying to maintain its integrity (Heyd, 2005, pp. 4–5). According to this teleological view, nature is autonomous from human beings. The autonomy of nature derives from its very existence. Nature is thus,

> what has come into existence, continues to exist, and finally, disintegrates/ decays, thereby going out of existence, in principle, entirely independent of human volition or intentionality, of human control, manipulation, or intervention.
>
> (Lee, 2005, p. 59)

Yet is this definition useful? Maybe not. Natural history is also social history, that is, one that has spread the human influence in so many ways that it is now difficult to tell whether human beings are *absent* or not from a given natural process or a certain natural entity. Are domesticated animals, human-designed rivers, or managed ecosystems still natural? If we stick to a strict distinction between the natural and the artificial, they are not. Not even the climate is completely 'natural' anymore!

This suggests that we should go beyond a definition of nature that relies on the absence of any trace of human influence. Nicole Karafyllis (2003) has proposed the term *biofact* to name those entities whose origin and formation have been anthropogenically influenced, directly or indirectly, irrespective of the actual *visibility* of that influence. This notion of the visibility of the anthropogenic influence is – as climate change again shows – more important than it seems, especially in regard to the public reaction to certain policies and socionatural possibilities (like transgenics, aquaculture or climate geoengineering). The wider historical process can also be referred to as one of hybridization, i.e. the environmental recombination that results after humanly originated processes and artefacts have exerted a variable degree of influence on natural beings and processes (see also Latour, 2004; Biesecker and Hofmeister, 2006, 2009).

For instance, the process of hybridization in the Anthropocene has resulted in altered patterns of biodiversity. A telling example is that of the rocks recently found on a Hawaiian beach: probably formed from melting plastic in fires lit by humans who were camping or fishing, they are cobbled together from plastic, volcanic rock, beach sand, seashells and corals. They have been dubbed, accordingly, 'plastiglomerate' (see Corcoran et al., 2014). Likewise, human predation on mammals has been recognized as the principal driver for changes in phenotypic traits of exploited species in many areas (Darimont et al., 2009). At the same time, species invasions have become normalized and constitute now one of the most significant anthropogenic changes in the biosphere. This process, by which some generalist species – those accommodating best to human systems – take over large portions of the planet, pushing out the specialist species that developed in isolation, has been named 'Homogocene', a term coined by zoologist Gordon Orians (see Rosenzweig, 2001). It is a term that rivals Anthropocene as an appropriate description of the current state of socionatural relations.

Hybridization thus refers to a view of the world as made up of heterogeneous materialities churned together in a way that breaks down the distinction between subject and object, the natural and the artificial, the digital and the analogical. Thus it identifies a whole set of agencies within a relational web, fostering a new way of seeing reality itself. In sum, nature is not just 'out there', nor is it found already 'made'. Rather it is a sociopolitical space or a technological artefact that is brought into being and gains meaning through representational practices and technologies (Baldwin, 2003). This view has become widespread in the social sciences, where simple 'nature' has been replaced by concepts such as social nature, second nature or hybrid nature, all them the product of a relational agency that involves both human and non-human 'actants' (Pollini, 2013, p. 30).

It has already been suggested that socionatural history can be read as a long process of hybridization by which nature becomes less and less autonomous, so that an increasing number of natural processes, beings and forms are innerly or outwardly – or both – influenced by human actions and social processes, whether intentionally or not. In this regard, the Anthropocene can be understood as the 'Great Hybridization'. At the same time, however, this socionatural intimacy means that nature is also a force in social history, since the co-production of nature is tantamount to the co-production of society, i.e. a socionatural co-production. In turn, this opens up all kind of interesting questions about agency: the agency of humanity and the agency of nature, as well as particular agencies and their relative weight. The climate, for instance, possesses agency – it influences social decisions and constrains human choices. But the latter have, in turn, changed the climate. So, who influences whom?

Therefore, the relational ontology that is associated with hybridization allows for multiple agencies distributed in networks and including non-human entities and processes (see Bakker and Bridge, 2006, pp. 17–18; Latour, 2004). There exists a network of agencies among which, though, the human one remains the most powerful, i.e. both the most disruptive *and* creative. Then again, this only makes sense if we can make distinctions and attribute *hierarchies of agency* when carefully observing particular assemblages and processes. Otherwise, everything is lost in an undifferentiated network of actors and influences. Asserting the primacy of human agency means recognizing (not necessarily *liking*) the exceptional extent of human transformative powers, as well as emphasizing a crucial difference between human actors and natural actants: a self-awareness that goes hand in hand with the conscious development of greater transformative powers and even the ability to measure the effects of them, in order to prevent its undesirable side-effects. In short, some associates within the assemblage are more relevant than others.

In sum, history matters more than ontology. Swyngedow (1999, p. 147) has emphasized this, pointing to the ontological priority of the process of hybridization over the hybrid itself, as 'a process of production, of becoming, of perpetual transgression'. As a metaphor, as Hinchliffe (2007, p. 51) argues, hybridity allows for change in all parties as they relate to one another, and for novelty to be produced – one that is not reducible to component parts. Consequently, there is much to be gained in replacing an ontology of division (nature/culture, body/mind and so on) by an ontology of configuration.

After all, neither naturalness nor hybridization are absolute categories. On the contrary, they are relative, depending on the degree of human influence upon each biological process, natural being or ecosystem. Naturalness is a gradable reality. Dieter Birnbacher's (2006) distinction between nature in a *genetic* sense and nature in a *qualitative* sense is very useful in this context. The former refers to the moment of nature's coming into existence without human intervention, whereas the latter alludes to the appearance of natural forms, which can be, and actually are, affected by human beings. Genetic nature's description is *historical*, whereas qualitative nature's description is *phenomenological*. Therefore, nature as an ahistoric essence is not the same as nature as an historic process. We are concerned about the constraints exerted by the former, as well as with our interactions with the latter.

To embrace the idea of the Anthropocene is thus to advance towards an understanding of nature that takes human influence on it seriously – before considering the moral implications of that influence. What the Anthropocene hypothesis states is that there is no way back for human beings, because we are not just *embedded* in nature, but actually *entangled* with it in an irreversible and complex way. We are living in the Anthropocene and we should just start making sense of it thinking within this new box.

Making sense of the Anthropocene

So far I have argued that the Anthropocene comes to confirm the plausibility of a view of nature that is informed by the history of socionatural relations. Therefore, we should distinguish between that which nature is *ontologically* and that which it becomes *historically*, i.e. after an ever-increasing interaction between human beings and societies. Such increase would have led to the actual transformation of nature into human environment and to a process of growing hybridization and recombination whose final result is an encompassing human influence on natural beings, processes and ecosystems. Of course, the influence of the latter on human beings has to be taken into account as well – since every relation operates both ways.

Again, climate is a telling example. By unwillingly changing the climate, we are forced to adapt ourselves to a phenomenon that exerts a massive influence on human life conditions. Yet the disturbed climate that acts as a constraint on us is not purely 'natural' anymore, without ceasing to be so: its current form is the product of our influence on it over the last centuries. Furthermore, we are also a part of nature. As it happens, we are a dominant species that goes beyond its ecological niche and transforms the environment. In that regard, there is nothing 'unnatural' about climate change.

Be that as it may, there are two important normative consequences stemming from the Anthropocene hypothesis: one is the idea that the human–nature dualism is untenable, the other the proposition that nature has ended. They are closely related to each other and revolve around the idea of the hybridity.

Dualism and the Anthropocene.

On the one hand, we have the deceivingly simple question of the human–natural dualism. How can any separation between human beings and nature be sustained in the light of the Anthropocene? The coupling of natural and social systems would precisely involve the opposite suggestion: that the human and the natural cannot be separated, because they have never been separated. Any distinction between these two realms would then be just a clever representation of the world that happens to meet human expectations as to what can be done *with* and *to* nature, but it possesses no rational ground whatsoever. Human beings are natural beings and the fact that the social and the natural are so intermingled comes to show that we cannot escape to natural constrictions and planetary boundaries. In other words, the Anthropocene would put an end to the typically modern assumption of human exceptionalism.

However, it might not be that simple. For one thing, the way in which socionatural history has unfolded complicates an outright refusal of the human–nature dualism. This is an important and subtle point that can be easily misunderstood. To begin with, it is difficult not to acknowledge that humans have in fact separated themselves from nature in a meaningful way. Human beings have proven exceptional, no matter which is the moral judgement that such exceptionalism and its 'products' may deserve. It is hard to deny that humans have been able to transcend their own ecological niche. They have done so by creating an artificial, human-made world that sets them apart from nature – between the natural and the artificial realms.

This aspect of human behaviour is linked to natural evolution by the niche-construction perspective on the latter, a theory introduced to evolutionary biology by Richard Lewontin in the 1980s. Instead of subscribing to the view that organisms always adapt to their environments and never vice versa, it recognizes the evidence that organisms *change* their environments, thus describing a dynamic, reciprocal interaction between the processes of natural selection and niche construction (see Laland and Brown, 2006). As it happens, culture is a key factor to explain the remarkable magnitude of *human* niche construction. Cultural niche construction is that in which learned and socially transmitted behaviour modifies environments, amplifying the evolutionary feedback loop generated by niche construction. Although niche construction is a general process observed in all living organisms, human beings are especially effective niche constructors due to their capacity for culture. And although it is debatable whether niche construction should be regarded one of the primary causes of evolution, there is an overwhelmingly compelling fact that supports the assertion that niche construction is, from the point of view of the species, adaptive: human population growth (ibid, p. 101) – an Anthropocene-friendly argument, if there ever was one! An evolutionary explanation of human behaviour and culture is thus compatible with the recognition of humanity's *exception* – that of a psycho-biological animal that is simultaneously inside nature *and* apart from it.

Needless to say, there was no original separation between humans and nature. Yet the human–nature division has *become* real with the passing of time, as human beings evolved and colonized and transformed nature in increasingly sophisticated ways. Such separation has been produced through processes such as the differentiation between the urban and the rural life and the digitalization of everyday life. Dualism is not so much *ontological* as it is *historical*, i.e. an emergent order that is produced by human beings in the course of their adaptation to nature. Crucially, such dualism is originated in the practical realm of socionatural relations, where the entanglement between the human, the social and the natural has never ceased to increase. Needless to say, humans remain subject to nature's laws, but they are also able to change some natural conditions which would have seemed immutable in the past – ranging from contraception to genetic manipulation. They are embedded in nature but can also detach themselves from nature.

Actually, this emergent dualism is completely consistent with the Anthropocene hypothesis. It is not ontological, but an emergent quality of socionatural relations that is produced via a double-edged process. On the one hand, humans penetrate in nature and the latter is more and more transformed and coupled with social systems, thus creating the kind of entanglement that sustains the very notion of the Anthropocene. On the other, as this mutual imbrication is reinforced, humans separate themselves from nature both cognitively and symbolically. This nuanced view of dualism allows us to avoid the conceptual trap of declaring dualism non-existent.

Moreover, an historical dualism is the logical derivation of the Anthropocene hypothesis, because the degree of human colonization described by the latter could not have been reached without such historical process – in short, that in which human beings separate gradually from nature in the act of aggressively adapting *themselves* to it by adapting *it* to them. Thus the corresponding proposition that nature is socially constructed.

Traditionally, the idea that nature is socially 'constructed' was meant to express that our perception of nature determines our relationship with it. In turn, this social condition would also mean that there is no *single* universal nature, because different contexts, cultures, social positions and historical moments will produce disparate visions of nature. Yet if we talk about socionatural history, we refer to the human penetration into the environment through nature's transformation, consumption and use. In other words, the social construction of nature implies not only a cultural apprehension of nature, but also a physical re-construction of it, a human impact in the surrounding world that never leaves nature unchanged (see Arias-Maldonado, 2011). The latter is literally re-constructed by human beings in deeper and deeper ways, hence affecting realms of nature so far considered beyond the human sphere of influence.

Of course, this social reconstruction produces unintended side-effects, as climate change dramatically shows. Yet both intentional and unintentional changes are embodied in the Anthropocene notion, which alludes to the final outcome of a process of reciprocal influence comprising: (i) intentional human modifications; (ii) unintentional side-effects of the latter; and (iii) natural influences on human beings and societies. Therefore, it is not inappropriate to argue that the Anthropocene is actually the result of the social construction of nature rightly understood.

The Anthropocene as the end of nature

Furthermore, the Anthropocene may be seen as the confirmation that nature has ended. Again, this is a provocative formulation that has to be carefully elaborated – yet there is more than provocation in it. If we leave aside the supposed end of nature as an idea or symbol, the most important sense in which this end can be argued for refers to nature's reality. The proposition is simple: as human intervention in nature has grown dramatically, it has become more and more difficult to speak of a nature that is free from human modification. Although nature was relatively independent from society, now, after history, it is not. The limits between the natural and the social are blurred. It can even be said that nature has morphed into human environment: the objective nature that existed long ago has been integrated into human history through labour and cultural appropriation. This process entails the end of nature.

But the latter is not so much the philosophical undermining of nature's vitality that took place under the rule of mechanicism, as it is an actual process of human colonization of the natural world. Again, obviously, although there is no such thing as an ontological end of nature, it is not ontology that matters when socionatural interaction is considered. On the contrary, what matters is the multiplicity of particular relations between nature and human beings. In this regard, the end of nature has a twofold meaning: (i) natural processes can no longer be defined as independent from human influence; and (ii) natural forms and processes have been influenced by humans to a very high degree. Sometimes, human intervention is manifest; sometimes, it is not. Some other times, as with the climate, is not even planned. But that hardly makes a *philosophical* difference: only a matter of degrees differentiate the urban park from the jungle. From this point of view, nature cannot be defined anymore by its independence from human beings and society.

There is no shortage of concepts to express this. It had been said that we live now in a 'post-natural world' (McKibben, 1990, p. 60), made of a 'created environment' (Giddens, 1991, p. 124) which has put an end to the antithesis between nature and society, so that nature is not understood anymore outside society and vice versa (Beck, 1992, p. 80). We face 'the end of the wild' (Meyer, 2006). Therefore, a trait that was exclusive to mankind – the hybrid position between nature and artefact – now encompasses nature at large. Admittedly, the interaction between nature and society has always existed, but it is the intensity of it that is unprecedented. This is precisely what the Anthropocene demonstrates, i.e. that the idea of nature as an independent entity is untenable in view of the degree in which natural and social systems are entangled. Biologist Earl Ellis concurs:

> From a philosophical point of view, nature is now human nature; there is no more wild nature to be found, just ecosystems in different states of human interaction, differing in wildness and humanness.
>
> (Ellis, 2011, p. 1027)

Apparently, it could be argued that the Anthropocene hypothesis fits *too well* in a number of assumptions about the socionatural relation. Because it does. But there is nothing suspicious about it, because those assumptions were already built upon the intuition that something like the Anthropocene – minus the name – was taking place. By linking the Anthropocene to these conceptualizations (an emergent dualism stemming from human exceptionalism, the social re-construction of nature, the proposition that nature has ended) we do more than making sense of the Anthropocene itself: we realize that the Anthropocene makes perfect sense.

Rethinking socionatural relations in the Anthropocene

If we take the Anthropocene hypothesis seriously, which are the practical consequences that follow for the rearrangement of socionatural relations? More to the point, does the Anthropocene entail a substantial change of our understanding of such relations and nature itself? These are relevant and complicated questions with no single answers. Mine is that the Anthropocene stresses the need for a postnatural understanding of nature and socionatural relations – a shift that does *not* preclude a call to the protection of that what is left of nature. Those who claim that the Anthropocene is not just a scientific issue, but also a moral and hence a political one, are right (see Ellis and Trachtenberg, 2013). Yet we need to understand what the Anthropocene says about socionatural relations before we can articulate a moral answer to it.

By recognizing the extent to which society and nature are entangled in irreversible ways and the fact that human beings have become major forces in natural change (without ceasing to be influenced by a natural environment that is also, in turn, a force in social change), the Anthropocene confirms that a human retreat from nature is but a delusion. Society and human beings are mixed up with nature. Paraphrasing Marx, human beings have not just thought about nature, they have transformed it. And they will keep doing it, because that seems to be their way of being-in-the-world.

Now, we reach a tricky point. However, if we claim that the occurrence of the Anthropocene is a confirmation for keeping business as usual regarding socionatural relations, we would be incurring in a naturalistic fallacy. Therefore, it is important to stress that, although the Anthropocene *does* confirm that no human retreat is possible anymore, a policy of retreat (for instance via a radical mitigation against climate change) might be defended. For those who consider that our past relations with nature were both mistaken and avoidable, a correction of the former might be precisely the point. In other words, a change in the human way of being-in-the-world would constitute a philosophical and political program for radical green change.

Yet it could as well be argued that the Anthropocene gives us a wider perspective about human relations with nature. As I have suggested, the end of nature has *already* occurred, as the logical consequence of a process of human colonization of nature which should be considered 'natural' rather than a matter of choice or a historical contingency. And it seems more realistic to depart from here than to propose a complete change in the human relation with the natural world. The latter can and should be changed – but it is doubtful that it can be radically reshaped. A more promising normative claim for the Anthropocene would then be to *refine* our domination of nature, which is not and neither can be absolute nor perfect, in order to achieve sustainability while maintaining the best features of our liberal, pluralistic societies.

Admittedly, human domination of nature is *complicated* by the Anthropocene. It signals a number of planetary boundaries that must be respected, points to several uncertainties regarding the coupling of social and natural systems, alerts to the possibility of reaching tipping points (see Röckstrom et al., 2009). All in all, it seems to confirm Eric Katz's warning: 'Nature's control is a dream, a delusion, a hallucination' (Katz, 1992, p. 267). For once, there are natural processes that remain inaccessible to us, interactions whose consequences we cannot predict, phenomena of such a range that we cannot influence them. The Anthropocene could actually be the proof of how dangerous it is to mess with nature – climate change being the most telling example of that general idea.

Precisely, one of the claims made by the counter-anthropocentrists – admittedly a loose group of critics rather than an organized opposition – is that the Anthropocene notion betrays a typically 'modern' language that insists on outdated notions of agency and control. The Anthropocene denotes the seemingly reprehensible language of modernity and the Enlightenment, presenting itself as a grand narrative (Dibley, 2012; Chakrabarty, 2009). This, in turn, puts the Anthropocene in connection with global capitalism as a characteristic modern force, whose role in the transformation of nature is hard to deny (see Worster, 1990). In that vein, a scientific approach that makes use of a quantitative metric homogenizes human agency and responsibility (Luke, 2009). As Malm and Hornborg put it, 'humanity seems far too slender an abstraction to carry the burden of causality' (Malm and Hornborg, 2014, p. 4). Many humans, for instance, are not party to the fossil fuel economy that is causing climate change. Universal narratives should then be avoided (Liverman, 2009; O'Brien and Barnett, 2013). After all, abstractions simplify agency – the greater the abstraction, the simpler the attribution. But there actually are different human societies, groups, even individuals: each with their own history of causation.

However, against the counter-anthropocentist claim, this a matter of perspective. A species viewpoint that stresses the universal impulse towards aggressive adaptation makes as much sense as the careful analysis of particular culturally driven sociohistorical processes in which different agencies can be identified. On the other hand, the inability to exert a complete control over socionatural relations is the logical consequence of our gains in knowledge: the more we know about socionatural relations, the more uncertainty we must face. As Innerarity puts it (2012, p. 5), we might rather be 'ignorance societies' instead of 'knowledge societies', that is, societies that 'make progress not by increasing their knowledge but by learning to manage various forms of ignorance: doubt, probability, risk, and uncertainty' (ibid, p. 5). Such is the language of the Anthropocene, one of complexity and interdependence that mirrors the main features of socionatural relations themselves. But the hardness of the task is no reason for abandoning it. Increasing our control of nature *and* refining it in order to reasonably protect natural forms is a feasible programme for environmental political theory and society at large.

Thus seen, domination can be rephrased as the control – a transformative control – of the human interaction with nature. Nature's processes and entities do not have to be thoroughly manipulated for that dominion to be carried out. Likewise, a domination so conceived does not have to be equated with nature's *destruction*, inasmuch as it can designate its active and conscious *transformation*. In fact, the history of socionatural relations is also the story of human stewardship and human–nature symbiosis (see Radkau, 2000). Insofar as a conscious and deliberate purpose is applied onto an inherently dynamic relationship, domination acquires a reflective condition that makes full sense in the context of a refined socionatural relationship (one which dominion itself has made possible). Maybe the problem lies partly in the word's connotations. We might then rather talk about human *control* of nature. We could even say that a blind domination of nature is replaced by a conscious effort to exert control of the socionatural entanglement.

Therefore, correcting the side-effects of the human colonization of nature involves the management of a system that has emerged from socionatural interactions and mixture. This, in turn, is a technologically mediated process – we would not even know about climate change had we not the scientific instruments that stem from the same process that provoked it in the first place. It is here that the notion of *technonatures* can be usefully employed. It is a term proposed by White and Wilbert in order to emphasize the central role that social power has played in the constitution of landscape and our environment, thus casting a sceptical eye 'over the idea that a politics of the environment can be usefully grounded in terms of the rhetoric of defending the pure, the authentic, or an idealized past' (White and Wilbert, 2009, p. 5). Such a term.

> seeks to highlight a growing range of voices ruminating over the claim not only that we are inhabiting diverse social natures but also that knowledges of our worlds are, within such social natures, ever more technologically mediated, produced, enacted, and contested, and, furthermore, that diverse peoples find themselves, or perceive themselves, as ever more *entangled* with

things – that is, with technological, ecological, cultural, urban, and ecological networks and diverse hybrid materialities and non-human agencies.

(White and Wilbert, 2009, p. 6)

As mentioned earlier, this perspective also underlines the fact that agency is not confined to human beings, because non-humans of all kinds can also be active in the production and reproduction of our world. Let us stick to our example: the climate has always been a major environmental factor in shaping social life and has forced humans to adapt to very different conditions. As a result of industrialization, it was unintentionally altered by human beings in a way that is forcing them to adopt radical measures if the catastrophic consequences of an ever-growing Earth temperature are to be avoided. It can be thus said that climate has become an agent of environmental *and* thus social change. Moreover, just as the natural world has become *the* human environment, climate itself has *become* a technonature, as it has been influenced– and is measured and studied – by technological means.

Therefore, human strategies to deal with this entanglement cannot be the traditional ones advocated by classical environmentalism. Anthropocene itself can be said to be a giant technonature. In fact, human beings are mostly cyborgs – but that is another story. Hybridization, fungible capital, ecological restoration, technological interventions, even climate engineering: these are the instruments that the control of socionatural relations in the Anthropocene seems to call for (see Arias-Maldonado, 2015). A more enticing narrative for environmentalism – or for sustainability beyond environmentalism – seems then to be in order. The richness of the human species should be emphasized, a richness that is material as much as it is intellectual (see Kersten, 2013). Up to now, the colonization of nature has helped to provide that wealth – the corollary of that historical process being, precisely, the Anthropocene. Now, it is time to *refine* the human control of nature, rearranging the socionatural entanglement in a more enlightened, reflective way. It will not 'liberate' nature, but it will protect the remaining natural forms in the context of a highly technological world that is rapidly in the making.

In sum, nature is ended, but the Anthropocene is born. It would be desirable that environmental thought does not shy away from the challenged posed by the latter.

Conclusion: An ending that makes sense

Although it may sounds preposterous, the Anthropocene is both the reminder that nature has ended and the best hope for its resurrection. By measuring and emphasizing the degree of the human colonization of nature, the Anthropocene states the obvious in a powerful way: that there is almost no nature left untouched. This is neither surprising nor absurd, but rather the logical consequence of the aggressive adaptation to the environment that signals the human presence on Earth. And although that also means that the separation between humanity and nature is ontologically untenable, it also explains the historical emergence of a dualism that the Anthropocene somewhat reverses: whereas human beings came out of nature, now nature becomes humanized and morphs into human environment. The whole socionatural entanglement that follows therefrom may end up being a gigantic maladaptation that leads to ecological apocalypse – but it may as well not.

Be that as it may, the normative implications of the Anthropocene are yet to be elucidated, after the notion itself is weighed and discussed. On my part, I have stressed the need to rearrange socionatural relations departing from the *fact* of hybridization, that is, taking into account that nature is a gradable reality mixed up with human beings and social products in an inextricable and promiscuous way. In that context, the Anthropocene calls for an enlightened control of nature, that is, a reflective control of socionatural relations that includes the protection of the remaining natural forms and processes (those that are less affected by social influence and retain a greater appearance of naturalness).

Such an option is not uncontroversial. On the contrary, a number of critics whose contributions amount to an alternative view of the Anthropocene – one that might be called the Counter-Anthropocene – openly contest this view. Emphasizing the urgency of the topic and allocating the responsibility in structural features of the capitalistic system, they tend to favour a radical democratic solution that opens up the political imagination, politicizing what apparently remains outside the political scope of democratic decisions, namely the economic system. What the particular alternatives are, is unclear, but de-growth and a reinforcement of local communities as privileged sites for making the transition towards sustainability seem to be among them (see Barry, 2012).

Notwithstanding the general validity of these arguments, this chapter has suggested that a realistic politics for the Anthropocene begins in the proper understanding of a complex phenomenon whose causation lies ultimately in the particular human way-of-being on Earth. In particular, I have emphasized how an aggressive human adaptation to nature culminates in the emergence of an historical – rather than ontological – dualism that ironically goes hand in hand with an ever-deeper socionatural entanglement whose final outcome is a general process of hybridization.

In that context, despite the recognition of multiple agencies and of a relational ontology that deprives human beings of their monopoly of influence, the latter continue to be the major actors in this planetary drama. Although this should translate into a clear attribution of responsibility, it should be remembered that the universal impulse towards adaptation and betterment has not properly been a reflective one until very recently. The Anthropocene might even be conceptualized as the final stage of such process of self-recognition. The corresponding effort to rearrange and refine socionatural relations is both relatively urgent and absolutely difficult. Relatively urgent, because human beings can adapt to new natural circumstance better than pessimists claim. Absolutely difficult, because the complexity involved cannot be minimised. That is why the modern tools of science and technology should not be set aside, but are, as they have always been in the course of the long evolutionary history of mankind, key to the survival and betterment of the species. The experiment, after all, cannot be stopped. It might thus better be successful.

References

Arias-Maldonado, M. (2011) Let's make it real: in defence of a realistic constructivism. *Environmental Ethics* 33(4): 377–393.

Arias-Maldonado, M. (2015) *Environment and Society. Socionatural Relations in the Anthropocene*. Heidelberg: Springer.

Bakker, K. and Bridge, G. (2006) Material worlds? Resource geographies and the "matter of nature". *Progress in Human Geography* 30(1): 5–27.

Baldwin, A. (2003) The nature of the boreal forest: Governmentality and forest-nature. *Space and Culture* 6(4): 415–428.

Barry, J. (2012) *The Politics of Actually Existing Unsustainability*. Oxford: Oxford University Press.

Beck, U. (1992) *Risk Society. Towards a New Modernity*. London: Sage.

Biesecker, A. and Hofmeister, S. (2006) *Die Neuerfindung des Ökonomischen. Ein (re) produktionstheoretischer Beitrag zur Sozialökolosgischen Forschung*. Munich: Oekom.

Biesecker, A. and Hofmeister, S. (2009) Starke Nachhaltigkeit fordert eine Ökonomie der (Re)Produktivität. In T. Egan-Krieger (ed), *Die Greifswalder Theorie starker Nachhaltigkeit*. Marburg: Metropolis-Verlag.

Birnbacher, D. (2006) *Natürlichkeit*. Berlin: Walter de Gruyter.

Chakrabarty, D. (2009) The climate of history: Four theses. *Critical Inquiry* 35(2): 197–222.

Corcoran, P., Moore, C. and Jazvac, K. (2014) An anthropogenic marker horizon in the future rock record. *Geological Society of America Toda* 24(6): 4–8.

Darimont, C., Carlson, S., Kinnison, M., Paquet, P., Reimchen, T. and Wilmers, C. (2009) Human predators outpace other agents of trait change in the wild. *Proceedings of the National Academy of Sciences* 106: 952–954.

Dibley B. (2012) The shape of things to come: Seven theses on the Anthropocene and attachment. *Australian Humanities Review* 52: 139–158.

Ellis, E. C. (2011) Anthropogenic transformation of the terrestrial biosphere. *Philosophical Transactions of the Royal Society* 369: 1010–1035.

Ellis, M. and Trachtenberg, Z. (2013) Which Anthropocene is it to be? Beyond geology to a moral and public discourse. *Earth's Future* 2(2): 122–125.

Ellis, E., Goldewijk, K., Siebert, S., Lightman, D. and Ramankutty, N. (2010) Anthropogenic transformation of the biomes, 1700 to 2000. *Global Ecology and Biogeography* 19: 589–606.

Giddens, A. (1991) *The Consequences of Modernity*. Cambridge: Polity.

Heyd, T. (ed) (2005) *Recognizing the Autonomy of Nature. Theory and Practice*. New York: Columbia University Press.

Hinchliffe, S. (2007) *Geographies of Nature. Societies, Environment, Ecologies*. London: Sage.

Innerarity, D. (2012) Power and knowledge: The politics of the knowledge society. *European Journal of Social Theory* 18(1): 3–16.

Karafyllis, N. (2003) Das Wesen der Biofakte. In Karafyllis, N. (ed), *Biofakte. Versuch über den Menschen zwischen Artefakf und Lebewesen*. Paderborn: Mentis, pp. 11–26.

Katz, E. (1992) The big lie: Human restoration of nature. *Research in Philosophy and Technology* 12: 231–241.

Kersten, J. (2013) The enjoyment of complexity: A new political anthropology for the Anthropocene. In Trischler, H. (ed), *Anthropocene. Envisioning the Future of the Age of Human*. Munich: Rachel Carson Center Perspectives, pp. 39–56.

Laland, K. and Brown, G. (2006) Niche construction, human behavior, and the adaptive-lag hypothesis. *Evolutionary Anthropology* 15: 95–104.

Latour, B. (2004) *Politics of Nature. How to Bring the Sciences into Democracy*. Cambridge, MA: Harvard University Press.

Lee, K. (2005) Is nature autonomous? In Heyd, T. (ed), *Recognizing the Autonomy of Nature. Theory and Practice*. New York: Columbia University Press, pp. 54–74.

Liu, J., Dietz, T., Carpenter, S., Alberti, M., Folke, C. et al. (2007) Complexity of coupled human and natural systems. *Science* 317: 1513.

Liverman, D. M. (2009) Conventions of climate change: Constructions of danger and the dispossession of the atmosphere. *Journal of Historical Geography* 35(2): 279–296.

Luke, T. W. (2009) Developing planetary accountancy: Fabricating nature as stock, service and system for green governmentality. *Current Perspectives in Social Theory* 26: 129–159.

Malm, A. and Hornborg, A. (2014) The geology of mankind? A critique of the Anthropocene narrative. *The Anthropocene Review* 1(1): 62–69.

McKibben, B. (1990) *The End of Nature*. New York: Anchor Books.

Meyer, S. (2006) *The End of the Wild*. Cambridge, MA: MIT Press/Boston Review.

Mill, J. S. (1998) *Three Essays on Religion*. Amherst: Prometheus Books.

O'Brien, K. and Barnett, J. (2013) Global environmental change and human security. *Annual Review of Environmental Resources* 38: 373–391.

Pollini, J. (2013) Bruno Latour and the ontological dissolution of nature in the social sciences: A critical review. *Environmental Values* 22: 25–42.

Radkau, J. (2000) *Natur und Macht. Eine Weltgeschichte der Umwelt*. Munich: C. H. Beck.

Röckstrom, J., Steffen, W., Noone, K., Perssson, A., Stuart, F. et al. (2009) A safe operating space for humanity. *Nature* 461: 472–475.

Rosenzweig, M. (2001) The four questions: What does the introduction of exotic species do to diversity? *Evolutionary Ecology Research* 3: 361–367.

Steffen, W., Grinevald, J., Crutzen, P. and McNeill, J. (2011) The Anthropocene: Conceptual and historical perspectives. *Philosophical Transactions of the Royal Society* 369: 842–867.

Swyngedow, E. (1999) Modernity and hybridity: Nature, *regeneracionismo*, and the production of the Spanish waterscape, 1890–1930. *Annals of the Association of American Geographers* 89: 443–465.

White, D. F. and Wilbert, C. (eds) (2009) *Technonatures. Environments, Technologies, Spaces, and Places in the Twenty-First Century*. Ontario: Wilfrid Laurier University Press.

Worster, D. (1990) Transformations of the Earth: Toward an agroecological perspective in history. *The Journal of American History* 76(4): 1087–1106.

4 Anthropocene

Delusion, celebration and concern

Simon Hailwood

Introduction

If we consider the facts reported by the relevant environmental sciences and other reputable monitors of environmental conditions, it seems reasonable to say they constitute an unprecedented, urgent and complex environmental crisis. Such facts include the reality and likely consequences of anthropogenic climate change; that we are living through the sixth Mass Extinction Event known to science (the first to be anthropogenic): loss of habitat, water acidification, soil erosion and so on. We are also often told that at least some of these facts are disputed. But because the majority of experts in the relevant scientific disciplines accept their general thrust it is reasonable to treat them as given. However, largely through the work of atmospheric chemist Paul Crutzen and others, including ecologist Erle Ellis, and geologists Jan Zalasiewicz and Michael Ellis, it is becoming popular to say the scale of the environmental crisis requires a reclassification of our geological era (see also Wissenburg, this volume). We should no longer take ourselves to be living in the Holocene (the interglacial period that succeeded the Pleistocene some 10–15,000 years BP). The scale and complexity of recent and ongoing anthropogenic impacts show that humanity is now one of the great forces shaping the Earth; and this means we live in the 'New Human' era, the *Anthropocene* (Crutzen, 2002). There is some disagreement over when exactly to place the onset of the Anthropocene within the confines of historical time, rather cramped as that is compared to the vastness of traditional geological timeframes. It is sometimes held to have begun 'around 1800 with the onset of industrialization' (Steffen et al., 2007). In this case James Watt's design of the steam engine in 1784 was a landmark in planetary, not just human, history. It is becoming more popular though to associate it with the 'Great Acceleration' in industrial output and appearance of radioactive residues of nuclear weapons testing 'around 1950' (cf. Baskin, 2015, p. 12).

The question I consider is *why should we want* to associate the environmental crisis situation with a new geological era – the Anthropocene? I am not questioning the natural scientific rationale for rebranding our geological era, although it is worth mentioning that the revision is currently only informal. Certainly, natural scientific proposers of the Anthropocene have not been shy about making prescriptive claims on the back of the proposed technical geological revision. Still, the revision is not yet formally accepted by the geological community; a matter presumably to be dealt with cautiously and coolly through the careful application of natural scientific method, especially regarding the kinds of stratigraphical considerations involved in the distinguishing and dating of geological periods (cf. Zalasiewicz et al., 2011). I am questioning the normative significance: the normative rationale for humanities and social scientific scholars interested in the ethical, political, policy and governance dimensions of our environmental situation to *welcome* the revision. I explore this by considering three broad kinds of reason for welcoming the Anthropocene proposal. For the sake of brevity I label these the 'end of nature' reason, the 'pro-mastery' reason and the 'anti-domination' reason. Maybe there are other, better reasons for embracing the proposal, but I argue that none of these three is tenable. I am not sceptical about the claim that facts such as those mentioned above constitute an urgent environmental crisis of great complexity. I am sceptical about those reasons for viewing the crisis through the lens of the Anthropocene. My argument touches on matters of conceptual definition (of nature, humanity and the Anthropocene), agency and justice and, I think, brings out that the Anthropocene is an unhelpful frame for thinking about the normative dimensions of relations between humans and between humans and nature.

However, putting aside the normative issues for a moment, notice that the question of *why* adopt the Anthropocene label for the current geological era is not out of order, partly because the facts of our environmental situation don't logically *entail* the Anthropocene label or idea. Nor is the Anthropocene 'empirically necessary' in the sense of being simply forced on us by self-evident environmental or other empirical facts. Thus we can ask surely meaningful, if somewhat naïve, questions like the following: If it is reasonable to name a geological epoch after a biological species because of its impact on Earth systems, are we sure that it is our species that should receive the honour? Why not find out which species of organism is responsible for the most photosynthesis, say, and name it after that, or that species which releases the most oxygen into the atmosphere? It is undeniable that human beings burn, chop down, alter the ambient acidity and otherwise impact decisively the photosynthesizing and oxygen-producing organisms and so we profoundly affect those processes ourselves. But in engaging in the practices that have those impacts we are using energy made available by the activity of the photosynthesizers and oxygen producers. We couldn't do what *we* do if they didn't do what *they* do, so why single us out for special mention in despatches? Moreover, our naïve questioner might continue, maybe human impact on Earth systems *is* greater than that of any other single species, but the impact of the others is surely greater than zero. So why not name the geological era after, say, the mammals: the impact of humans plus the rest of the mammals must be greater than that of humans alone? Or the vertebrates? In other words, why not name the era after another taxonomic rank in the biological classificatory hierarchy, rather than a species; whether genus, family, order, or whatever as the case may be? No doubt there are good, scientifically respectable answers to these questions and reasons not to combine biological and geological taxonomies in the ways just suggested. It is important to my own discussion and argument that the questions are meaningful, not that they are unanswerable. In sum, as I have said, I am interested in the following (non-scientific, non-taxonomic) answers to the question of *why we should want to* associate the environmental crisis with the Anthropocene: the end of nature reason; the pro-mastery reasons; and the anti-domination reason. I will discuss each in turn and argue that none of them is tenable.

The end of nature

First, talk of the Anthropocene can be taken as a way of reinforcing claims about the 'end of nature' and radical constructionism about nature. Some environmental thinkers urge us to focus environmental concern onto the human constructed environment rather than something called 'nature' – a nonhuman realm distinguishable meaningfully from humanity and its products (for example, Vogel, 2002). The Anthropocene proposal could be welcome from this perspective as evidence that even the natural sciences are coming around to the view that there is no (longer) any such thing as nature in that sense, at least on Earth, whose systems are now shaped by the impact of human activity. 'Environmentalists' should stop talking about 'respecting or protecting nature', or the like, because such talk is confused, or at least now otiose, and directs attention away from the real task of making a better job of creating and sustaining a just and stable human environment. The environmental facts constitute a crisis inasmuch as they show that humanity is making a very bad job of that task. Presumably, comments like these of ecologist and Anthropocene proposer Erle Ellis are very welcome from this perspective:

> From a philosophical point of view, nature is now human nature; there is no more wild nature to be found, just ecosystems in different states of human interaction, differing in wildness and humanness ... Environmentalist traditions have long called for a halt to human interference in ecology and the Earth system. In the Anthropocene the anthropogenic biosphere is permanent ... making the call to avoid human interference in the biosphere irrelevant.
>
> (Ellis, 2011a, p. 1027)

Let us adopt the phrase popularized by environmentalist and journalist Bill McKibben (1990) and call this motivation for embracing the Anthropocene the 'end of nature' reason. It seems to me to be delusional. I think this is shown by the meaningfulness of the naïve questions raised above about the Anthropocene proposal. For example, given that it is a genuine question whether our species' impact on Earth systems is greater than that of any other species, the impact of nonhuman species being greater than zero, then we cannot have ended nature. Indeed, given that the idea of the Anthropocene is defined in terms of impact on

Earth systems, systems that are held still to exist and that no one believes were created by humanity, the Anthropocene idea itself presupposes that we have not ended nature. Thus both the Anthropocene idea and the proposal to adopt it presuppose the continued existence of nonhuman nature. The former is the case in virtue of immediate conceptual necessity. The latter is the case in virtue of the intelligibility of the naïve questions, the answerability of which Anthropocene proposers must presuppose. Therefore the conjunction of the Anthropocene idea and proposal with the end of nature rationale for embracing them is incoherent. I want to say 'delusional', rather than merely incoherent, because it seems to me that the incoherence is so obvious that only a delusional hubris could prevent its appreciation: not only are we a *very* powerful – the *most* powerful – species; we are *so* powerful that we have *ended nature*. Here I agree with philosopher Val Plumwood's comment that,

> It may be reasonable, in the present context, to doubt that there is any part of the earth that has not felt human influence, but to doubt that the world itself has elements of independence is an indicator of the need for therapy, philosophical (Wittgenstein) or personal, depending on the kind of doubt it is.

(Plumwood, 2006, p. 135)

Perhaps this is too quick. A thoroughgoing constructionist about 'nature' might object that I have missed the point: there is not, and never has been, any such thing as a genuinely 'independent nature', or 'nature as such'; like everything else these are social constructions. We cannot 'step outside' our social constructions to perceive, know, or say anything meaningful about 'things in themselves', including any putative 'nature' supposedly independent of them. What the Anthropocene idea and proposal underline in a welcome way is an increasing recognition that such constructions as 'independent nature' are untenable: again, even 'natural scientists' are coming around to this conclusion. But this won't do. If we accept that 'everything is a social construction' then the issue becomes that of what constructions we should adopt. In these terms my point is what seems to me to be the obvious one that we cannot coherently run the construction that is the Anthropocene without also running the construction that is nature.

Another response to me here might be that I am ignoring the scale and scope of our impacts on the Earth: the point is there is nowhere on Earth that is not influenced more or less significantly by anthropogenic impacts. Thus we *have* ended nature; or at least terrestrial nature, which is what we care about. The Anthropocene proposal is welcome because of its dramatic emphasis of this important 'post-natural' feature of our environmental situation.

But this response won't do either. It presupposes that 'nature' means something like 'pure, wilderness'; something whose being is by definition so fragile that it ceases to exist once it suffers any human contact or 'interference'. That is one idea of nature, to be sure, and we do acquire a certain status in the world by defining 'nature' in that way and then pointing out that we have ended it. Yet 'nature' is not just one thing; it has many different senses (for classic discussions see, for example, Lewis, 1967; Mill, 1904). They don't all have that 'pure untouched' implication. One such is the 'natural world' of empirical regularities ('laws of nature'). We and our doings are inescapably a part of nature in this sense and clearly we haven't ended that. More pertinently, the natural world also incorporates 'nonhuman nature', in the sense of what is not human and has not been brought about by human activity. This need not be understood in a 'pure' way, but in a way that admits of degrees and hybrid cases and that invites precisely the kind of scientific investigations associated with the Anthropocene proposal. In the case of climate change, for instance, there are questions about the extent of the change *and the extent to which the change is anthropogenic*. No-one in this scientific debate proposes that the average temperature at any level of the atmosphere is a function *only* of anthropogenic factors; that solar radiation, for example, plays no role at all. *Insofar as* the temperature is the result of anthropogenic factors then it is not 'natural' in this sense of nonhuman nature; insofar as it is not the result of anthropogenic factors then it is, to that degree, (still) natural in this sense. The same goes for the other observed behaviours and properties of the fluid that is the Earth's atmosphere. And this remains so even when the complexity and dynamism of the forces and processes involved preclude absolute precision (or easy consensus) about the relative weight of anthropogenic and non-anthropogenic factors. Thus, for example, Steffen and colleagues raise this question: 'How does the magnitude and rate of human impact compare with the *natural* variability of the Earth's environment? Are human effects similar to or greater than the great forces of nature in terms of their influence on Earth System functioning?' (2007, p. 614, my emphasis).

Thus the 'philosophical point of view' Ellis reports as holding that 'nature is now human nature' is either just false or trades misleadingly on the idea of nature as pure wilderness. Of course, there have been radical forms of 'environmentalism' asserting the need to 'get in touch with' or 'return to' nature in that sense. That 'pure' idea of nature, along with the call to 'return to it', is highly problematic and probably always has been. But why replace one absurdity with another? Consider that Ellis ascribes the view that 'nature is now human nature' to the position adopted by the environmental historian William Cronon in his classic (1995) article, 'The trouble with wilderness; or, getting back to the wrong nature' (Ellis, 2011a, p. 1027, p. 1035n132). In this article, which was a major spur to the North American 'Great Wilderness Debate', Cronon provides a powerful and influential critique of the ideological role played by ideas of 'pure wilderness', for example in denying or hiding the fact that putative wildernesses were in fact home to indigenous civilizations. But he also makes clear that in urging us to reject the idea of pure wilderness he is not urging us to drop the idea of nonhuman nature. He is urging us to be careful in our handling of it and he explicitly refutes the 'end of nature' claim because it equates nonhuman nature with pure, untouched wilderness (Cronon, 1995, p. 82). Indeed, other parts of Ellis's discussion commit him to agreeing with this. For example, shortly after claiming 'nature is now human nature' he says, human transformation of terrestrial ecology is always incomplete: some native species flourish even in the most densely populated cities ... [the] transformation remains incomplete, as significant wildlands persist and much of the anthropogenic biosphere consists of novel ecosystems altered significantly but not completely.

(Ellis, 2011a, p. 1029)

I discuss matters relating to the end of nature thesis and the social construction of nature more thoroughly than here in Hailwood (2015b).

Pro-mastery

So much for the end of nature reason for embracing the Anthropocene. What of the second, pro-mastery, reason? The Anthropocene proposal might be taken to be a way of emphasizing increased human mastery of nature as something to be celebrated. We are now so powerfully dominant as a species that we deserve to have a geological epoch named after us. The environmental facts don't constitute a crisis after all. Or, if they do then, as with the end of nature rationale, this is only insofar as they constitute a situation that is far from perfect from the point of view of controlling the impacts so that they maximally satisfy human interests. It is this sort of motivation for welcoming, indeed *celebrating*, the Anthropocene proposal as a way of framing the environmental situation that I am labelling the 'pro-mastery' rationale. Climate change for example serves to underline both humanity's power to impact Earth systems and the need to control this power better for the sake of human interests. It can seem obvious then that the required control in turn requires the power be extended through the development of large-scale climate engineering technologies (see for example, Crutzen, 2002; Ellis, 2011b). Not so much a crisis then, as an opportunity. Because natural scientific proposers of the Anthropocene often wrap it up with prescriptions of overall management and utopian levels of technological optimism, Jeremy Baskin suggests it should be understood as an ideology: 'as such it is not so much a geological epoch as a paradigm or, more accurately, a paradigm presented as an epoch' (2015, pp. 10–11).

Anthropocene proposers do sometimes seem to incline to this way of thinking in addition to any purely scientific rationale for revising the taxonomy of geological epochs. For example, Erle Ellis who, as we have seen, is tempted also by the end of nature reason, has spoken in the *Guardian* newspaper of our living in the Anthropocene as meaning that, 'We need to think differently and globally, to take ownership of the planet' (*Guardian*, 2011). It is unclear what 'take ownership' means here. Consider these two possible interpretations:

a   'Own up to' something or some process; acknowledge that one is involved in it, and take responsibility for how it is turning out. It is possible that Ellis meant something like this: we should face up to the scale of human impacts on Earth systems, take responsibility for it and exercise more control over the impact to shape it in more benign ways. Or maybe even lessen it. On this reading, the phrase is consistent with the third, anti-domination reason for welcoming talk of the Anthropocene I discuss below. Yet although this chimes with some of his comments elsewhere (2011a, p. 1028f), Ellis is not reported in that newspaper interview as saying take ownership of *our impact* on the planet; he says take ownership *of the planet*. And this suggests a quite different sense of 'take ownership':

b   'Possess' it: view it as our own exclusive property to use and modify as we see fit for our own interests. This more definitely belongs with the pro-mastery reason for talking of the Anthropocene, or to an uneasy combination of that with the first, end of nature, reason. I say 'uneasy' here because if we have already ended nature then what is there left to master but each other? This makes the question of who 'we' are quite an urgent one.

Whatever Ellis's meaning, and it is unfair and poor scholarly practice, of course, to give much weight to remarks made in a newspaper interview, presumably everyone agrees it is important that we 'take ownership' in the first sense: something like, acknowledge responsibility for the world we're making, insofar as 'we' are making it. But the second, possessive, sense of take ownership presupposes a domineering attitude, the analogue to which in inter-personal human relations is the hierarchical and egoist attitude of the slave master.

Now, because it is couched in terms of a purely anthropocentric domination, while also presupposing the existence of (nonhuman) nature, the pro-mastery rationale seems to me to partake of something of the delusional quality of the end of nature rationale. A project of total mastery *under the banner of the Anthropocene* risks incoherence because, as we have seen, the idea of the Anthropocene and the intelligibility of the Anthropocene proposal presuppose some non-mastered nature; some nonhuman beings and processes that are not anthropogenic or subject to human control.

In this respect the idea of the Anthropocene is like the idea of human labour on Ted Benton's plausible 'eco-regulatory' conception of the latter (Benton, 1992). Benton explains this notion in the context of discussing the green critique of Marx as committed to the mastery of nature. Marx gave this impression because he tended to understand the human labour process as purely transformative: labour is all about using instruments to transform raw materials into objects with 'use value'. This is false as a general conception, Benton argues, because human labour generally occurs against a background of conditions that are not themselves transformed but have to be accommodated to. This seems clear in the case of agricultural and horticultural labour, for example, where the labour is 'primarily devoted to optimizing and maintaining the *conditions* under which some organic transformations take place'. Here human labour optimizes the conditions for things to occur otherwise by themselves (ibid., p. 60). These conditions and associated causal mechanisms are not themselves transformed into commodities or products with use value. Nor are they utterly non-manipulable 'untouched nature': the point is that such labour presupposes the '*relative* non-manipulability of certain contextual conditions and causal mechanisms'. However, the point is generalizable and applies even to such relatively transformative labour processes as genetic engineering (ibid., p. 66). Benton draws this general conclusion: 'For any given socio-technological organization of the labour process, some things can be altered but others just have to be taken as "given" and adapted to as well as possible' (ibid., p. 61). This general fact is not something we can coherently envisage transcending through further 'socio-technological developments'. The idea of human mastery over all nonhuman processes is 'the purest idealism', Benton says, and to attempt it is 'to court ecological catastrophe' (ibid., p. 63). Let us say that it is at least incoherent to combine a project of pure mastery with an adequate (eco-regulatory) conception of human labour. Similarly, because the Anthropocene presupposes the continued existence of some nonhuman nature it is incoherent to combine *that* with a project of pure mastery. It cannot now or ever denote a situation in which humanity's mastery of nature is complete.

Still, it might be said that even if *total* mastery is out of the question, what we (should) want is as much control and transformation as *possible*. This seems consistent in principle with an eco-regulatory conception of human labour. And again, the Anthropocene proposal is a welcome sign that the mastery project is proceeding apace and will continue as our impact on Earth systems continues to intensify. Of course, we must acknowledge here that to impact or affect something, even profoundly, is not necessarily to master or dominate it in the sense of controlling it. It is important to remember that the environmental crisis is generally a matter of the unintended consequences of human activity in an arena – let us call it nature – that is highly complex and unpredictable. The relevant environmental facts do not generally concern the foreseen and intended consequences of courses of action pursued as part of a worked-out master plan to control the Earth's systems to produce the best overall consequences in terms of human interests. The *crisis* is a matter of the unintended consequences piling up more and more. These points remain consistent with the pro-mastery rationale. The crisis is one of insufficient control, rather than excessive power or impact, and we might envisage better control by pursuing certain avenues of socio-technological development. Not everything such leading proponents of the Anthropocene as Crutzen and Ellis say suggests this pro-mastery agenda, but there is no mistaking the occasional relish at the prospect of an ever-tightening grip on a more and more humanized world: 'We most certainly can create a better Anthropocene ... The first step will be in our own minds. The Holocene is gone. In the Anthropocene we are the creators, engineers and permanent global stewards of a sustainable human nature' (Ellis, 2011b).

There are, however, reasons to suppose an agenda of *maximizing* mastery of nature for the sake of human interests is incoherent, or at least self-defeating, even if detached from the dream of total control over everything. This points us towards the third, anti-domination, reason for embracing the Anthropocene discourse.

Anti-domination

This rationale for talk of the Anthropocene presents itself as a way of emphasizing the scale of impacts as a matter of unambiguous concern: a way of representing the situation to emphasize the seriousness of impacts on both human interests *and nonhuman nature*. It is a way of packaging the facts associated with the environmental crisis to emphasize their urgency and seriousness, both in terms of negative impact on human interests and negative impact on nature, 'in its own right', independently of human interests. Other things being equal, anthropogenic destruction of ecosystems, species and so on is always regrettable on this view. It is the vast scale of the destruction, as well as the harm to human interests involved and threatened by destruction on this scale, which justifies the belief that they constitute a crisis. The Anthropocene proposal emphasizes the vastness of the scale; it is so vast as to usher in a whole new geological era, so something new needs to be done. For example, the philosopher Dale Jamieson has called for a 'new ethic for the Anthropocene' (Jamieson, 2014, p. 155ff). This is partly because of the complexity of the process of anthropogenic impact. The fragmented, non-linear causality involved in climate change, for instance, overstretches the resources of traditional ethics, including with regard to moral psychological demands and the allocation of responsibility. It thwarts time-honoured solutions to collective action problems. The complexity of the problems in these terms is unprecedented; such as to require a new ethic for a new era, the Anthropocene. But so, Jamieson holds, is the *scale* of the impacts, impacts *on nature* as well as humanity. Thus one of the 'green virtues' Jamieson identifies as having particular salience in the Anthropocene is non-dominating 'respect for nature' (2014, p. 188ff). I am calling this sort of motivation for associating the environmental crisis with the Anthropocene idea the 'anti-domination' reason.

Unsurprisingly, such an anti-mastery line is usually unpacked via a critique of pro-mastery perspectives. There are various ways to do this; ways it should be emphasized that either don't, or don't need to, trade naïvely on ideas of nature as pure wilderness or as exhibiting forms of harmony with which we should get 'in touch' or to which we should 'get back'. See for example Robert Goodin's 'green theory of value' (Goodin, 1992) or David Schlosberg's account of extending recognitional justice to nonhuman beings and systems (Schlosberg, 2007). One way to go that seems particularly pertinent to the Anthropocene debate is to argue that the pro-mastery view perpetuates problematic 'dualist' assumptions embedded in many traditional views of nature. As Val Plumwood has explained, 'dualism' here refers to the drawing of (a network of) distinctions as dichotomies in which the terms are coloured normatively as 'superior' and 'inferior' (e.g. Plumwood, 1993, ch. 2). Examples of this include male and female, the mind and the body, reason and emotion, the West and the Rest and, of course, humanity and nature. Take Descartes' famous mind/body dualism: the mind is an utterly distinct 'substance' to the body. The point here is not so much that Descartes' strict separation between 'thinking things' (minds or souls) and 'extended things' (bodies or material objects) is metaphysically dubious as such (though it is problematic in various ways, for example in making interaction between mind and body a mystery calling for divine intervention); rather, the point is that his distinction is drawn within a deeply questionable network of background normative assumptions. The mind is not just distinct from the body but 'higher' than it. Bodies are *mere* material objects, there to serve the interests of the mind, which, as the site of reason, cognition and subjectivity, is closer to the divine, and properly in charge of the material body.

With respect to (nonhuman) nature the anti-mastery thought here is that this sort of hierarchical dualism is often at play, perhaps as a hidden assumption, when we mention or fail to mention nature. Thus it might be assumed that not only are we different from nature, but 'higher' than it, properly masters of it: it is only right, and maybe just inevitable, to view nature simply as an instrument to our purpose. But that assumption is problematic partly because of the tendency of such a dualistic instrumentalizing attitude to push into the background what is viewed as lower or of merely instrumental significance: 'but I am so much more interesting and important', says the higher, master side of the dualism, '*surely* I don't need to care about *that* (the lower side of the dualism)' (e.g. Plumwood, 1993, p. 48f). Such an attitude of mastery and superiority makes it harder to sustain attention on our dependence on nature: for example on the fact that we are not lordly creators, the be-all and end-all of everything we survey, but vulnerable, evolved, embodied organisms with ecological needs ourselves. Sustained attention on such dependencies, as opposed to occasional intellectual assent to issues temporarily intruding on one's grand projects, *requires a degree of humility*. Indeed, Jamieson considers humility to be another virtue with special salience in the Anthropocene, and draws upon Thomas Hill Jr's classic treatment of this virtue as an environmental virtue: 'Indifference to nature "is likely to reflect either ignorance, self-importance or a lack of self-acceptance which we must overcome to have proper humility"' (Hill Jr, 1983, p. 222, cited by Jamieson, 2014, p. 187).

Also important here is that the attitude of mastery, with its instrumentalizing and backgrounding of nature expressed through a humanity/nature dualism, makes it harder to resist similar arrogant, self-aggrandizing and hierarchical attitudes *within human relations*. It makes it more difficult to resist any tendency to view other humans (especially if they are seen as somehow 'closer to nature') only as means to one's own glorious ends, or those of one's own group, class, gender or nation. If others are discounted or instrumentalized in this way then clearly one or more of the various forms of injustice, including distributive, recognitional and deliberative injustice (cf. Schlosberg, 2007, for environmental applications of these) will be present.

Presumably humans have important interests in both sustained attention on ecological dependencies and in just social relations. Thus, although superficially it may seem paradoxical, enlightened, self-interested anthropocentrism requires some 'non-anthropocentric respect for nature', at least to the extent of refraining from a thoroughly dualistic, purely instrumental stance regarding nature. This is to say that at the end of the day there is not a strict, stable dichotomy between (tenable) anthropocentric and non-anthropocentric perspectives: only the most narrow, cramped, egoistic forms of anthropocentrism don't require a dose of nonanthropocentric respect for nature. Notice that it is not a strong objection to this line of thought to assert what is sometimes called 'perspectival anthropocentrism': we are human so obviously we have to see things entirely through the lens of human interests (i.e. anthropocentrically and instrumentally). The problem with this objection is that it doesn't follow from the fact that we are us, and so can only see and think from our own perspective, that we can only consider things in terms of their impact on *our interests*. To see this we need only put aside for a moment the matter of our relations to nature and consider the same argument in terms of interpersonal relations: I can see and think about you only from my own perspective; therefore I can only consider you in terms of how I can use you for my own interests.

With regard to the pro-mastery reason for embracing the Anthropocene then the pertinent conclusion to draw from a critique of dualism is that the project of maximizing the mastery of nature for the sake of human interests is self-defeating. This is partly because in embodying a humanity/nature dualism it is at odds with the humility required for a sustained appreciation of dependency. It is self-defeating also because the humanity/nature dualism is a central plank of a network of interrelated dualisms and running it will perpetuate the rest, including those expressed through unjust human class and gender relations (e.g. Plumwood, 1993, p. 44ff). The argument here is similar to the critical theoretic critique of the domination of nature: the thorough instrumentalization and domination of 'external nature' is self-defeating because it requires the instrumentalization and domination of 'internal nature', thereby undermining the subjective conditions of the human freedom for the sake of which the project is pursued in the first place (see for example Bìro, 2005). Maximizing mastery is therefore inimical to human interests. Therefore the pro-mastery rationale for welcoming the Anthropocene proposal is inimical to human interests.

It is probably better to say inimical to the interests of *many*, if not all, humans. Anti-dualist arguments are highly pertinent here also because the Anthropocene idea itself suggests a dualist picture that focuses on the agency of an exclusive, particularly 'enterprising' and powerful subset of humanity. This is then made to stand for all humanity – *Anthropos* as such – as if all of humanity were equally involved in and responsible for the socio-economic, political and technological developments of the early Industrial Revolution or the Great Acceleration, as the case may be (cf. Malm and Hornborg, 2014). The Rest (of humanity), those not responsible for the transformations held to inaugurate the New Era, are homogenized and backgrounded, as if submerged within the nature *upon which* the *human* transformative agency is exercised. Nor of course is all of contemporary humanity equally responsible for the ongoing environmental impacts of our present technological civilization. These considerations raise again the question of whether it is reasonable to name a geological era after our particular biological species *as such*; only this time the question seems less naïve.

But what of the anti-domination reason for embracing talk of the Anthropocene? Has that not been strengthened by the anti-dualist considerations I have been setting out? To my mind the smoothing away of the unevenness of the responsibilities for the anthropogenic environmental crisis, making them instead a function of the development of human potential as such, problematizes the anti-domination reason for embracing talk of the Anthropocene, no less than it does the pro-mastery reason. This third rationale, remember, focuses on the Anthropocene's dramatic emphasis of the scale and complexity of anthropogenic impacts as greatly worrying urgent threats to both nature and human interests. Take the latter first. Assuming that we don't want to posit the End of Justice any more than the End of Nature it is unclear how it could be in *the* human interest to adopt an overarching framing concept that, taken literally, implies that all humans are equally responsible for the situation. Perhaps the point is that we are not supposed to take it literally. But then it is not clear why we should take it at all, rather than employ one of these seemingly no less empirically valid alternative metaphors Baskin takes from the critical literature on the Anthropocene (Baskin, 2015, p. 15): '*Capitalocene*', '*Econocene*', or '*Shiva-cene*' ('after the Indian deity's characterization as "destroyer" or "transformer"'); or '*The Eremozoic*' ('The Age of Loneliness or Emptiness, in order to acknowledge the existential impact on humanity of the immense losses resulting from the major extinction event that is underway').

Consider now the concern for nature component of the anti-domination approach. In its definitional emphasis on the role of human agency the Anthropocene idea also backgrounds the *nonhuman* agency involved in the production of our surroundings. Adopting it as an overall framing concept seems problematic then if the aim is to emphasize concern for nonhuman nature. It suggests a picture of the latter as homogenized inert stuff with no form of agency of its own, no *vitality*. In this respect it has more affinity with the pro-mastery perspective than with a perspective of respect for nature. If the current Earth era is produced by specifically human agency then presumably there is little nonhuman around worth respecting. But again we are not supposing that nature has ended. The point is that the Anthropocene framework makes it *more* difficult to focus on the nonhuman as something in any way to be respected, rather than something we are simply using or ignoring. Here also my point is similar to an argument of Plumwood's, this time regarding the concept of 'cultural landscape' employed by many human geographers. By entirely reducing our surroundings to a cultural artefact or construction this concept gives a spurious unqualified ascendency to human agency, removing from attention the contributions of nonhuman beings and processes to the production of the environments we inhabit (Plumwood, 2006). Similarly with the Anthropocene: using the idea to emphasize the urgency of the plight of a nature to which we owe some more respectful treatment seems a way of shooting oneself in the foot.

To see this point in more detail consider Marcello Di Paola's recent work on developing Jamieson's project of 'an ethic for the Anthropocene' (Di Paola,

2015). Di Paola interprets the massive scale and complexity of anthropogenic impacts on Earth systems as requiring a form of environmental protection delivered through an ethic of virtuous stewardship. The virtues involved are those exemplified in food-producing urban gardening. For example, this practice helps inculcate the virtue of 'mindfulness' understood as the disposition to acknowledge responsibility for outcomes even when these are spatio-temporally diffuse (ibid., p. 199ff). This is particularly important in the face of phenomena such as anthropogenic climate change which involve non-linear causal pathways and fragmentation of responsibility. The mindful person accepts some responsibility for outcomes to which she only contributes alongside other agents and processes. In this way she retains access to the source of meaning and value that is the acknowledgement of her 'place in a wider working of things' (ibid., p. 201). 'Cheerfulness' is another important virtue here, Di Paola explains (ibid., p. 201ff). The cheerful person affirms her freedom and dignity by appreciating temporary local successes in tasks the renewal of which is necessitated by her own efforts in performing them. One has to weed the garden and thereby contribute to the need for further weeding (by spreading the weeds' seeds), and so on (ibid., p. 202). A telling question here is why Di Paola focuses on gardening, rather than other practices with similar characteristics calling for cheerfulness rather than despair, such as, say, housework: one dusts the book shelves and in doing so sheds the skin that will contribute to the need for further dusting, and so on. At least part of the answer is that in gardening we are more obviously 'working *with nature*' to produce a desired outcome, mindful that the outcome depends on more than our own agency. It is more like 'eco-regulatory' labour in Benton's sense. But then, given that awareness of (relatively) nonhuman nature's active contribution is a condition of such virtuous practice, employing the Anthropocene idea to frame the overall context as the result of specifically anthropogenic agency seems to be at serious odds with the mindfulness. The latter seems to require the virtues of humility and respect for nature (as co-contributor, rather than mastered slave) that Jamieson emphasizes. Di Paola's picture of the virtuous practices called for by our complex environmental situation thus seems to be undercut by the backgrounding of nonhuman agency implicit in the overall Anthropocene frame. None of this is meant to deny the urgency and complexity of the environmental crisis as a situation requiring a new or refocused ethic that allows us to take better responsibility for our role. I am not disagreeing with Jamieson, for example, that we need an ethic for our situation. It is worth pointing out though that Jamieson's own earlier case for viewing certain 'green virtues' as particularly salient for our time made no mention at all of the Anthropocene. Instead he used such traditional phrases as 'the problem of global environmental change' to summarize the challenges of anthropogenic climate change, mass extinction and so on (Jamieson, 2007). If what I have just argued is right then his earlier case was *more* powerful for that, not less powerful (cf. Hailwood, 2015a).

Conclusions

I have argued that none of the reasons discussed above for welcoming the Anthropocene proposal are tenable. They are either delusional or self-defeating. Insofar as the first, end of nature, reason is running alongside one of the others the result is both delusional and self-defeating. I should re-emphasize that my argument does not concern any *purely* natural scientific case for naming the current geological epoch the Anthropocene. Rather it addresses some normative reasons for doing so; matters of interest to humanities and social science scholars concerned with the ethical and political dimensions of our environmental situation. Why *should* such scholars embrace the Anthropocene discourse? I don't think they should, at least not for the reasons I have discussed. The guiding question of this volume – how should we understand and develop effective and equitable governance in the unfolding environmental crisis situation – speaks to a project that is largely normative. This project is *weakened* by adopting the Anthropocene discourse as a discourse entangled with the reasons I have discussed. In the case of the first two (end of nature and pro-mastery) reasons this is because of inherent flaws in their underlying perspectives: they are inherently delusional and/or self-defeating and viewing them (or their furtherance) as reasons for embracing the Anthropocene is simply another way of bringing out those flaws. With regard to the third rationale, that it can express or further the cause of anti-domination perspectives is not a good reason for embracing the Anthropocene proposal either. This is because the Anthropocene is a not a helpful framework within which to articulate humility, respect for nature and concern for justice in a highly complex world. On the face of it, the Anthropocene expresses urgency in an appropriately dramatic, eye-catching way, but considered more deeply and viewed as a potential frame for anti-domination perspectives it actually delivers a homogenizing and reductive simplification of the normative complexity of our environmental situation.

References

Baskin, J. (2015) Paradigm dressed as epoch: The ideology of the Anthropocene. *Environmental Values* 24(1): 9–29.

Benton, T. (1992) Ecology, socialism and the mastery of mature: A reply to Reiner Grundmann. *New Left Review* 194(1): 55–74.

Biro, A. (2005) *Denaturalizing Ecological Politics: Alienation from Nature from Rousseau to the Frankfurt School and Beyond.* Toronto: University of Toronto Press.

Cronon, W. (1995) The trouble with wilderness; or, getting back to the wrong nature. In Cronon, W. (ed), *Uncommon Ground: Rethinking the Human Place in Nature.* New York: W. W. Norton & Co., pp. 69–90.

Crutzen, P. (2002) Geology of mankind. *Nature* 415: 23.

Di Paola, M. (2015) Virtues for the Anthropocene: Taking action in the garden. *Environmental Values* 24(2): 183–207.

Ellis, E. C. (2011a) Anthropogenic transformation of the terrestrial biosphere. *Philosophical Transactions of the Royal Society A: Mathematical, Physical and Engineering, Sciences* 369: 1010–1035.

Ellis, E. C. (2011b) A world of our making. *New Scientist* 210 (2816): 26–27.

Goodin, R. (1992) *Green Political Theory*. London: Polity Press.

Hailwood, S. (2015a) Depending on something bigger. *Environmental Values* 24(2): 141–144.

Hailwood, S. (2015b) *Alienation and Nature in Environmental Philosophy*. Cambridge: Cambridge University Press.

Hill Jr, T. (1983) Ideals of human excellence and preserving the natural environment. *Environmental Ethics* 5(3): 211–224.

Jamieson, D. (2007) When utilitarians should be virtue ethicists. *Utilitas* 19(2): 160–183.

Jamieson, D. (2014) *Reason in a Dark Time: Why the Struggle Against Climate Change Failed and What it Means for Our Future*. Oxford: Oxford University Press.

Lewis, C. S. (1967) *Studies in Words*, 2nd ed. Cambridge: Cambridge University Press.

Malm, A. and Hornborg, A. (2014) The geology of mankind? A critique of the Anthropocene narrative. *The Anthropocene Review* 1(1): 62–69.

McKibben, W. (1990) *The End of Nature*. London: Viking.

Mill, J. S. (1904) *Nature, the Utility of Religion and Theism*. London: Rationalist Press.

Plumwood, V. (1993) *Feminism and the Master of Nature*. London: Routledge.

Plumwood, V. (2006) The concept of a cultural landscape: Nature, culture and agency in the land. *Ethics & the Environment* 11(2): 115–150.

Schlosberg, D. (2007) *Defining Environmental Justice: Theories, Movements and Nature*. Oxford: Oxford University Press.

Steffen, W., Crutzen, P. and McNeill, J. (2007) The Anthropocene: Are humans now overwhelming the great forces of nature? *Ambio* 36(8): 614–621.

The *Guardian*. (2011) Geologists press for recognition of earth-changing "human epoch". The *Guardian*. [Online]. 11 June. Available from: http://www.theguardian.com/science/2011/jun/03/geologists-human-epoch-anthropocene [accessed 30 July 2014].

Vogel, S. (2002) Environmental philosophy after the end of nature. *Environmental Ethics* 24(1): 23–39.

Zalasiewicz, J., Williams, M., Fortey, R., Smith, A., Barry, T., Coe, A., Bown, P., Rawson, P., Gale, A., Gibbard, P., Gregory, F. J., Hounslow, M., Kerr, A., Pearson, P., Knox, R., Powell, J., Waters, C., Marshall, J., Oates, M. and Stone, P. (2011) Stratigraphy of the Anthropocene. *Philosophical Transactions of the Royal Society A: Mathematical, Physical and Engineering Sciences* 369: 1036–1055.

5 Fair distribution in the Anthropocene

Towards a normative conception of sustainable development

Simon Meisch

Introduction

Academic and public debates increasingly refer to the Anthropocene concept (Lundershausen, 2015) introduced to describe a geological time period that has been predominantly shaped by the human species since the beginning of the Industrial Revolution in the eighteenth century (Crutzen, 2002; Zalasiewicz et al., 2011). Empirical evidence that would allow classifying the Anthropocene as a new geological epoch is still debated (ICS, 2013).

Yet, regardless of contested issues, global challenges such as ever decreasing natural resources, ecosystems' limited capacity to absorb human emissions, and ongoing environmental destruction are evident and create a sense of urgency to act. The present critical state of environment and ecosystems is reflected in the concept of planetary boundaries (Rockström et al., 2009). At the same time, a fair human development is at risk. About 1 billion people worldwide do not have access to clean drinking water, 1.3 billion people do not have access to electricity, and more than 1 billion people suffer from hunger. Moreover, projected population growth will put further stress on resources and ecosystems. Regions already suffering from water scarcity will see their populations increase threefold (Leese and Meisch, 2015, pp. 698–700). Meanwhile, global inequality in income and consumption has increased dramatically in the last 50 years (Biermann, 2014, pp. 145–146).

Earth system governance is a social science research programme that faces these inequalities in resources and entitlements and aims to provide modes and mechanisms of fair access and allocation in the Anthropocene (Biermann, 2014, p. 146). It defines access as 'meeting the basic needs of humans to live a life of dignity' and allocation as 'allocating benefits, responsibilities, and involuntary risks between countries and actors' (Biermann et al., 2009, p. 60). Building an understanding of access on human dignity requires a universalistic moral approach (respecting the dignity of *all* human beings) while still being open for different ways and designs of life. Philosophically, this is an ambitious challenge. On the one hand, one makes claims about 'the basic rights and freedoms of *every* human being' (Gupta and Lebel, 2010, p. 379, italics added), on the other hand one would have to 'tangle with issues of cultural imperialism and be sensitive to the contexts in which injustice and justice are framed' (Biermann et al., 2009, p. 60). The task would be to elaborate and justify those parts of a life of dignity (e.g. health, education, employment) that have overriding priority over other practical considerations and that therefore need political and legal protection. With this, collective and state action can be legitimized and at the same time limits to its scope be defined. This directs attention to governance approaches being built on (distributional) justice and dealing with effective protective, corrective and counter actions to global environmental change (mitigation, adaptation, geo-engineering). They have to provide answers to questions posed by the Anthropocene concept, namely how to create social orders adequate to steer societies through the challenges of 'earth system transformation, within the normative context of sustainable development' (Schröder, 2014, p. A2). Yet, governance approaches aimed at both achieving a fair social order and effective political measures against climate change and environmental destruction have to be within the same normative framework, i.e. sustainable development. If one assumes that all political programs designed to keep human action within planetary boundaries are grounded in the belief that humans today and in the future should be able to live a life of dignity there cannot be a gap between both aims in principle. Yet, resulting debates will precisely be on which institutions and policies will secure fair allocation and access best. An approach dealing with the actual functioning of governance systems as well as providing fundamental critiques of underlying systemic forces of non-sustainable development is analytical and normative at the same time (Biermann, 2014, p. 59).

This chapter contributes to the political philosophy of global environmental governance and policy. It argues that in order to make claims with regard to access and allocation, one needs a moral theory to justify these claims. The normative theory related to the Anthropocene is the concept of sustainable development that needs to be elaborated by means of a theory of justice. This theory has to specify individuals' rights and duties as well as social institutions that protect and support the exercise of these rights and duties. With this, a justified groundwork is laid for claims with regard to access and allocation in the Anthropocene. This chapter relates these normative considerations to urgency, responsibility and institutional complexity, which are regarded as three central characteristics of the Anthropocene. Its argument will be developed in four steps. First, the Anthropocene concept makes normative claims with regard to human agency: human–nature relationship and capacity to act. With this, the concept implies a questionable idea of responsibility. By addressing this idea, sustainable development will be presented as the normative idea to deal with problems of the Anthropocene, some of which have become urgent. Second, any conception of sustainable development requires a theory of justice to specify moral claims. Third, Martha Nussbaum's *Capability Approach* and Alan Gewirth's *Principle of Generic Consistency* will be presented as promising theories of justice by means of which claims for goods and corresponding moral, political and legal obligations can be formulated. Both approaches conceptualize justice in terms of human-dignity-related rights that allow determining issues of access and allocation.

Fourth, both approaches can help to address issues of overarching principles of and institutional settings for fair access and allocation in the Anthropocene. A concluding section will relate the normative argument of this chapter to urgency, responsibility and institutional complexity.

The Anthropocene: Normative implications

Conceptually, the term Anthropocene implies more than empirical knowledge about specific characteristics of a geological era. The concept also encompasses a normative component calling for social and political action in order to counteract global environmental changes and their detrimental effects on humans and nature. By describing and evaluating states of the world and fields of action, the concept makes normative claims. It stresses 'the enormity of humanity's responsibility as stewards of the Earth' (Crutzen and Schwägerl, 2013). A business-as-usual strategy does not seem possible any longer, because continuing with the status quo would be 'detrimental or even catastrophic for large parts of the world' (Rockström et al., 2009, p. 472). An integral part of the Anthropocene concept is a political agenda (Steffen et al., 2011; Zalasiewicz et al., 2011).

The Anthropocene can therefore be described as a 'thick moral concept', that is a concept comprising descriptive as well as normative and evaluative elements, i.e. facts and value judgements (Meisch, 2014a). Both are closely intertwined in common language usage ('thick') but can nevertheless be separated analytically (Williams, 1985, pp.129–130). For instance, the mere fact of global environmental changes does not itself create obligations for (political and legal) action unless there is a normative concept such as justice claiming that detrimental effects on human life and nature are to be prevented.

With regard to normative implications of the Anthropocene concept, many different queries have been voiced (Lövbrand et al., 2015; Hailwood, this volume; Wissemburg, this volume). Some refer to the concept's image(s) of world and humanity and the role some social actors will or ought to play in it. While this strand of ethical reasoning critically discusses the concept and its implicit or explicit normative presuppositions, others affirm the concept and aim to argue for legitimate individual and collective actions within the Anthropocene. The Anthropocene concept attributes special importance to the role of human agency. Actually, it is one of its defining features: 'humans have interfered with the Earth's biological, chemical and geological processes to such an extent that anthropological forces now seem to be the dominant drivers of global environmental change' (Schröder, 2014, p. A1).

It is argued that humanity has the responsibility and to a certain degree the capacity to act. This raises several epistemological and ethical questions that cannot be dealt with here in detail. As the concept of Anthropocene emphasizes the importance and relevance of responsibility, this issue will be used here to sketch some ethical criticism of the concept. Ascribing responsibility necessitates free moral agents who on the basis of legitimate values and norms have the duty (moral Ought) as well as the capacity to act. Agency needs to have an effect, i.e.

no one is obligated beyond what he or she is able to do: an Ought presupposes a Can (cf. Meisch, 2013a). So, two issues are raised here, the first refers to what is (or ought to be) the goal of action within the Anthropocene, while the second deals with the question of agency.

First, Anthropocene concepts are often not explicit with regard to their normativity. It appears that the Anthropocene is about managing earth, nature or ecosystems respectively and keeping the scope of human action within planetary boundaries. Therefore, humanity needs to know more about the material basis of human life on earth and to create new political institutions (e.g. Crutzen and Schwägerl, 2013; Rockström et al., 2009). This engineering and managerial approach focuses political and scientific debate on what to sustain and how, yet, to a lesser degree on why and for whom. However, the last two questions are essential for issues of access and allocation.

Furthermore, it seems that some Anthropocene concepts attribute rights to ecosystems, Gaia or nature. For instance, arguments that aim for 'balancing the needs of humans and nature' or viewing ecosystems as 'legitimate "user" of water, just like human society' (Vörösmarty et al., 2013, p. 537) might get into trouble when protecting ecosystems conflicts with human needs. Then, they would have to justify why the needs of nature have equal moral relevance – or in some cases even overriding priority. The argument made in this chapter is built on moral anthropocentrism. In line with the Rio Declaration, it regards '[h]uman beings … at the centre of concerns for sustainable development. They are entitled to a healthy and productive life in harmony with nature' (UN, 1992, Principle 1). With regard to nature, there are direct and indirect human claims and these rights justify protective, corrective and counter actions with regard to nature. In this reading, nature would not be protected for its own sake but as a necessary precondition for *every* human to live a life of dignity. This can be regarded as a starting point for a normative analysis of human influence on the earth system and a reform of the global political system.

Second, as human agency is understood as the main driver for global environmental change, humans are credited with the responsibility to act and to use all measures available up to large-scale geo-engineering projects (Crutzen, 2002). However, this very optimistic view on the possibilities of human agency is debatable. Even though the destructions and overexploitations the Anthropocene concept refers to are caused by human action they are nevertheless the result (and unintended consequence) of uncoordinated collective actions. It is a phenomenon already described by the Scottish philosopher and social scientist Adam Ferguson in 1767 as 'the result of human action, but not the execution of any human design' (Ferguson, 1782, p. 205). This is no plea for sitting back and taking things easy, as it can't be helped anyway. However, the repairing and stewarding approach might just be a prolongation of the failed Cartesian paradigm that sees humans as masters and possessors of nature and that promotes a philosophically and methodologically reductionist science and innovation (Pereira and Funtowicz, 2015). At the same time, it would be utterly misleading to blame humanity as such or the human species for all the deficiencies related with the Anthropocene when it is quite obvious that some people (in the Global North) supported by a specific social order (global capitalism) have contributed more to the problem than others. In spite of arguing for humanity's potency, one might as well say that the Anthropocene demonstrates both human ignorance and the fragility of a single human being in the face of ongoing global changes.

According to Biermann (2014, p. 57), the Anthropocene's classification as a new geological epoch will fundamentally change the understanding of current political systems. Yet, social and environmental problems will remain the same with or without the classification and what is more, the Anthropocene concept carries difficult implicit notions – as discussed above. Added to this, it rekindles a crisis rhetoric that legitimizes extraordinary political measures (Leese and Meisch, 2015). However, one does not have to buy the grandeur of Biermann's statement to admit that there are many urgent present and future challenges for global environmental politics. Due to social organization, environmental change and the interplay of both, there are manifold limitations to humans worldwide to live a life of dignity. One does not have to agree to the Anthropocene concept nor the way it conceptualizes reality to acknowledge these challenges and the need for political action. The normative and social concept that aimed to address these issues is sustainable development. It constitutes the moral basis to formulate duties and reflect on responsibilities to act.

Sustainable development

Since the Brundtland report in 1987, the concept of sustainable development is the political strategy to deal with human development and nature protection (Meadowcroft, 2000). From its beginnings, the concept was popular as well as contested. Biermann et al. (2009, p. 59) describe it somewhat ironically as 'something almost everyone agrees with, at least until it is carefully defined and one starts working on achieving it'.

Voget-Kleschin and Meisch (2015) argue that sustainable development will for two reasons always be contested and that this does not need to be a reason against its usage. First, it is '*appraisive* in the sense that it signifies or accredits some kind of valued achievement' (Gallie, 1956, p. 171, italics in original), i.e. it comprises descriptive and normative elements. Knowing the value-ladenness of some concepts allows addressing contestation explicitly. By making implicit normative claims transparent, they can become subject to ethical reflection. Second, contestation can and will also arise when it comes to specifying a concept by means of conceptions. This insight draws on John Rawls and Ronald Dworkin who distinguish between concepts that are ideal or abstract notions and different conceptions that are the realizations of an ideal. While there might be consensus on the ideal itself, the choice of a particular conception and its elaboration might be contested. For instance, Sandel (2010) demonstrates how the concept of justice can be realized by different ethical conceptions such as libertarianism, utilitarianism, deontology or communitarianism. Both Rawls and

Dworkin highlight the importance of conceptions as they also determine the relationship and the meaning of the constituting elements a concept consists of. By comparing different concepts of sustainable development, Voget-Kleschin and Meisch (2015) show that there is actually a broad consensus on its constituting elements.

The concept's normative core is the idea of inter- and intra-generational justice in the face of decreasing natural resources, the ecosystems' limited capacity to absorb human emissions, and the ongoing environmental destruction. Briefly stated, humans are obligated to ensure that everyone has the right to live a good life. In this endeavour, humanity proceeds in such a way that the natural basis necessary to live such a life is at least retained (and in the best case extended) for all contemporary and future humans. Furthermore, as a good life also depends on social preconditions, it would be inconsistent only to protect the natural but not the social basis. Therefore, sustainable development specifies claims for justice. These comprise claims for intra- and intergenerational justice as well as direct and indirect claims for justice. While the first refers to the claims that everybody today and in the future should be able to live a life of dignity, the second refers to direct obligations with regard to other humans as well as indirect obligations with regard to the necessary natural and social preconditions to live a life of dignity (Meisch, 2013a; Voget-Kleschin and Meisch, 2015).

Conceptions of sustainable development need to be multi-layered. On the one hand, they have to specify the concept of sustainable development by means of a theory of justice. On the other hand, they need to argue how these theories apply to a specific social context. With regard to earth system governance in the Anthropocene, this means that specifying a concept of sustainable development can generate those overarching principles that determine access and allocation. In an application-oriented political and scientific discourse, these principles can help to elaborate those effective governance mechanisms that reconcile addressing fair access and allocation and environmental consequences and drivers of global change. This conceptualization of sustainable development needs to be done in interdisciplinary collaborations.

Normative conceptions of sustainable development

Any conception of (and any political programme building on) sustainable development has to refer to a theory of justice in order to determine which moral, legal and political obligations emerge from the concept of sustainable development – for instance with regard to access and allocation. In other words, all conceptions of sustainable development do actually refer to a normative theory of some kind in order to specify rights and duties addressed to individual and state action. Actual conceptions in academic and political discourses differ to the extent that they make their reference to an ethical approach and resulting specification of legitimate courses of action explicit and thereby open to ethical debate.

Within the conceptual core of sustainable development, the idea of justice needs to be specified in terms of obligations and corresponding rights and duties.

Drawing on Claassen and Düwell (2013), this chapter uses two ethical approaches to conceptualize sustainable development: Martha Nussbaum's *Capability Approach* and Alan Gewirth's *Principle of Generic Consistency*. Both bring forward ethical approaches that regard human rights as based on a universalistic moral understanding of human dignity (Claassen and Düwell, 2013; Düwell, 2013). With this, the normative claim is asserted that human dignity possesses an overriding priority over other practical considerations. Dignity signifies what humans owe each other and what can legitimately claim to be put into political and legal rules. However, Nussbaum and Gewirth go one step further. They aim to specify which aspects of human life are indispensable parts of human dignity and therefore create direct obligations to other humans and the state. Both employ different methods of justification. In spite of this difference, both come to defining capabilities that are morally relevant and whose protection and support are morally, politically and legally obligatory. Both approaches claim that they can respect the plurality of various ways of living while at the same time they can identify morally relevant capabilities necessary to live a life of dignity. These capabilities are to be protected by human rights. Therefore, Nussbaum's as well as Gewirth's approach can be used to deal with normative issues of access and allocation in earth system governance.

Martha Nussbaum: Capability Approach

The social philosopher Martha Nussbaum and the economist Amartya Sen developed an ethical approach called the Capability Approach which is based on two normative claims: first, the freedom to achieve well-being is of primary moral and political importance. This freedom has to be respected by all governments and constitutes the basis of the political order. Second, the Capability Approach understands the 'freedom to achieve well-being … in terms of people's capabilities, that is, their real opportunities to do and be what they have reason to value' (Robeyns, 2011; cf. also Nussbaum, 2006, p. 70). With this, it makes a universal moral claim for core human entitlements that are 'a true minimum of what respect for human dignity requires' (Nussbaum, 2006, p. 70). By reasoning over constituent parts of a human life, Nussbaum developed capabilities humans need in order to live a life worthy of human dignity. Subsequently, she puts forward a list of morally relevant capabilities whose protection and support have an overriding priority over other practical considerations. These are, for instance, being able to live to the end of a human life of normal length or being able to have good health or being able to laugh and play. Nussbaum claims that it is necessary that at least a 'threshold level of each capability is reached, beneath which it is held that truly human functioning is not available to citizens; the social goal should be understood in terms of getting citizens above this capabilities threshold' (ibid., p. 71).

Therefore, she does not rank capabilities or provide a principle on the basis of which one could prioritize capabilities. All capabilities are equally necessary to live a life of dignity. As it is the duty of the social order to protect and support capabilities, the state and state action are legitimized. Nussbaum explicitly justifies positive rights. It follows from her approach that the corresponding political order needs to be a democracy.

The Capability Approach distinguishes between capabilities and functionings. Functionings are understood as '"beings and doings", that is, various states of human beings and activities that a person can undertake', while capabilities 'are a person's real freedoms or opportunities to achieve functionings' (Robeyns, 2006). Sen illustrates this difference, by using the example of a fasting person (Sen, 1992, p. 52). Although he/she might be able of being adequately nourished (capability), he/she chooses to fast and not to eat (functioning). That is completely different from a starving person who does not have this option and is therefore capability deprived.

The Capability Approach tries to give a universal account of morally relevant capabilities that is still culturally open and flexible. Therefore, the approach focuses on capabilities rather than on functionings because it does not want to 'privilege a particular account of good lives but instead aim at a range of possible ways of life from which each person can choose' (Robeyns, 2006). Consequently, it regards goods and resources as important because they are means to an end, i.e. developing capabilities. However, they are not seen as means in themselves. The Capability Approach deliberately contrasts with approaches that make claims with regard to specific goods or utilities.

Alan Gewirth: Principle of Generic Consistency

Gewirth introduces the Principle of Generic Consistency (PGC) as a supreme moral principle (Gewirth, 1978, pp. 129–199) that reads as follows: 'Act in accord with the generic rights of your recipients as well as of yourself' (ibid., p. 135). It is not necessary here to reconstruct the justification of the Principle of Generic Consistency in detail. Basically, in line with Kant, Gewirth attempts to argue for a categorical imperative by means of a transcendental argument. By applying the dialectically necessary method, he aims to demonstrate that 'an agent would contradict its status as an agent if it did not accept that it was bound to the PGC' (Beyleveld and Brownsword, 1998, p. 670, italics in original).

Gewirth focuses on human agents and their reciprocal rights and duties. Generic rights are rights to the necessary conditions an agent needs for purposeful action (Gewirth, 1978, p. 64). These rights are freedom and well-being. The right of freedom consists of non-coercion and the ability to act according to one's own choice, while the right of well-being encompasses those general abilities and conditions that are necessary for an agent to reach the purpose of his/her action (ibid., p. 64). Both rights are to be respected, protected and supported by other agents and by political institutions.

With regard to safeguarding an agent's capacity to act Gewirth distinguishes positive and negative rights. Negative rights mean the freedom from interference by others, while positive rights imply legitimate claims to those goods necessary to realize prospective agency. Gewirth distinguishes three kinds of goods an agent requires to achieve the purpose of his/her action (ibid., pp. 53–58): basic, nonsubtractive and additive goods.

Basic goods are the generally necessary preconditions for all purposive action and 'comprise certain physical and psychological dispositions ranging from life and physical integrity (including such of their means as food, clothing, and shelter) to mental equilibrium and a feeling of confidence as to the general possibility of attaining one's goals' (ibid., p. 54). Nonsubtractive goods are goods an agent also values and which he/she needs to maintain his/her level of purpose-fulfilment. Gewirth introduces 'level of purpose-fulfilment' as a reference point. It is the status quo of what an agent already has acquired (Steigleder, 1999, p. 53): 'Since he regards each of the particular purposes for which he acts as good, he regards as good in each case an increase in his level of purpose-fulfilment whereby he achieves the goal for which he acts' (Gewirth, 1978, p. 53). Therefore, an agent would be harmed if he/she loses (some of) these abilities in the course of an action. While the loss of a basic good would inflict basic harm on an agent, the loss of a nonsubtractive good would cause a specific harm (ibid., p. 230). Additive goods are acquired in acting for a purpose and raise an agent's level of purpose-fulfilment. They cannot be basic or nonsubtractive. For instance, an agent struggling for life does not acquire additive goods as his/her actions deal either with maintaining the necessary preconditions of his/her agency (basic good) or with retaining what he/she already has (nonsubtractive good) (ibid., p. 56).

With reference to the Principle of Generic Consistency, it becomes possible to prioritize goods (relative to the needs of agency) that deserve moral protection: 'If the normative idea is that we should be enabled to act as prospective agents, then the hierarchy follows from the relative necessity of each good for acting as a prospective agent' (Claassen and Düwell, 2013, p. 502). Therefore, the Principle of Generic Consistency allows one to prioritize some goods over others and to deal with conflicts of duties of some agents to respect their recipient's generic rights. In that regard, the Principle of Generic Consistency 'functions as the organizing principle for determining the scope and the relative importance of the basic capabilities that are forming the basis of rights and entitlements' (ibid., p. 503).

As the generic rights are to be respected, protected and supported by other agents and by political institutions, the Principle of Generic Consistency also legitimizes protective and supportive state action (Gewirth, 1978, 1996). In this regard, Gewirth distinguishes direct and indirect applications of the PGC (Gewirth, 1978, p. 200). The direct application refers to individual actions. An agent acts freely without interference by others (negative rights) or legitimately claims those goods required to realize prospective agency (positive rights). It might also imply that an agent fulfils his/her obligations with regard to other agents' generic rights. The indirect application refers to the state and its institutions insofar as they protect the negative rights of individual agents and promote the positive rights of developing basic capabilities and basic goods. With this, Gewirth distinguishes a static and dynamic justification of social rules. The first focuses on the protection and restoration of every person's equal possession of generic rights. The second acknowledges a disproportional inequality in people's ability to exercise their generic rights and aims to remove this inequality (ibid., p. 292).

Fair access and allocation in the Anthropocene

The approaches of Nussbaum and in particular of Gewirth can generate answers to the questions of earth system governance with regard to access and allocation. Their main contribution lies in identifying and justifying overarching principles and in linking normative and governance issues. A comparison of both approaches will provide the basis for a discussion of their contribution to normative issues of access and allocation.

Comparing theories of justice

Nussbaum and Gewirth give an answer to the question of what humans need and have legitimate claims to in order to live a life of dignity. Table 5.1 gives a summarizing overview of both approaches (Claassen and Düwell, 2013; Düwell, 2013).

Both regard human dignity as the normative foundation of human rights and aim to justify universal moral obligations in order to protect these rights. Resulting normative duties encompass the protection and support of necessary preconditions of human life. While Nussbaum aims to seek criteria of a truly human life, Gewirth refers to prospective agency. Both try to specify what

Table 5.1 Nussbaum and Gewirth: Similarities and differences

Similarities

- Conceptualization of justice in term of rights connected to human dignity
- Justification of universal moral obligations to protect these rights
- Justification of universal moral obligations to protect and support the necessary preconditions of human life
- Legitimation of the state and state action
- Formulation of negative as well as positive rights

Differences

Nussbaum	Gewirth
• Justification of normative claims with 'overlapping consensus' (J. Rawls)	• Justification of normative claims with transcendental argument
• Capabilities that cannot be hierarchically ranked	• Hierarchy between rights
• Therefore, no supreme principle to justify a hierarchy	• Supreme principle to justify a hierarchy

Source: Author's table (based on Claassen and Düwell, 2013; Düwell, 2013).

humans need for a truly human life or prospective agency and justify universal moral obligations that protect and support these preconditions. As universal moral obligations neither refer to the realization of specific goals nor the maximization of goods or utilities (Düwell, 2013, p. 114; Claassen and Düwell, 2013, p. 494) both approaches remain open to diverse ways of living. Finally, both approaches highlight negative as well as positive rights. Thereby, they indicate a scope of legitimate state action, i.e. supporting and protecting the preconditions for a life of dignity as defined by the respective approaches. It follows from both approaches that Nussbaum as well as Gewirth demand a democratic political order, as it is the precondition for a life of dignity.

Both differ with regard to the justification of their claims and a possible hierarchy of capabilities. Nussbaum seems to use different methods in order to justify her list of capabilities. While she uses a 'self-validating' strategy of argumentation in her early works, in her recent writings she refers to the Rawlsian 'overlapping consensus'. By applying the dialectically necessary method Gewirth uses a transcendental justification. Both approaches are contested with regard to their justification. It is a matter of debate (and philosophical affiliation) whether Gewirth proved convincingly enough the universalist claim of his approach (Beyleveld, 2013, 2012). Claassen and Düwell (2013, pp. 506–508) doubt that Nussbaum's justification is strong enough in order to legitimate universal moral obligations and indicate how Gewirth's moral theory could improve her approach with regard to the selection of capabilities, the question of hierarchy and the method of justification. In its present form, Nussbaum precludes a hierarchy of capabilities and therefore she does not offer a principle to rank them. As Gewirth starts from a supreme principle, he can build a hierarchy of rights (relative to the needs of agency).

Possible answers to questions in earth system governance

Earth system governance seeks to create policy solutions that aim at 'meeting the basic needs of humans to live a life of dignity'. So far, this chapter has presented an argumentative structure to determine principles that might underlie access and allocation in the Anthropocene. It has done so by employing two theories of justice that specified those constituent parts of human dignity that create overriding priority over other practical considerations and that therefore deserve moral, legal and political protection and support. With this, human dignity avoids being an empty term and can become the normative basis for policies with regard to access and allocation.

Nussbaum and Gewirth offer solutions to determine what humans need to live a life of dignity. Humans ought to have access to those goods that allow them to develop their capabilities or to be a prospective agent. As Nussbaum does not rank capabilities, it becomes difficult for policymakers to deal with situations in which not all capabilities can be promoted at the same time. As she argues for a threshold level of each capability, there would be a greater obligation to promote those capabilities that are still beneath the level. Gewirth's approach explicitly allows the building of a hierarchy of rights by promoting those goods necessary for prospective agency. The Principle of Generic Consistency might therefore be a promising approach to further elaborate specific claims in policy fields.

What both approaches mean for policy advice depends on their specification in concrete social contexts. Both approaches (and especially the Principle of Generic Consistency) work well in determining principles for access and allocation and justifying legitimate state action. Taking the Principle of Generic Consistency or the Capability Approach as a starting point, governance research and policy recommendations would look for governance models that respect people's generic rights of freedom and well-being or human capabilities. At this theoretical level, no governance model can be excluded *prima facie*. Most likely, there will be no single solution but many – in line with human capabilities or people's generic rights of freedom and well-being. Politics and social research will have to deal with polycentric governance and the interaction of different governance models (Ostrom, 2014). With this, the approach presented here stands in stark contrast to dominant, present understandings of access and allocation that build on welfare economics and favour (libertarian) notions of market solutions and minimal state. It seems that current approaches such as the Water Energy Food Security Nexus favour market solutions in the first place without asking for institutional alternatives (Leese and Meisch, 2015). Yet, in deliberations on principles of access and allocation, proponents of economic utilitarianism and market solutions would have to give reasons how and why market solutions are better suited to protect and support the necessary preconditions of a life of dignity (Meisch, 2014b). While it is in the capacity of social ethics (the main disciplinary focus of this chapter) to criticize existing normative policy frameworks and to justify other solutions, (failed) implementation of these alternative principles is an issue of empirical research. Studying power relations, overcoming institutional lock-ins and creating new opportunities will then become a crucial task for the earth system governance analytical approach.

Finding policy solutions with regard to access and allocation in the Anthropocene can be achieved by means of an interdisciplinary conceptualization of justice. What justice means in general and with regard to sustainable development in particular has to be argumentatively specified. Gupta and Lebel (2010) pointed to a disharmony in this respect. In a way, that does not come as a surprise. Social science theories (such as law, economics, political geography, sociology or international relations) do not only focus on specific causal mechanisms in the social world connecting aims and means, they also have underlying (normative) assumptions about which role (successful) human agency plays and ought to play in their models (Streeck, 2009, pp. 6–7; Biermann et al., 2009, p. 59). This does become a problem when in the course of scientific overspecialization particular institutional models are declared superior and made the normative basis of 'overly stylized policy prescriptions' – a danger seen by Ostrom with regard to economists and political scientists (Aligica, 2009). An interdisciplinary understanding of access and allocation would first need an understanding of what humans have a right to and second of what are the appropriate governance mechanisms to achieve these rights (Mayntz, 2009). That will challenge belief systems within disciplines when the taken-for-granted preferability of one's own model is questioned and its scope becomes limited – as would be the case with economists' belief in the superiority of markets (Streeck, 2009). In this respect, the normative theory of earth system governance can provide a critique of existing practices as well guidance for possible pathways to institutional reform.

In theory, issues of access and allocation should create no problem for governance 'effectiveness in addressing environmental consequences and drivers of global change' (Biermann et al., 2009, p. 63). It can be argued that consequences and drivers of global change are only interesting and relevant if one wants to ensure that everyone has the right to live a life of dignity. If this right weren't endangered then probably global change would be not be an issue at all. One could even argue that initiatives dealing with consequences and drivers of global change would not be effective if they did not promote fair access and allocation. On a theoretical level, problems would result if one attributed rights in themselves to nature. However, that is difficult to justify – and, maybe, politically problematic as it might weaken the human rights movements.

This chapter cannot deal with the relevance of allocation and access for global environmental governance and policy as this is mainly an empirical question. However, it is highly morally relevant, as it deals for instance with the reasons and consequences of poverty (Robeyns, 2011). In this case, it is of course relevant how poverty is defined, e.g. either with reference to an amount of resources or as lacking the necessary preconditions to act.

Conclusion

The term Anthropocene was introduced to describe a new geological time period, which sees humanity as a geological force. It is used to call attention to the many and diverse effects humans have had on the earth system since the late eighteenth century but also to legitimize protective, corrective or counter actions (adaptation, mitigation, geo-engineering). A normative foundation for action within the Anthropocene is the concept of sustainable development that calls for justice for present and future humans in the face of decreasing natural resources, ecosystems' limited capacity to absorb human emissions and ongoing environmental destruction. In spite of contestation over sustainable development, it encompasses relatively uncontroversial elements that need to be specified argumentatively in conceptions. Specifying conceptions of sustainable development is an interdisciplinary task as many disciplines contribute to judgements on what ought to be done, e.g. acting for fair access and allocation.

The approaches of Martha Nussbaum and Alan Gewirth were presented and discussed with regard to their contribution to normative challenges for global environmental governance and policy in the Anthropocene. It was suggested that both approaches could strongly inspire debate on principles governing access and allocation by specifying and justifying what humans need for a life of dignity. In an anthropocentric moral framework, tensions between issues of access and allocation and governance effectiveness in addressing causes and drivers of global change could be reconciled in principle.

How does the normative approach presented in this chapter relate to urgency, responsibility and complexity as constituting features of the Anthropocene concept? Ongoing academic discussions on whether or not there is enough scientific evidence to finally declare the Anthropocene a new geological time period cannot hide the fact that many of the problems associated with the Anthropocene are already present and urgent. These multiple problems range from Pacific islands endangered by sea level rise, global hunger, the daily loss of biodiversity, to refugees dying every day in the Mediterranean. The approach presented in this chapter focuses on what *every human* is entitled to in order to live a life of dignity. Thereby, it diverges from other approaches that take humanity's survival in the face of crises on the centre stage and that link a good life to a specific amount of resources. However, if the Anthropocene concept does not want to (further) risk being accused of extrapolating and solidifying (non-sustainable) Western lifestyles and solving global challenges (under the disguise of humanity's progress and well-being) by techno-fix solutions and high capital investments (Leese and Meisch, 2015; Pereira and Funtowicz, 2015), the normative approach presented in this chapter might help to identify and prioritize the most urgent problems. Accordingly, global environmental governance and policy would have to focus on those who cannot exercise their generic rights or who are capability-deprived. Then, it would look for individual and collective action that supports these rights and capabilities respectively and protects their necessary natural and social preconditions.

This chapter dealt with the questionable notion of responsibility implied by the Anthropocene concept. It criticized the vague and ambivalent normative basis of underlying moral norms and questioned its idea of human agency. The approach presented here established a normative basis in order to determine what global environmental governance and policy have a responsibility for: respecting and protecting the generic rights of other agents and enhancing other human's capabilities respectively. Both ethical approaches make a case for collective and state action as means of exercising this responsibility.

That brings institutions into focus. As this chapter elaborated a normative argument, it can not make empirical statements or predictions on real or prospective institutional complexity. Both ethical approaches introduced to specify sustainable development as the normative basis of global environmental governance and policy claim to provide an argument for a human rights regime. On the global level, institutions, probably linked to the UN, would be necessary to protect and support human rights. If institutional fragmentation weakens the human rights regime, this would not be the preferable way to choose. Yet, it is not clear why there should be one global institutional structure to secure and protect generic rights or capabilities designed for the many different social contexts worldwide. If one respects people's freedoms one would expect an institutional diversity – as long as it stayed within the human rights regime.

This chapter is theoretical and normative in focus. It agrees with Gupta and Lebel (2010, p. 391) that access and allocation 'are contentious political issues in earth system governance because they challenge existing property rights and claims'. And one might add that they are also contested issues in inter- and transdisciplinary collaborations when normative assumptions on how the world ought to be underlying social sciences theories become questioned. It does not delegitimize the argument presented here that attempts to realize and implement it will face political and scientific resistance. Furthermore, the chapter also agrees with Dryzek (2014) that instead of creating great political designs, social science research should start with the analysis of institutions and path dependencies. Yet, it believes that strategic agency trying to overcome path dependency and create dynamics for change to a more sustainable development requires knowledge about institutional (in-)stability *as well as* normative guidance (Meisch, 2013b). With this in mind, next steps would be to bring together this contribution to the normative theory of earth system governance with analytical approaches.

References

Aligica, P. D. (2009) *Rethinking Institutional Analysis: Interviews with Vincent and Elinor Ostrom*. [Online] Available from: http://ppe.mercatus.org/publication/rethinking-institutional-analysis-interviews-vincent-and-elinor-ostrom [accessed 26 February 2015].

Beyleveld, D. (2012) The Principle of Generic Consistency as the supreme principle of human rights. *Human Rights Review* 13: 1–18.

Beyleveld, D. (2013) Korsgaard v. Gewirth on universalization: Why Gewirthians are Kantians and Kantians ought to be Gewirthians. *Journal of Moral Philosophy*, June 2013. DOI: 10.1163/17455243-4681026.

Beyleveld, D. and Brownsword, R. (1998) Human dignity, human rights, and human genetics. *The Modern Law Review* 61: 661–680.

Biermann, F. (2014) The Anthropocene: A governance perspective. *The Anthropocene Review* 1: 57–61.

Biermann, F., Betsill, M., Gupta, J., Kanie, N., Lebel, L., Liverman, D., Schroeder, H. and Siebenhüner, B. (2009) *Earth System Governance: People, Places and the Planet*. Science and Implementation Plan of the Earth System Governance Project. Earth System Governance Report 1, IHDP Report 20. Bonn, IHDP: The Earth System Governance Project.

Claassen, R. and Düwell, M. (2013) The foundations of Capability Theory: Comparing Nussbaum and Gewirth. *Ethical Theory and Moral Practice* 16: 493–510.

Crutzen, P. (2002) The geology of mankind. *Nature* 415: 23.

Crutzen, P. and Schwägerl, C. (2013) Living in the Anthropocene: Towards a new global ethos. *Environment 360*. [Online] Available from: http://e360.yale.edu/feature/living_in_the_anthropocene_toward_a_new_global_ ethos/2363/ [accessed 17 August 2014].

Dryzek, J. (2014) Institutions for the Anthropocene: Governance in a changing earth system. *British Journal of Political Science*. 28 November 2014. DOI: 10.1017/S0007123414000453.

Düwell, M. (2013) Fähigkeiten – Rechte – Menschenwürde. Ethische Begründung und anthropologische Dimensionen der Menschenwürde bei Martha Nussbaum und Alan Gewirth. In Joerden, J., Hilgendorf, E. and Thiele, F. (eds), *Menschenwürde und Medizin. Ein interdisziplinäres Handbuch.* Berlin: Duncker & Humblot, pp. 99–118.

Ferguson, A. (1782) *An Essay on the History of Civil Society,* 5th ed. London: T. Cadell.

Gallie, W. B. (1956) Essentially contested concepts. *Proceedings of the Aristotelian Society* 56: 167–198.

Gewirth, A. (1978) *Reason and Morality.* Chicago: University of Chicago Press.

Gewirth, A. (1996) *The Community of Rights.* Chicago; London: University of Chicago Press.

Gupta, J. and Lebel, L. (2010) Access and allocation in earth system governance: Water and climate change compared. *International Environmental Agreements* 10: 377–395.

ICS (International Commission on Stratigraphy) (2013) *Subcommission on Quaternary Stratigraphy, Working Group on the 'Anthropocene'.* [Online] Available from: http://quaternary.stratigraphy.org/workinggroups/anthropocene/ [accessed 17 August 2014].

Leese, M. and Meisch, S. (2015) Securitising sustainability? Questioning the 'water, energy and food-security nexus'. *Water Alternatives* 8: 695–709.

Lövbrand, E., Beck, S., Chilvers, J., Forsyth, T., Hedrén, J., Hulme, M., Lidskog, R. and Vasileiadou, E. (2015) Who speaks for the future of Earth? How critical social science can extend the conversation on the Anthropocene. *Global Environmental Change* 32: 211–218.

Lunderhausen, J. (2015) Defining the Anthropocene. In Meisch, S., Lundershausen, J., Bossert, L. and Rockoff, M. (eds), *Ethics of Science in the Research for Sustainable Development.* Baden-Baden: Nomos, pp. 295–316.

Mayntz, R. (2009) New Challenges to Governance Theory (1998). In Mayntz, R., *Über Governance. Institutionen und Prozesse politischer Regelung.* Frankfurt/Main: Campus, pp. 13–27.

Meadowcroft, J. (2000) Sustainable Development: a New(ish) Idea for a New Century? *Political Studies* 48, pp. 370–387.

Meisch, S. (2013a) Green food consumption: Whose responsibility? In Röcklinsberg, H. and Sandin, P. (eds), *The Ethics of Consumption. The Citizen, the Market and the Law.* Wageningen: Wageningen Academic Publishers, pp. 160–165.

Meisch, S. (2013b) Devolution in Scotland – A historical institutionalist approach for the explanation of intergovernmental relations. In López Basaguren, A. and Escajedo San-Epifanio, L. (eds), *The Ways of Federalism in Western Countries and the Horizon of Territorial Autonomy in Spain,* Vol. 2. Berlin, Heidelberg: Springer, pp. 315–328.

Meisch, S. (2014a) The need for a value-reflexive governance of water in the Anthropocene. In Bhaduri, A., Bogardi, J., Leentvaar, J. and Marx, S. (eds), *The Global Water System in the Anthropocene. Challenges for Science and Governance.* Cham: Springer, pp. 427–437.

Meisch, S. (2014b) Bewusster Fleischkonsum – wie kann Politik gestaltend eingreifen? In Voget-Kleschin, L., Bossert, L. and Ott, K. (eds), *Nachhaltige Lebensstile,* Marburg: Metropolis, pp. 411–436.

Nussbaum, M. (2006) *Frontiers of Justice. Disability, Nationality, Species Membership.* Cambridge, MA; London: Belknap.

Ostrom, E. (2014) Beyond markets and states: Polycentric governance of complex economic systems. In Sabetti, F. and Dragos, A. (eds), *Choice, Rules and Collective Action. The Ostroms on the Study of Institutions and Governance.* Cholcester: ECPR Press, pp. 167–209.

Pereira, A. and Funtowicz, S. (2015) *Science, Philosophy and Sustainability. The End of the Cartesian Dream*. London: Routledge.

Robeyns, I. (2011) The Capability Approach. *The Stanford Encyclopedia of Philosophy*. [Online] Summer 2011 Edition. Available from: http://plato.stanford.edu/archives/sum2011/entries/capability-approach/ [accessed 17 August 2014].

Rockström, J., Steffen, W., Noone, K., Persson, Å., Chapin, III, F. S., Lambin, E., Lenton, T. M., Scheffer, M., Folke, C., Schellnhuber, H., Nykvist, B., De Wit, C. A., Hughes, T., van der Leeuw, S., Rodhe, H., Sörlin, S., Snyder, P. K., Costanza, R., Svedin, U., Falkenmark, M., Karlberg, L., Corell, R. W., Fabry, V. J., Hansen, J., Walker, B. H., Liverman, D., Richardson, K., Crutzen, C. and Foley. J. (2009) A safe operating space for humanity. *Nature* 461: 472–475.

Sandel, M. (2010) *Justice: What's the Right Thing to Do?* New York: Farrar, Straus and Giroux.

Schröder, H. (2014) Governing access and allocation in the Anthropocene. *Global Environmental Change* 26: A1–A3.

Sen, A. (1992) *Inequality Re-examined*. Oxford: Clarendon Press.

Steffen, W., Grinevald, J., Crutzen, P., and McNeill, J. (2011) The Anthropocene: Conceptual and historical perspectives. *Philosophical Transactions of the Royal Society A* 369: 842–867.

Steigleder, K. (1999) *Grundlegung der normativen Ethik. Der Ansatz von Alan Gewirth*. Freiburg i. Br.; München: Alber.

Streeck, W. (2009) *Von der gesteuerten Demokratie zum selbststeuernden Kapitalismus: Die Sozialwissenschaften in der Liberalisierung*. MPIfG Working Paper 08/7. Available from: http://www.mpifg.de/pu/workpap/wp08-7.pdf [accessed 26 February 2015].

UN (United Nations) (1992) *Report of the United Nations Conference on Environment and Development*. Rio Declaration on Environment and Development. Rio de Janeiro, 3–14 June 1992. Available from: http://www.un.org/documents/ga/conf151/ aconf 15126-1annex1.htm [accessed 17 August 2014].

Voget-Kleschin, L. and Meisch, S. (2015) Concepts and conceptions of sustainable development: A comparative perspective. In Meisch, S., Lundershausen, J., Bossert, L. and Rockoff, M. (eds.) *Ethics of Science in the Research for Sustainable Development*. Baden-Baden: Nomos, pp. 45–72.

Vörösmarty, C. J., Pahl-Wostl, C. and Bhaduri, A. (2013) Water in the Anthropocene: New perspectives for global sustainability. *Current Opinion in Environmental Sustainability* 5: 535–538.

Williams, B. (1985) *Ethics and the Limits of Philosophy*. London: Fontana.

Zalasiewicz, J., Williams, M., Haywood, A. and Ellis, M. (2011) The Anthropocene: A new epoch of geological time? *Philosophical Transactions of the Royal Society A* 369: 835–841.

Part II

Institutions in the Anthropocene

6 Mapping institutional complexity in the Anthropocene

A network approach

Oscar Widerberg

Introduction

By some accounts, the Anthropocene is the result of what has been called 'the Great Acceleration' (Lewis and Maslin, 2015). It describes how processes in social systems such as population growth, fertilizer consumption, and the number of McDonald's restaurants have increased exponentially since the 1950s resulting in large adverse effects on natural systems such as climate change and biodiversity loss (Steffen et al., 2005).

New institutions are needed to cope with large-scale and complex socio-ecological challenges in the Anthropocene (Biermann et al., 2012). However, rulemaking on environmental issues has undergone a Great Acceleration of its own. At the time of writing, Mitchell's (2015) database on international environmental agreements contains more than 1190 entries of multilateral treaties, up from only three agreements in 1950. Also, the emergence of transnational institutions engaging companies, non-governmental organizations (NGOs), international organizations (IOs), philanthropists, cities and regions, adds new governance layers to environmental decision-making (Biermann and Pattberg, 2012; Green, 2013a). Thus, governance in the Anthropocene (Maldonado, this volume) has become a maze of institutions and norms – and we have little understanding on how to navigate this fragmented landscape towards effective and fair outcomes.

The institutional fragmentation mirrors and affects the three key aspects of the Anthropocene informing the contributions to this book: complexity, responsibility and urgency (see Pattberg and Zelli, this volume). First, the sheer number and diversity of institutions reflect institutional complexity in the Anthropocene. Second, spreading authority across multiple state and non-state institutions, creating both political and functional overlaps, tends to cloud who bears the responsibility, willingness, capacity and legitimacy to address emerging challenges. Third, the question arises to what extent fragmented institutional complexes are capable of addressing urgent global problems.

To address these challenges, institutional complexity demands good maps for navigating the Anthropocene. How do, for example, different structures of institutional complexes and varying degrees of fragmentation affect the problem-solving capacity, legitimacy, accountability and effectiveness of governance arrangements in the Anthropocene? Such maps are currently unavailable. In this chapter, I suggest an approach for mapping institutional complexity based on network theory. It follows recent popularizations of network analysis and marries international relations theory with concepts from network science. The approach is illustrated for the case of global climate governance.

The first section defines and conceptualizes key concepts including 'institutional complex', 'complexity' and 'fragmentation'. The second section outlines the state of the art in mapping and measuring institutional complexity and identifies the main shortcomings. The third section introduces network analysis as an appropriate tool for analysing institutional complexity, which is further illustrated in the fourth section on institutional complexity in global climate governance.

Defining key concepts: Institutional complexes, complexity and fragmentation

Three central concepts in this chapter – complexes, complexity and fragmentation – are subject to vivid scholarly debate on institutional complexity (e.g. Orsini et al., 2013). I explain my take on these concepts in the coming paragraphs.

An 'institutional complex' comprises all institutions governing an issue area in global governance. The concept emerged from empirical observations of proliferating international and transnational global governance institutions, making the study of isolated single regimes – defined as subsets of international institutions that constrain state-behaviour (Oberthür and Stokke, 2011, p.2) – untenable. In global climate governance, for example, the UNFCCC has been complemented by hundreds of public, private and hybrid institutions demanding authority on a variety of issues (Keohane and Victor, 2011; Bulkeley et al., 2012). '[I]nternational regime complexity', write Alter and Meunier (2009, p.13), 'refers to the presence of nested, partially overlapping, and parallel international regimes that are not hierarchically ordered'. Institutional complexity is, thus, a quality of institutional complexes.

All institutional complexes are to some degree fragmented (Biermann et al., 2009). And fragmentation is likely to be a function of multiple variables of which at least four have been identified in literature. Biermann and colleagues (2009, p. 19) have suggested the problem structure of the institutional complex, the level of integration among norms, and the configuration of actor-constellations. Zelli (2011) adds discursive structures in relation to fragmentation to accommodate theories of discursive institutionalism (Zelli and Van Asselt, 2013). Accordingly, fragmentation can be said to vary in function of the degree of material, functional, normative and discursive overlap between the institutions forming an institutional complex.

Finally, it is not given that fragmentation leads to something complex, intricate or complicated. As Galaz and colleagues (2011, p. 2) note, 'fragmentation at the international level does not imply anarchy'. It remains an empirical question. Zürn and Faude (2013) for instance, suggest that institutional complexity could produce functional differentiation and division of labour between institutions creating coherency rather than disorganization. For this chapter, this is a crucial insight since, in order to establish the consequences of a specific structure, we need to know what that structure actually looks like.

State of the art: Mappings of institutional complexity in global environmental governance

Previous mappings of institutional complexes can be distinguished by their focus on either states collaborating through intergovernmental regimes, or non-state actors and hybrid arrangements between public and private actors collaborating through transnational institutions. In this chapter, current mappings are discussed along these lines.

Intergovernmental institutions

Mappings of intergovernmental institutions take their starting point in international law and international relations scholarship, notably regime theory. Here, the mere increase in number of multilateral and bilateral environmental agreements between states is an indicator for how institutional complexity has been an emerging property of international law for some time (Brown Weiss, 1993; International Law Commission, 2006; Raustiala and Victor, 2004). Legal scholars termed it 'treaty congestion' (Brown Weiss, 1993), referring to how legalization at the international level has consequences that are difficult to foresee for the drafters and negotiators. This overall expansion and diversification of international law has led to what the International Law Commission termed 'fragmentation', characterized by functional overlaps and potential conflicts between different rules and rule-systems (International Law Commission, 2006).

To capture fragmentation, scholars have developed conceptual models and coined new terms such as 'global governance architectures' (Biermann et al., 2009) and 'regime complexes' (Raustiala and Victor, 2004) to describe the meta-level situated somewhere between the broader concept of 'order' and the more specific concept of 'regimes' (Biermann et al., 2009, p. 18). Problems could arise when institutions start to interact. Multilateral agreements on climate change for example, interact with environmental legislation, e.g. on biodiversity, but also with legislation on non-environmental issues such as trade (Zelli et al., 2013). Fragmentation then increases when the number and/or strength of interactions increase.

The work carried out through the regime theory lens has significantly enhanced our understanding of institutional complexity by moving away from analysing regimes in isolation towards perceiving them as part of wider regime complexes (Raustiala and Victor, 2004; Orsini et al., 2013). These merits notwithstanding, the respective mappings of institutional complexes have limited scope, either arriving at theory-based typologies on different characteristics of inter-regime relations (e.g. Young, 1996); or, under the heading 'institutional interplay', as empirical investigations of dyadic interactions between two regimes, for instance between the climate and trade regimes (Young et al., 2006; Oberthür and Gehring, 2006).

System-level mappings of an issue area or between issue areas, however, are largely missing and few quantitative tools are available to compare the degree and severity of fragmentation. Moreover, attempts to display the regime complex of an issue area have generally resulted in crude visualizations of little analytical value beyond heuristics (e.g. Keohane and Victor, 2011; Zelli, 2011). Finally, studies starting from regime theory have largely remained silent on the interaction between the emerging landscape of non-state public and private actors on the one hand, and the international, state-dominated level on the other.

Transnational institutions

Besides examining intergovernmental governance arrangements, another analytical theme which informs studies on institutional complexity capitalizes on the regime theorists' bias towards state-based, multilateral and formal institutions. Addressing the theoretical and empirical gap, more recent writings focus on the emerging plethora of transnational governance initiatives. These initiatives operate in more than one country and 'include private actors and/or subnational units of government as well as, or rather than, states and interstate organizations (IOs)' (Abbott, 2012, p. 572).

Institutional complexity is compounded by the rise of private and hybrid authority manifested by collaborative governance arrangements such as voluntary standards, market-based trading schemes, and codes of conduct. This trans-nationalization of global governance (Pattberg and Stripple, 2008; Andonova et al., 2009) involves a motley crew of international organizations, sub-national public authorities, NGOs, companies, philanthropists and individual citizens. More often than not, these initiatives are hybrid, i.e. linking state and non-state actors. For instance, the various stages and functions of global carbon markets – including certification, monitoring, verification and reporting – are moulded by both public and private actors. One study identifies 30 private carbon standards which interact with public international standards in one way or another (Green, 2013b).

There are several academic and policy-oriented mappings of transnational institutions in different issue areas. In sustainable development, for example, Pattberg et al. (2012) examined over 330 partnerships registered with the United Nations at the time. Scholars and organizations working on climate change have been particularly proliferate in creating databases and lists on transnational actors and institutions working on different aspects of mitigation and adaptation (e.g. Bulkeley et al., 2012; Abbott, 2012; UNFCCC, 2014). These mappings create data entries based on expert judgements; their analyses rely on descriptive statistics of attributes such as governance function, type and origin of members and type of institutions. Bulkeley and colleagues, for example, list 60 transnational climate initiatives and divide them into two distinct groups: one group, including many hybrid initiatives, dedicated to financing, and a second group, with mostly private initiatives, focusing on rule setting (Bulkeley et al., 2012, p. 609). Several other scholars such as Hoffman (2011), Weischer et al. (2012) and Hale and Roger (2014) have engaged in similar exercises of listing institutions. Abbott (2012), based on a list of 67 transnational initiatives, moves one step beyond simply listing and describing the institutions by placing them into a 'governance triangle' (Abbott and Snidal, 2009) which improves our overall understanding of how the global transnational governance complex on climate is structured.

Shortcomings in current mappings of institutional complexity

Current mappings of institutional complexity suffer from three important shortcomings. First, the division between international and transnational levels might be analytically pragmatic but conceptually problematic. Only a few scholars link state and non-state actors in institutional complexes, for example, by suggesting the possibility for non-state actors to manage problematic relationships between regimes (Orsini et al., 2013). However, noting the relationship and showcasing it with a limited number of case studies is insufficient to establish an overall measure of fragmentation of the institutional complex. Hence, if fragmentation partly is a result of proliferating non-state actors and shifts in authority away from states, then the two levels should be linked or, at least, part of the same mapping exercise to show the dynamics between the different players.

Second, mappings have hitherto been unable to analyse or even plot the relationships between the different actors for an entire institutional complex. International regime theory has made important strides in identifying different types of dyadic interactions and relations between individual institutions, predominantly examining the interplay between norms and rules. However, it is possible to conceive of a large number of other relationships and connections such as shared memberships, information exchange or discursive interactions between institutions.

Third, the methods used for mapping institutional complexes to date provide few tools to compare the degree of fragmentation across issue areas in a replicable and valid manner. In particular when the number of institutions exceeds a certain threshold, qualitative and in-depth analysis of institutional complexity become difficult to manage and call for a methodology apt for larger data sets.

To address these three shortcomings new methods are needed to connect the dots. In the coming sections I outline one such method and illustrate its added value by applying it to global climate change governance.

Towards a network approach for mapping institutional complexity

Fragmentation is a structural quality of an institutional complex. The *Oxford English Dictionary* defines structure as a 'combination or network of mutually connected and dependent parts or elements; an organized body or system' (OED, n.d.). A focus on structure must hence accommodate both parts and elements as well as the connections and relations linking them. For this chapter's purposes, I assume that the analytical glue binding institutions together to form an institutional complex are the material and functional linkages to the issue area itself. Measuring the degree of fragmentation then requires us to identify overlap between the institutions forming an institutional complex.

By conceptualizing institutional complexes as networks I explicitly focus on the relationships between institutions. Institutional complexity can then be examined as a global property of the network and allows for network analysis to compare structures in different institutional complexes and compute the degree of fragmentation. It also enables us to draw insights from applications of network analysis in a wide range of disciplines such as computer science, biology, economics, sociology and, increasingly, international relations (Kahler, 2009; Hafner-Burton et al., 2009).

Network theory and institutional complexity

Network theory studies networks created by patterns of interconnections between sets of things. In social network analysis (SNA), the interconnections comprise relations between social entities or actors (Wasserman and Faust, 1994). In SNA, the actors – also called 'nodes' – could be individuals, organizations or institutions, connected via repeated patterns of interactions – also called 'edges' – such as friendship, membership or co-attendance of events.

In international relations theory, the use of network theory has at times been confusing because of the dual meaning of networks. First, in line with SNA, networks can be understood as structures which influence actors' behaviour (Kahler, 2009, p. 7). Second, networks can be understood as actors in their own right (ibid., p. 5). Policy networks such as the World Commission on Dams are good examples of multi-stakeholder collaborations with vertical decision-making, relying on an exchange of resources between the actors in the network to be effective (Streck, 2002). As a result, networks as actors can be part of networks as structures.

In SNA, a common type of network is called two-mode 'affiliation networks'. Two-mode networks are different from one-mode networks since they connect two different types of nodes. In sociology, for example, affiliation networks are commonly used to study social behaviour by linking actors and events. From researching behavioural similarities of actors that participate in the same events, we can infer the 'social circles' or 'social groups' to which they belong (Wasserman and Faust, 1994). Classic cases include sets of people joining different meetings, but affiliation networks have also been applied to a much wider range of subjects including corporate board networks, club memberships, or author affiliations in scientific networks (ibid.). Another interesting feature of affiliation networks is their duality, which enables us to study three different types of relations: between events and actors, between events and events, and between actors and actors.

Using a method called 'projection' we can select one of the two node-sets (actors and events) and link them if they share at least one connection to the other node-set (Opsahl, 2015).

Finally, whether the network represents an electricity grid, the World Wide Web, or strategic alliances between countries, it is assumed (and proven) that it is driven by common organizing principles and behaviour (Barabási, 2015). Based on this notion, network analysis provides tools to compute and describe the structure of a network, disregarding what it represents. Two such measures, density and centrality, are also found in theorization around institutional complexity. Measuring them could allow for testing hypotheses on the degree of fragmentation or identifying key players in institutional complexes.

Density

Institutional complexity is marked by a densification of institutions governing an issue area. But what is 'density' in the context of institutions and can we measure the degree of density across time and space in different institutional complexes?

Most authors seem to have taken densification for granted without much discussion on how to measure it. Among the rare conceptual approaches to the term, one can roughly discern two understandings of density: increases in the sheer number of institutions, and increases in functional overlaps between institutions. Morin and Orsini (2013) suggest that regime complexes are expected to densify over time because the efforts of managing this complexity will involve further institutional processes such as negotiation and implementation. Testing their claim however, would require a measure of density in institutional complexes. Moreover, changes in density could have important repercussions for the functioning of the institutional complex. Abbott and colleagues (2014), for instance, argue from an organizational ecology perspective that the degree of institutional density determines the competition for resources in the population of arrangements. Others have suggested that large numbers of institutions negatively impact actors without the capacity to sustain negotiations in multiple fora (Brown Weiss, 1993, p. 697). Hence, the density of the institutional complex could prove an important structural variable for explaining the possibility for actors to engage in global governance as well as the problem-solving capacity of the institutional complex.

How can density be indicated and measured? In network analysis, density in a network with dichotomous relations is understood as the proportion of all the edges that are present in a network (Hanneman and Riddle, 2005). Density is usually given as a percentage. For instance, if density equals 20 per cent then that is the proportion of edges present compared to all possible edge formations between nodes. To arrive at a meaningful measure of density, researchers need to define what connects the institutions in an institutional complex.

On the one hand, institutional complexity is characterized by the increase in number of institutions. A network can be constructed by defining different types of connections between institutions, for example: shared membership; common board-members, authorship or sponsoring of reports; or any other measure showing a repeated pattern of communication between different actors across institutions. However, institutional density can also be understood in other ways of institutional interaction. Functional overlaps conceptualized as situations where the functional scope of one institution protrudes into the functional scope of another institution (Rosendal, 2001), for example, could also lead to complexity in situations with few institutions. Density could also increase when a few organizations carry out extensive and complex activities occupying the governance space (Abbott et al., 2014). In sum, the type of edges used depends on the definition and indication of institutional density chosen by the researcher.

Centrality

The shapes of institutional complexes are not the outcome of some organic process driven by natural forces independent of the actors occupying them (Orsini et al., 2013). On the contrary, institutional complexity and fragmentation are the result of political bargaining involving agents with different interests, capacity and belief-systems.

Some would argue that fragmentation is the result of strategic behaviour and practical considerations of a few powerful states (Benvenisti and Downs, 2007). Also, the decentralized structure of global decision-making could favour the already strong, spreading the number of negotiation venues and enabling forum-shopping or forum-shifting for actors to evade previously agreed terms (Benvenisti and Downs, 2007; Alter and Meunier, 2009; see also Walbott, this volume). Similar lines of critique have been aimed towards the active involvement of international organizations in public–private partnerships for promoting business influence on global governance at the expense of social protection and development (Zammit, 2003). Also civil society engagement could increase the legitimacy of multi-stakeholder governance arrangements while power tends to stay with the already powerful (Ponte, 2014).

To explore these arguments on the role of different actors it is essential to identify key players in institutional complexes. For identifying central actors in a network several measures of centrality are available. Degree centrality, for instance, measures how many connections an actor has and provides a crude measure of status in the network and level of activity. An actor with many connections could be considered more engaged in the institutional complex than others. Betweenness centrality measures to what extent a node is vital to the transactions between other nodes. An actor with high betweenness centrality could, for example, act as a bridge between different actors or groups of actors and thus facilitate (or obstruct) exchanges. Such 'bridging organizations' have been identified as potentially important actors to manage fragmentation (Gupta et al., 2015).

Mapping an institutional complex as a network and calculating metrics such as density and centrality could yield information on the structure and agents governing an issue area. In the coming sections this approach is illustrated on the global climate governance complex and findings are contrasted with theories on institutional complexity.

An illustration: Mapping the institutional complex of global climate governance

Global climate governance is probably the most researched issue area in terms of fragmentation, institutional interplay and regime complexes, providing a rich body of literature to build upon for illustrating the mapping method (e.g. Zelli, 2011; van Asselt, 2014; Abbott, 2012). In the first sub-section, I set the stage with a brief background on the emergence of institutional complexity on climate change. Second, I illustrate an approach by operationalizing the climate regime complex as an affiliation network. Finally, building on the previous conceptualization of both terms, I compute and discuss different measures of density and centrality.

Setting the stage

International climate politics was long concentrated to a single regime, the UNFCCC, as the central forum for negotiating multilateral responses to climate change. In 1997, the regime was expanded when parties to the UNFCCC adopted the Kyoto Protocol, devising a global market-based system of rights and obligations concerning the mitigation of greenhouse gases (GHGs). Through 'flexible mechanisms' consisting of emissions trading, the Clean Development Mechanism (CDM) and Joint Implementation (JI), a global market was to be created, putting a price on carbon. Developed countries would take on a larger role in mitigating emissions than developing countries. This top-down 'target-and-timetable' approach to international climate action was initially hailed as a role model for collective multilateral action.

However, implementing the vision behind the UNFCCC soon turned out to be much harder than expected. Important GHG emitters such as the US never fully committed to the convention's rules and regulations (see Kühner, this volume). Moreover, the global market of GHG emissions failed to materialize beyond regional pockets, with the European Union providing the largest system to date. After the 15th Conference of Parties (COP) in Copenhagen in 2009 had failed to agree on a successor to the Kyoto Protocol, a new paradigm for climate policy seemed to emerge (Dimitrov, 2010). The new discourse promoted voluntary, flexible and context-based approaches rather than top-down steering. A narrative of bottom-up 'pledge-and-review' was born in which countries would simply state their preferred mitigation contributions and the UNFCCC would analyse and review them.

In the context of waning trust in concerted governmental efforts to address climate change, alternative institutions gained traction. In an increasingly rapid tempo after Copenhagen, the UNFCCC has been complemented by numerous cross-border initiatives comprising both public and private actors, such as states, international organizations, NGOs, companies, epistemic communities and cities (Biermann et al., 2009; Keohane and Victor, 2011; Abbott, 2012; Bulkeley et al., 2014). In parallel, since its inception the UNFCCC has expanded its agenda several times to include areas such as forestry and land use. What is more, already existing institutions such as the World Bank have substantially increased their activity on climate change issues.

Altogether, global climate governance has developed into an institutional complex, and is now characterized by fragmentation and functional overlaps rather than by coherence and hierarchy (Keohane and Victor, 2011, p. 15; Biermann et al., 2009). Ostrom even argued that global climate governance is best described as a polycentric system with 'multiple governing authorities at different scales rather than a monocentric unit' (2010, p. 552).

There are several descriptions of the current institutional complex for climate change governance and its effects on performance. Keohane and Victor (2011, p. 7) suggest that the global climate regime complex comprises a 'loosely coupled set of specific regimes' where elements are linked 'more or less close to one another'. They argue that the degree of fragmentation can be situated on a continuum ranging from coherent to fragmented, but provide little guidance on how to measure it. The effectiveness of the complex can be better than a single integrated regime if it meets a set of six criteria, of which one is coherency which occurs when 'the components are compatible and mutually reinforcing' (ibid., p. 16).

Biermann and colleagues suggest another structure to global climate governance where the UNFCCC takes a central position in the global climate governance architecture with other multilateral forums, institutions and international organizations forming concentric circles to the institutional complex, adding layers of fragmentation (Zelli, 2011). They also describe the institutional complex as fragmented. But instead of placing it on a continuum, they suggest three different types of fragmentation: synergistic, cooperative and conflictive (Biermann et al., 2009). Degree of fragmentation is thus established *ex-post*, for instance, conflictive fragmentation can occur when core norms conflict, a statement which is difficult to evaluate *ex-ante*. Regarding the consequences of fragmentation, the authors conclude, perhaps unsurprisingly, that conflictive fragmentation 'appears to bring more harm than positive effects' (ibid., p. 33), and that synergistic fragmentation might be a second-best option to 'purely universal governance architectures', revealing a slight preference for monocentric structures.

A third perspective perceives global climate governance as polycentric where many different, independent centres of gravity are at work (Ostrom, 2010; Cole, 2011). Proponents suggest polycentrism to be superior to monocentric approaches for global governance since they spur experimentation and learning as well as communication and interaction to build trust (Cole, 2011). Galaz and colleagues (2011) have started to theorize the relationship between density, performance and coordination, arguing that polycentrism is 'a matter of degree, ranging from weak coordination to strong polycentric order' and that '[d]egrees of polycentric order are defined by variables such as communication dynamics, degree of formalization, and network structural patterns' (ibid., p. 11).

All three perspectives suggest that the institutional structure affects the problem-solving performance of the complex as a whole. However, despite fragmentation being linked to performance, few methods exist for measuring it and/or for tracking it over time or across issue areas.

The institutional complex for global climate change governance as an affiliation network

To conceptualize an institutional complex as a network, the nodes and edges need to be defined. The coming paragraphs first outline the network data collected. Then the structure of the network is presented visually and discussed in terms of density. Finally, central actors in the network are identified by measures of centrality.

Data collection

A two-mode affiliation network – where nodes are represented by institutions and their members and edges represent membership in institutions – forms the basis of the illustration. To select the institutions, previous mappings of international and transnational climate institutions in academic databases (e.g. Hoffmann, 2011; Bulkeley et al., 2012; Abbott, 2012) and policy-oriented databases (e.g. UNFCCC, 2014; 2015; Ecofys, 2014) have been scanned and updated according to four criteria. Institutions are included that: (1) are either international or transnational; (2) intend to steer the behaviour of members; (3) explicitly mention a governance goal; and (4) display significant governance functions (Pattberg et al., 2014, p.11). For this illustration, only public institutions with state or sub-state members such as cities and regions have been selected.

The members are defined as actors with the formal position to influence the rules, norms, operations or performance of an institution. They have access to the network an institution provides and benefit from the privileges it may accrue. Those actors that merely support an institution or ascribe to its values, rules, norms or mission, without the ability to influence the governance of the institution, are excluded.

The sample used in this illustration has been collected in the CONNECT-project (http://www.fragmentation.eu) and consists of 31 public international and transnational institutions with 8850 unique members (see Table 6.1).

The sample contains four types of institutions based on main member characteristics arranged by states, cities, regions and hybrid (mixed membership). The distribution between the types is fairly even with states, cities and regions accounting for 39 per cent, 29 per cent and 26 per cent respectively of the total sample. Only two institutions, the International Carbon Action Partnership (ICAP) and the Partnership for Market Readiness (PMR), are considered true hybrid institutions since they allow for both states and regions to participate and

Table 6.1 Sample of international and transnational institutions in the institutional complex for global climate change governance

Institution	Abbreviation	Type	Membership
Climate Alliance of European Cities with Indigenous Rainforest Peoples	Climate_Alliance	Cities	1716
Carbonn	cCR	Cities	3
Covenant of Mayors	CoM	Cities	5717
ICLEI – Local Governments for Sustainability	ICLEI	Cities	1102
EUROCITIES	EUROCITIES	Cities	45
C40	C40	Cities	75
Energy Cities	EnergyCities	Cities	184
Union of Baltic Cities	UBC	Cities	93
R20	R20	Regions	46
New England Governors and Eastern Canadian Premiers' Annual Conference	NEG_ECP	Regions	11
World Mayors Council on Climate Change	WMCCC	Regions	88
The Climate Group States and Regions	TCG	Regions	27
North America 2050	NA2050	Regions	20
Solar Cities	SolarCities	Regions	5
Western Climate Initiative	WCI	Regions	5
Clean Energy Ministerial	CEM	States	22
United Nations Framework Convention on Climate Change	UNFCCC	States	196
Kyoto Protocol	KP	States	193
Forest Carbon Partnership Facility	FCPC	States	59
Global Methane Initiative	GMI	States	59
International Carbon Action Partnership	ICAP	Hybrid	58
Major Economies Forum	MEF	States	17
Carbon Sequestration Leadership Forum	CSLF	States	23
International Partnership for Energy Efficiency Cooperation	IPEEC	States	16
The UN-REDD Programme	UN_REDD	States	73
The Climate Registry	TCReg	Regions	60
Global Mayors Compact	GMC	Cities	9
International Renewable Energy Agency	IRENA	States	135
Partnership for Market Readiness	PMR	Hybrid	33
Climate Investment Funds	CIF	States	27
GLOBE International	GLOBE	States	79

govern. The size of the institutions in terms of membership is heavily skewed towards three large city networks with the Covenant of Mayors (CoM), Climate Alliance and ICLEI – Local Governments for Sustainability having more than 1000 members each. Through the UNFCCC, the membership data also contains nearly all countries on earth.

In the coming two sub-sections, the results of computing density and centrality are presented and discussed.

Density in the institutional complex for global climate change governance

Examining density in the institutional complex can be carried out both visually and computationally. For a visual representation, the affiliation network has been compressed to a one-mode network of institutions connected by shared membership. Figure 6.1 shows the resulting one-mode projection where each node represents an institution and each edge indicates that the institutions share at least one common member.

The network forms a single component without any isolates meaning that all institutions are connected to each other by at least one member. Nodes are also fairly densely connected with an average degree of the network of 11.3 and 37.6 per cent of the edges being present. Edges are unevenly distributed across the network creating a 'core-periphery' structure with state institutions forming a core by being more densely connected than the rest.

Moreover, three clusters can be observed divided by type of membership. State institutions form a highly connected cluster with large sharing of members and few connections to the institutions with cities and regions. The two other main types of institutions also form fairly cohesive clusters with a number of shared members both within and between the respective clusters. Perhaps unsurprisingly, the network shows a high degree of 'homophily', i.e. actors similar to each other tend to cluster together.

The size of the network can be thought of in terms of length between nodes, also called 'geodesic distance'. The largest geodesic distance in the network, also called the 'diameter of the network', is three, meaning that within a maximum of three steps, all nodes can reach each other. For most nodes however, this distance is much shorter since the average distance is a mere 1.82. This means that actors that are part of several institutions have short distances for reaching other actors via their respective institutions.

Both visual and computational examinations of the institutional complex for global climate governance suggest that the network is densely connected by membership. This finding questions some of the accounts of global climate governance as consisting of independent or loosely coupled elements and instead displays a structure where institutions are closely linked. The data supports the proposition that the UNFCCC remains an important institution complemented by a number of other institutions.

What do the network data tell us about performance? According to network theory, closely knit networks should allow for information and change to travel

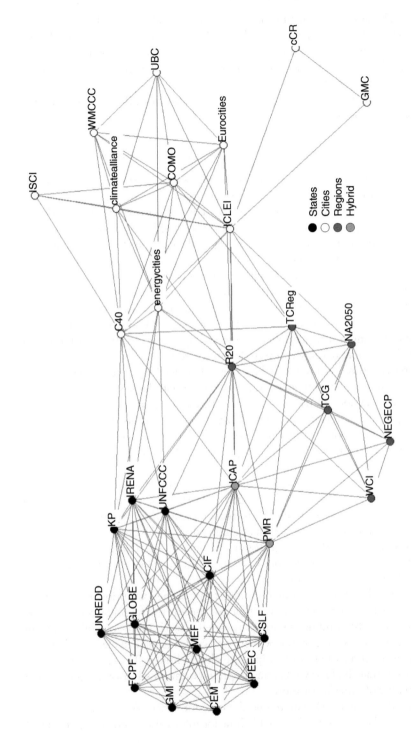

Figure 6.1 The institutional complex of global climate governance (public institutions only)

fast along the nodes (Hanneman and Riddle, 2005). The presence of clusters hints towards high centrality for those nodes connecting the different groups since these can facilitate (or obstruct) transactions in the network. In the next sub-section on centrality, these important nodes are identified.

Centrality

Several measures for identifying central nodes are available such as degree and betweenness centrality. Node degree measures who has the most edges and node betweenness identifies nodes positioned between other nodes.

To test which actors are particularly active in the network, we can calculate the node degree. Of the 8850 members in the network only 6.7 per cent are part of more than one institution. The degree distribution also follows a power law suggesting that the network has scale-free properties. These types of networks are characterized by the presence of a few nodes that have far above average degree, also called hubs. These nodes are probable candidates for taking up central positions in the network, for instance, by connecting different clusters.

The top four hubs are countries, including Germany, Japan, Mexico and the United Kingdom, which are all part of 13 institutions, or 42 per cent of all the institutions in the sample. They are closely followed by Australia, France and the United States, which are part of 12 institutions. The first non-state hubs are the North American regions of California and Quebec, and the European Commission, which all are part of seven institutions. The first hubs of cities on the list are Barcelona and Malmö, both members of six institutions.

Testing the presence of hubs could support statements and case studies suggesting that global climate governance is driven by a small number of 'orchestrators' or 'regime entrepreneurs' (Hale and Roger, 2014; Abbott and Hale, 2014). The data corroborates some of the findings from qualitative research identifying the United Kingdom (Hale and Roger, 2014) and Germany (Van de Graaf, 2013) as central nodes. By expanding the dataset to include other non-state actors such as international organizations one would expect to reveal more hubs, which could further test claims on who are the orchestrators – for instance, international organizations such as the World Bank or the United Nations Environment Programme (UNEP).

To identify which institutions attract actors and facilitate cooperation between clusters, I compute the degree and betweenness centrality in the one-mode network. The results are plotted against each other in a line graph in Figure 6.2.

The measures reveal institutions that are both popular and potential gate keepers between clusters. The nodes with the highest degree are those that share the most members with other institutions. The highest scorers are ICAP, PMR, the R20 Regions of Climate Action, UNFCCC, KP and the International Renewable Energy Agency (IRENA). The nodes with the highest betweenness connect other institutions with each other through membership. These include ICAP, ICLEI, R20, the C40 Cities Climate Leadership Group, EnergyCities and PMR.

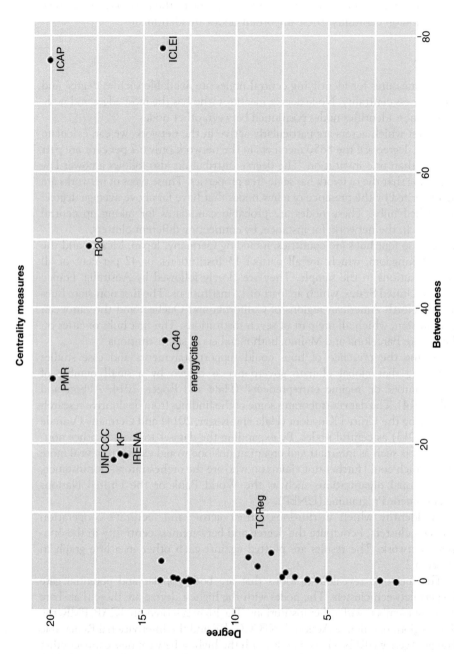

Centrality measures

Figure 6.2 Betweenness and degree in the institutional complex for global climate change

ICAP and PMR both score high on degree and betweenness. These institutions are partnerships that to different degrees comprise states and regions collaborating on carbon markets. They are issue-specific institutions within the overall complex where a smaller number of actors have decided to work jointly on matters that interest them, sometimes referred to as 'clubs' (Weischer et al., 2012). PMR, for instance, engages both countries that are part of the European Emission Trading Scheme (EU-ETS), such as Sweden and the Netherlands, as well as North American regions including California and Quebec, which have their own trading systems.

The regions and cities institutions R20, ICLEI and C40 also score high on both degree and betweenness centrality. Examining the network in Figure 6.1, all three institutions can be considered central nodes since they connect to most of the city and regional institutions. ICLEI, for instance, clearly stands out as a local hub in the cities cluster where it connects to all other city networks. The institutions of regions R20 and C40 both connect to cities and state institutions, making them central in the network. Some of these connections are relatively tenuous. For example, C40 and the UNFCCC only share Singapore, which could be considered a 'city state' with the state institutions. However, network theory has repeatedly shown the strength of weak ties in connecting different clusters and proving valuable nodes for transfer and exchange of communication (Granovetter, 1973).

Traditional state-based institutions, the UNFCCC, KP as well as IRENA, emerge as local hubs in the state cluster, likely due to their near universal membership. Figures 6.1 and 6.2 thus both corroborate the propositions made by scholars on the sprawling institutional complex around the UNFCCC.

Methodological caveats

Using approaches from network theory to examine fragmentation in global governance holds much promise. A broad range of tools become available for the researcher to build theories and test claims on both structure and agency in institutional complexes. It also allows for building dynamic databases over time and conducting comparative research across issue areas. However, with every method comes caveats, of which I would like to highlight three.

First, fragmentation is a matter of scale. Biermann and colleagues (2009) note that empirical research on fragmentation is highly dependent on the scale of the problem. Simply put, the larger the scale, the more fragmentation one can expect. To remedy the problem, clear definitions of central concepts including institutional complex, issue area, institutions and members are needed.

Second, the results are highly dependent on the type of relation (edge) used. In this chapter I have used membership in institutions as a central relation, which clearly demands a number of assumptions to be made, most importantly about who qualifies as a member and which are the institutions. Complementing the membership network with other types of relations, such as norms or discourses, could accomplish a more complete mapping, allowing for robust and nuanced measurement of fragmentation.

Third, conceptualizing the institutional complex as a network is only part of the puzzle to explain the causes and consequences of a particular structure. Describing the network can provide avenues for further research, such as identifying central actors that could be of interest for case studies. But it is merely one part of the researcher's tool-box.

Nevertheless, network approaches move us towards a relational perspective where transactions are central units for analysis and, according to Emirbayer, actors 'derive their meaning, significance, and identity from the (changing) functional roles they play within the transaction' (1997, p. 287). Hence, the method could have large potential when exploring how norms, resources and discourses travel and change throughout a network.

Conclusions

The Great Acceleration in global environmental institutions – driven by both state and non-state actors – makes institutional complexity a ubiquitous characteristic to global governance in the Anthropocene. The emerging structure challenges researchers to revisit methods and perspectives on how to carry out research on institutions designed to address complex problems such as climate change, biodiversity loss and air pollution. In this chapter, I have presented a network-based approach for mapping institutional complexity that enables different ways to measure the degree of fragmentation and to identify key actors and institutions.

While network theory and analysis have been common practice in other disciplines such as sociology, they are only slowly gaining traction in international relations scholarship and have almost never been used in relation to institutional complexity in global governance. The illustrative case study on climate change showed a fraction of the potential of conceptualizing fragmentation in network terminology but still yielded some important insights. First, the results question recent scholarship characterizing the structure of global climate governance as 'loosely coupled' (Keohane and Victor, 2011) or polycentric (Ostrom, 2010; Cole, 2011) by portraying it as rather dense and well connected. They show that institutions at different administrative public levels – state, regions and cities – are connected through hybrid institutions and any one member can reach any other member through a maximum of three steps in the network. Second, the identification of key actors corroborates research on orchestrators and pinpoints a few countries, state and cities, such as Germany, California and Barcelona, as important nodes in the institutional complex of global climate change. These actors are, for one reason or another, highly active in several institutions besides the UNFCCC and thus contribute to creating and perpetuating the institutional complex.

Returning to the central themes in this book – complexity, urgency and responsibility in the Anthropocene – I draw three conclusions. First, network analysis could help untangle complex relations and enable a structured and formal way to study institutional complexity in the Anthropocene. Second, the urgency of resolving issues such as climate change and biodiversity loss in the Anthropocene requires fast and clear approaches to communicate complex relations to audiences beyond academia. I believe that network visualizations, such as the ones made in this chapter, can improve the way researchers present data to third parties and that they go beyond mere 'illustration' (Brandes et al., 1999). Showing what complexity looks like becomes increasingly important as connections and interrelations between institutions increase. Third, the presence of institution and actor hubs in institutional complexes brings up questions on responsibility and leadership, legitimacy and accountability in governance (see also Isailovic, this volume). By identifying central players and forums for negotiation we can trace the increasing complexity to a few nodes. For example, the illustrative case showed how the institutional complex of global climate governance contains at least 31 institutions (not counting private or hybrid institutional arrangements). All G20 countries except Turkey and Saudi Arabia are among the top 30 countries in terms of degree count in the network, suggesting a correlation between activity in number of international climate institutions and wealth in terms of GDP.

Finally, I propose two avenues for future research. First, tying structural characteristics of networks to the causes and consequences of institutional fragmentation. For example, Rydin (2012) has suggested that a 'hub-and-spoke' structure of a policy network – where most nodes in the network could be reached with only a few steps – could be superior to other structures for efficacy of the resource exchange that is a pivotal activity for networks. Second, a comparative research program on institutional complexity across issue-areas – using methodologies such as the one suggested in this chapter – could generate more generalizable theory-building and testing to strengthen our understanding of governance in the Anthropocene.

References

Abbott, K. W. (2012) The transnational regime complex for climate change. *Environment & Planning C: Government & Policy* 30(4): 571–590.

Abbott, K. W. and Hale, T. (2014) Orchestrating global solutions networks: A guide for organizational entrepreneurs. *Innovations* 9(1–2): 195–212.

Abbott, K. W. and Snidal, D. (2009) The governance triangle: Regulatory standards institutions and the shadow of the state. In Mattli, W. and Woods, N. (eds), *The Politics of Global Regulation*. Princeton, NJ: Princeton University Press.

Abbott, K. W., Green, J. and Keohane, R. O. (2014) Organizational ecology and organizational diversity in global governance. [Online] Available from: http://www.princeton.edu/~rkeohane/publications/Organizational%20Ecology%20and%20Organizational%20Diversity%20in%20Global%20Governance.pdf [accessed 25 June 2015].

Alter, K. J. and Meunier, S. (2009) The politics of international regime complexity. *Perspectives on Politics* 7(1): 13–24.

Andonova, L. B., Betsill, M. and Bulkeley, H. (2009) Transnational climate governance. *Global Environmental Politics* 9(2): 52–73.

Barabási, A.-L. (2015) *Network Science*. Available from: http://barabasi.com/network sciencebook/content/book_chapter_1.pdf [accessed 25 June 2015].

Benvenisti, E. and Downs, G. W. (2007) The empire's new clothes: Political economy and the fragmentation of international law. *Tel Aviv University Legal Working Paper Series* 41.

Biermann, F. and Pattberg, P. (2012) *Global Environmental Governance Reconsidered*. Cambridge, MA: MIT Press.

Biermann, F., Pattberg, P., Van Asselt, H. and Zelli, F. (2009) The fragmentation of global governance architectures: A framework for analysis. *Global Environmental Politics* 9(4): 14–40.

Biermann, F., Abbott, K. W., Andresen, S., Bäckstrand, K., Bernstein, S., Betsill, M. M., Bulkeley, B., Cashore, B., Clapp, J. and Folke, C. (2012) Navigating the Anthropocene: Improving earth system governance. *Science* 335(6074): 1306–1307.

Brandes, U., Kenis, P., Raab, J., Schneider, V. and Wagner, D. (1999) Explorations into the visualization of policy networks. *Journal of Theoretical Politics* 11(1): 75–106.

Brown Weiss, E. (1993) International environmental law: Contemporary issues and the emergence of a new world order. *Georgetown Law Journal* 81: 675–710.

Bulkeley, H., Andonova, L., Bäckstrand, K., Betsill, M., Compagnon, D., Duffy, R., Kolk, A. et al. (2012) Governing climate change transnationally: Assessing the evidence from a database of sixty initiatives. *Environment and Planning-Part C* 30(4): 591–612.

Bulkeley, H., Andonova, L., Betsill, M. M., Compagnon, D., Hale, T., Hoffmann, M. J., Newell, P., Paterson, M., Roger, C. and VanDeveer, S. D. (2014) *Transnational Climate Change Governance*. New York: Cambridge University Press.

Cole, D. H. (2011) From global to polycentric climate governance. *Climate Law* 2(3): 395–413.

Dimitrov, R. S. (2010) Inside Copenhagen: The state of climate governance. *Global Environmental Politics* 10(2): 18–24.

Ecofys (2014) *Climate Initiatives Database*. Available from: http://www.climateinitiativesdatabase.org/ [accessed 25 June 2015].

Emirbayer, M. (1997) Manifesto for a relational sociology. *American Journal of Sociology* 103(2): 281–317.

Galaz, V., Crona, B., Österblom, H., Olsson, P. and Folke, C. (2011) Polycentric systems and interacting planetary boundaries–emerging governance of climate change–ocean acidification–marine biodiversity. *Ecological Economics* 81: 21–32.

Granovetter, M. S. (1973) The strength of weak ties. *American Journal of Sociology* 78(6): 1360–1380.

Green, J. F. (2013a) *Rethinking Private Authority: Agents and Entrepreneurs in Global Environmental Governance*. Princeton, NJ: Princeton University Press.

Green, J. F. (2013b) Order out of chaos: Public and private rules for managing carbon. *Global Environmental Politics* 13(2): 1–25.

Gupta, A., Pistorius, T. and Vijge, M. J. (2015) Managing fragmentation in global environmental governance: The REDD+ partnership as bridge organization. *International Environmental Agreements: Politics, Law and Economics*. 1–20. DOI: 10.1007/s10784-015-9274-9.

Hafner-Burton, E. M., Kahler, M. and Montgomery, A. H. (2009) Network analysis for international relations. *International Organization* 63(03): 559–592.

Hale, T. N. and Roger, C. (2014) Orchestration and transnational climate governance. *The Review of International Organizations* 9(1): 59–82.

Hanneman, R. A. and Riddle, M. (2005) Introduction to social network methods. Available from: http://www.citeulike.org/group/1840/article/1192030 [accessed 25 June 2015].

Hoffmann, M. (2011) *Climate Governance at the Crossroads: Experimenting with a Global Response after Kyoto.* New York: Oxford University Press.

International Law Commission (2006) Fragmentation of international law: Difficulties arising from the diversification and expansion of international law. *Report of the Study Group of the International Law Commission. UN Doc. A/CN 4.*

Kahler, M. (ed.) (2009) *Networked Politics: Agency, Power, and Governance.* Ithaca: Cornell University Press.

Keohane, R. O and Victor, D. G. (2011) The regime complex for climate change. *Perspectives on Politics* 9(1): 7–23.

Lewis, S. L. and Maslin, M. A. (2015) Defining the Anthropocene. *Nature* 519(7542): 171–180.

Mitchell, R. B. (2015) *International Environmental Agreements Database Project (Version 2014.3).* Available from: http:/iea.uoregon.edu [accessed 25 June 2015].

Morin, J.-F. and Orsini, A. (2013) Regime complexity and policy coherency: Introducing a co-adjustments model. *Global Governance: A Review of Multilateralism and International Organizations* 19(1): 41–51.

Oberthür, S. and Gehring, T. (2006) *Institutional Interaction in Global Environmental Governance: Synergy and Conflict among International and EU Policies.* Cambridge, MA: MIT Press.

Oberthür, S. and Stokke, O. S. (2011) *Managing Institutional Complexity: Regime Interplay and Global Environmental Change.* Cambridge, MA: MIT Press.

OED (n.d.) Structure. In *Oxford English Dictionary: 3rd Edition.* Oxford, UK. Available from: http://www.oed.com/view/Entry/191895?rskey=Ho9yGS&result=1#eid. [accessed 25 June 2015].

Opsahl, T. (2015) Defining two-mode networks. Available from: http://toreopsahl.com/tnet/two-mode-networks/defining-two-mode-networks/ [accessed 25 June 2015].

Orsini, A., Morin, J.-F. and Young, O. R. (2013) Regime complexes: A buzz, a boom, or a boost for global governance? *Global Governance: A Review of Multilateralism and International Organizations* 19(1): 27–39.

Ostrom, E. (2010) Polycentric systems for coping with collective action and global environmental change. *Global Environmental Change* 20(4): 550–557.

Pattberg, P. and Stripple, J. (2008) Beyond the public and private divide: Remapping transnational climate governance in the 21st century. *International Environmental Agreements: Politics, Law and Economics* 8(4): 367–388.

Pattberg, P., Biermann, F., Chan, S. and Mert, A. (2012) *Public-Private Partnerships for Sustainable Development: Emergence, Influence and Legitimacy.* Cheltenham, UK and Northampton, MA: Edward Elgar Publishing.

Pattberg, P, Widerberg, O., Isailovic, M. and Guerra, F. D. (2014) *Mapping and measuring fragmentation in global governance architectures: A framework for analysis.* Report R-14/34. Amsterdam: IVM Institute for Environmental Studies.

Ponte, S. (2014) "Roundtabling" sustainability: Lessons from the biofuel industry. *Geoforum* 54 (July): 261–271.

Raustiala, K. and Victor, D. G. (2004) The regime complex for plant genetic resources. *International Organization* 52(2): 277–309.

Rosendal, G. K. (2001) Impacts of overlapping international regimes: The case of biodiversity. *Global Governance* 7(1): 95–117.

Rydin, Y. (2012) The issue network of zero-carbon built environments: A quantitative and qualitative analysis. *Environmental Politics* 22(3): 496–517.

Steffen, W., Jäger, J., Matson, P., Moore, B., Oldfield, F., Richardson, K., Sanderson, A. et al. (2005) *Global Change and the Earth System: A Planet Under Pressure*. Global Change – The IGBstreP Series. Berlin, Heidelberg: Springer-Verlag.

Streck, C. (2002) Global public policy networks as coalitions for change. In Esty, D. C. and Ivanova, M. H. (eds), *Global Environmental Governance: Options and Opportunities*: New Haven, CT: Yale School of Forestry and Environmental Studies, pp. 121–140.

UNFCCC (2014) Portal on cooperative initiatives. Available from: http://unfccc.int/focus/mitigation/items/7785.php [accessed 25 June 2015].

UNFCCC (2015) The Non-State Actor Zone for Climate Action (NAZCA). Available from: http://climateaction.unfccc.int/ [accessed 25 June 2015].

Van Asselt, H. (2014) *The Fragmentation of Global Climate Governance: Consequences and Management of Regime Interactions*. Cheltenham, UK and Northampton, MA: Edward Elgar Publishing.

Van de Graaf, T. (2013) Fragmentation in global energy governance: Explaining the creation of IRENA. *Global Environmental Politics* 13(3): 14–33.

Wasserman, S. and Faust, K. (1994) *Social Network Analysis: Methods and Applications*, Vol. 8. Cambridge: Cambridge University Press.

Weischer, L., Morgan, J. and Patel, M. (2012) Climate clubs: Can small groups of countries make a big difference in addressing climate change? *Review of European Community & International Environmental Law* 21(3): 177–192.

Young, O. R. (1996) Institutional linkages in international society: Polar perspectives. *Global Governance* 2: 1–24.

Young, O. R., Oberthür, S. and Gehring, T. (2006) *Institutional Interaction in Global Environmental Governance: Synergy and Conflict among International and EU Policies*. Cambridge, MA: MIT Press.

Zammit, A. (2003) *Development at Risk: Rethinking UN-Business Partnerships*. Geneva, Switzerland: UNRISD.

Zelli, F. (2011) The fragmentation of the global climate governance architecture. *Wiley Interdisciplinary Reviews: Climate Change* 2(2): 255–270.

Zelli, F. and Van Asselt, H. (2013) Introduction: The institutional fragmentation of global environmental governance. *Global Environmental Politics* 13(3): 1–13.

Zelli, F., Gupta, A. and Van Asselt, H. (2013) Institutional interactions at the crossroads of trade and environment: The dominance of liberal environmentalism? *Global Governance: A Review of Multilateralism and International Organizations* 19(1): 105–118.

Zürn, M. and Faude, B. (2013) Commentary: On fragmentation, differentiation, and coordination. *Global Environmental Politics* 13(3): 119–130.

7   Transnational governance towards sustainable biofuels

Exploring a polycentric view

Christine Moser and Robert Bailis

Introduction

The Anthropocene concept poses a revised understanding of humanity's roles and responsibilities in the natural world. Many of the environmental problems we face today, however, are not the responsibility of a homogenized humanity, nor do they affect all humans in the same way (Lövbrand et al., 2015). Placing 'the human' (*anthropos*) at the centre of environmental change and aiming at mobilizing social change, the Anthropocene programme requires differentiated social analyses that account for spatial and sociocultural differences of human agency and impacts. Beyond the complexity of biophysical processes, such a radical understanding of the Anthropocene means a more nuanced understanding of the various conflicts between and within communities and their objectives (ibid.). Critical questions are: how can transformative change be facilitated, and what institutions ensure effective and equitable environmental governance?

The global environmental governance arena has been portrayed as staging a 'Cambrian explosion' (Keohane and Victor, 2011), a proliferation of rules, organizations and initiatives at several levels of governance (Widerberg, this volume). Transnational governance in particular is framed as decentralized, with a multitude of governance arrangements emerging bottom-up as problem-driven responses to environmental challenges (Abbott, 2011). Here, environmental standards and certification programmes have become a particularly prominent form of intervention for enhancing sustainability in commodity supply chains. Yet, despite scholarly calls for increased articulation between the public and the private, little is known about whether and how such governance arrangements become effective (Lambin et al., 2014).

Governance of land-based biofuels exemplifies the dimensions of responsibility, complexity as well as urgency of environmental governance in the Anthropocene. Governments around the world created demand for biofuel production through subsidies, policy programmes and mandates. Climate change mitigation, energy security and rural development have been presented as the main, co-beneficial objectives of deployment programmes (Bailis et al., 2015). Consequently, the demand for land-based biofuels and biofuel feedstock has increased substantially in the last decade. Rising food prices and food riots, conflicts arising from large-scale land investments, environmental degradation and adverse greenhouse-gas (GHG) emissions effects, however, casted serious doubts regarding the sustainability of biofuels. In response to growing evidence for negative impacts from biofuel demand, public and private actors on different scales developed regulations, standards and codes of conduct to mitigate or minimize the negative impacts of biofuels and their production processes (Moser et al., 2014). Sustainability governance in biofuel production is exemplary for 'increasing segmentation of different layers and clusters of rule-making and rule-implementing' (Biermann and Pattberg, 2012).

Drawing on an example of transnational governance for biofuel sustainability, the objective of this chapter is to explore the potential of the polycentricity concept to orientate investigations of transnational governance. Polycentricity refers to multi-level responses to public good provision and production that 'include the self-organizing relationship between many centres of decision-making that are formally independent of each other' (Galaz et al., 2012, p. 22). It is hence not only about multiplicity of governance units, but also about how interactions between these are organized in order to provide for collective goals.

The functional and normative concept suggests that polycentric governance succeeds to the extent that it enables the flexible and adaptive provision of problem solutions grounded in institutionalized accountability relationships. The resulting institutional diversity is akin to complex problems and multiple responsibilities in the Anthropocene. Based on an institutional analysis that looks at functional and structural components of governance systems as well as key institutional properties, we argue, the polycentricity concept can contribute analytical as well as critical ways to understand the nexus between design and performance in institutional diversity.

This argument is pursued as follows. First, we sketch out a basic understanding, analytical properties and critical implications of the polycentricity concept (section 2). Building on this, we portray transnational governance based on multi-stakeholder standards and certification as polycentric systems (section 3). Addressing collective action problems of transnational commodity chains, certification standards take a joint production approach – in which private benefits subsidize the voluntary provision of public goods, but which also poses inherent tensions between private and public benefits. In the absence of state-based authority, the polycentric field has evolved to account for these trade-offs by institutionalizing multi-stakeholder decision-making procedures, transparency and accountability. Governance for sustainable biofuels in the European Union (EU) relies on certification standards and is an illustrative case of a novel form of hybrid transnational governance with an articulate role for the state. Mapping this governance solution and practice (section 4), we find that the *de jure* re-regulation of the sector, by ways of its institutional design has led to a *de facto* de-regulation in the procedural dimension of biofuel certification – with problematic implications for the effectiveness and legitimacy of the overall governance approach.

Conceptualizing polycentric governance

In this section we delineate an understanding of the polycentricity concept, focusing on its relational, functional and context-dependent aspects. There are several related concepts and analyses that enhance our understanding of institutional complexity in the international realm, including work on regime complexes, institutional fragmentation, institutional interplay and interplay management (Zelli and van Asselt, 2013). While we acknowledge the contributions they provide to polycentricity, this chapter, due to space limitations, focuses on outlining elements of a polycentricity concept as developed by Vincent Ostrom and colleagues (Ostrom et al., 1961; Ostrom, 1999).

Multiplicity of governance units, we argue, is not a goal in itself. Studies on polycentric governance emerged because scholars were interested in the performance of different governance arrangements in providing a governance function, with performance as the dependent variable and polycentric form as the independent variable. The concept is based on the fundamental assumption that different public goods require different scales and modes of their provision and production. Polycentric configurations of interrelated actors and structures can provide for governance responses catering in such a way to specific problem characteristics (Ostrom et al., 1961), resulting in what we might refer to as 'institutional fit', i.e. a governance system in which multiple institutions can effectively operate with each other across spatial and temporal scales (Young, 2002).

While we stress that polycentric governance needs to be characterized and distinguished in specific contexts based on empirical inquiry, this would exceed the scope of this contribution. Nevertheless, in what follows, we lay conceptual and empirical groundwork, delineate analytical categories and shed light on underlying assumptions and critical aspects that should be considered in a more comprehensive framework.

The role of institutions

We follow Ostrom (2005) in our understanding of institutions as formal and informal rules, norms and customs, as well as strategies that shape human interactions. They are devices that can be designed and hence are subject to intervention and change. In that vein, environmental governance in the Anthropocene can be described as 'establishment, reaffirmation or change of institutions to resolve conflicts [of interest] over environmental resources' (Paavola, 2007, p. 94).

This understanding draws attention to authority, to design rules that steer conduct and to impact on behaviour, i.e. institutional performance. Importantly in this context, rules are not hierarchical, but affect behaviour by structuring action situations. Further, rules combine in configurations and interplays, meaning that they cannot be studied in isolation (Ostrom, 2005; Oberthür, 2009). For governance institutions, three functional levels can be distinguished: constitutional, collective and operational (Figure 7.1). While the levels refer to

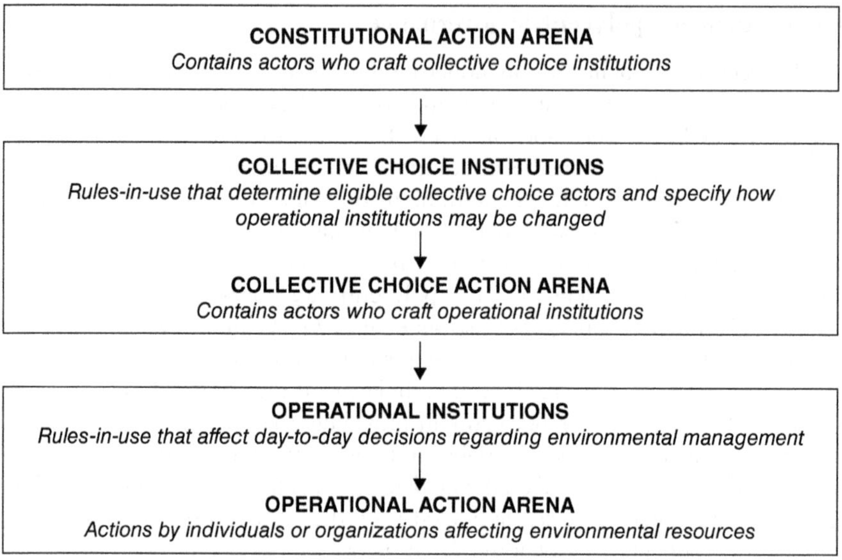

Figure 7.1 Three tiers of institutions. (Source: Adapted from Paavola, 2007; cf. Gruby and Basurto, 2013.)

institutional functions rather than to the vertical structure of a governance chain, 'today many governance solutions have both the three functional levels and a multi-level structure' that may emerge top-down or bottom-up, as Paavola elaborates (2007, p. 99).

The three-tier structure provides a useful analytical tool for mapping governance arrangements in 'higher resolution'. That is, it guides institutional analysis to disentangle the relative positions of actors and institutions in critical arenas of 'rule-making' and 'rule-taking'. Organizing analyses of polycentric systems around the three-level structure, we argue, furthermore enables interlinking different levels of governance and concrete environmental management behaviour. The approach displays the functional roles taken by actors and institutions in the respective action arenas in which they collaborate, compete or encounter conflicts.

Attributes of polycentric governance

According to Ostrom et al. (1961), a polycentric governance system occurs when 'many centres of decision-making which are formally independent of each other … take each other into account in competitive relationships, enter into various contractual and cooperative undertakings or have recourse to central mechanisms to resolve conflicts … with consistent and predictable patterns of interacting behaviour' (ibid., p. 831). Based on this definition, four attributes of inter-organizational arrangements in polycentric systems can be characterized (van Zeben, 2013).

The first attribute refers to a pluralism of independent governance units. They can exist on multiple levels (e.g. local, national, global), across different sectors (e.g. public, private), with multiple purposes (e.g. general, issue-specific, cross-jurisdictional) and with different governance functions (e.g. rule-making, enforcement). Importantly, these governance units are functionally interrelated. This is either by way of horizontal (e.g. intergovernmental initiatives) or vertical (e.g. in differentiated governance functions from supranational to national-level government) coordination, or by way of conflict (e.g. national-level policies violating international treaties).

Second, the interactions within the system generally do not follow a principal-agent model, but rather emerge in self-generating and self-organizing activities (Ostrom, 1999). However, in reality governance arrangements often interlink hierarchical and polycentric systems (Skelcher, 2005).

Third, an evolutionary process of 'competitive rivalry' and 'conflict resolution' marks polycentric systems (Ostrom, 1999). This idea is well captured by the term 'democratic destabilization' (Brassett et al., 2012). 'Destabilizing' effects occur based on competition between decision-making units, undermining existing sources of authority. 'Democratic' then refers to contestation based on some sort of performance review – triggering deliberation between authorities and affected publics, and, if necessary, institutional change. In this regard, multiplicity is as well a precondition as outcome of such societal processes.

Hence, and fourth, the relationships are institutionalized, i.e. they are staged in some sort of institutional architecture or 'general systems of rules' (Ostrom, 1999), which makes behaviour predictable and consistent. Herein, recourse to 'central mechanisms' of conflict resolution furthermore implies a nested structure with overarching rules.

Polycentricity thus is at least as much about 'means' as about 'ends'. Here, a normative dimension of the concept becomes visible that refers to aspects of democracy. Polycentric governance as outlined above implies certain 'institutional essentials' (van Zeben, 2013, p. 23) that facilitate particular societal processes, which in turn enable the emergence of a polycentric governance structure, capable of maintaining itself (Ostrom, 1999). Specifically, these include the freedom to organize and to enter or exit organizational forms that result in the availability of competing alternatives. Further, participating in deliberation, the process through which relationships are 'updated' in polycentricity necessitates procedural rules. Articulating criticism and nudging change to safeguard requires regular access to information, i.e. an institutionalized accountability relationship (Keohane, 2006). These types of institutions can be referred to as collective choice institutions (Figure 7.1). 'The safeguarding of these institutional essentials', van Zeben (2013, p. 23) summarizes, 'implies a certain amount of design and deliberation'. In our three-tier structure, this would take place in constitutional action arenas.

Performance, accountability and legitimacy in polycentric governance

Polycentricity has been portrayed as a functional governance structure in which individuals and organizational actors have the incentive to become 'public entrepreneurs', with the objective 'to realize a public benefit for a discrete community of people' (Ostrom, 1999, p. 70). This viewpoint emphasizes a view of polycentric governance as a response to specific problems, and hence as functional and dependent on specific contexts.

It also refers to performance. Consistent with its roots in rational-choice theory, foundational polycentricity literature refers to efficiency and cost-effectiveness as central performance criteria of bounded but intentionally rational actors (Ostrom et al., 1961). However, efficiency here is a function of responsiveness to preferences. As outlined earlier, processes of rivalry and consolidation ('democratic destabilization') are critical drivers for the adaptability of governance systems, with the 'consumer' of governance functions being the central force by means of articulation of preferences. Henceforth, the polycentric view prescribes neither form nor measure of performance for a polycentric governance system. Instead, whether a system takes adequate form depends on specific problems to be solved and their characteristics. The evaluation of outcomes is left to the targeted beneficiaries in a specific polycentric governance system (van Zeben, 2013), which might place more value on other objectives than efficiency, such as social justice or environmental sustainability (McGinnis and Ostrom, 2011, p. 20f.). Thus, by virtue of its flexibility, polycentricity leads to opportunities of governing at different spatial scales, responding to different preferences and addressing contingency in impacts and capacities among different places (Pahl-Wostl et al., 2012).

Clearly, this reading of polycentricity brings to the fore the need to construct legitimacy in order to motivate responses of compliance or change – constructed (and contested) in accountability relationships (Black, 2008). Legitimacy is provided on the grounds of its desirability, appropriateness and aptness of actions within a particular socially constructed system. Black (2008) calls transnational governance the 'hard case' in this context, as non-state actors cannot rely on the authority of law or nestedness in a wider legal order.

First, and especially when polycentric governance transcends jurisdictional boundaries, mandates become uncertain, i.e. it may be not clear who acts on whose behalf, and who is accountable to whom. Second, polycentric governance at any level (sub-national, national, international) has to deal with the problem of 'many hands' as different functions from rule-formulation to monitoring and enforcement are dispersed among many, making it difficult to identify who is accountable for what (Black, 2008, p. 143). Third, interdependencies between 'rulers' within polycentric systems cause 'inward' expansion of legitimacy communities, whose claims may have to be met. From the perspective of governance bodies, accountability is about 'navigational competence': making 'proper use of authority to range freely across a multi-relationship terrain in search of the most advantageous path to success' (Considine, 2002, p. 26).

Consequently, polycentricity has to deal with problems regarding the democratic quality of governance (Huitema et al., 2009), for example with regard to questions of representation: who should different governance bodies involve in decision-making; to whom should they to be accountable and how (Black, 2008)? Further normative challenges arise regarding objectives and operations of polycentric governance systems, where we can expect competing ideas of what goals should be pursued, and how. Complex, interdependent governance networks with no central locus of authority face further functional challenges that relate to coordination: with no steering or centrally coordinating part, how can a governance system move towards solving the problem, which it defines and by which it is defined? Besides strategic inconsistency, multiplicity of decision-centres increases the likelihood for 'forum shopping' and 'regime shifting' (Raustiala and Victor, 2004). Such problems are of course not limited to polycentric governance, but likely to be enhanced by it (Black, 2008).

There is, it should be noted, criticism that applies to the concept of polycentricity which points to, for example, the difficulty to determine or measure performance and the overreliance on decentralization (Huitema et al., 2009). A comprehensive discussion is beyond the scope of this chapter. However, particularly relevant given our research interest, critics challenge an important assumption: that transparency secures multi-directional accountability, leads to empowerment of the 'ruled' to hold the 'rulers' accountable, to participate in collective decision-making, and to make informed choices (Gupta and Mason, 2014). Similar presuppositions are engrained in contemporary environmental governance discourse and practice of a neoliberal environmentalism (Zelli et al., 2013) – of which certification schemes are a prominent manifestation. In this context, polycentricity can be criticized as indifferent to these problematic trends.

Polycentricity, as we apply it here, is an open-ended framework that refers to three interrelated dimensions of empirical analysis. On a conceptual level, we understand polycentric governance as functional, that is: contingent on the (nature of the) problems that it is concerned with, and emergent from dialectical relationships within organizational arrangements as well as between organizational and societal actors. On an organizational level, relational aspects of multiple, independent decision-making centres that interact by means of coordination and competition are in the focus. In a behavioural dimension, decision-making is strategic and affected by the institutional environment in which individual actors as well as the governance system as a whole are embedded. Critical analysis can be obtained through its diagnostic capacity, i.e. by scrutinizing organizational arrangements and key institutional rules regarding their ability to provide for and balance multiple accountability relationships.

Polycentricity in the transnational arena

Environmental standards and certification schemes are an increasingly important mode of transnational governance (Dingwerth and Pattberg, 2009). Standards are sets of environmental (and sometimes also social) specifications (i.e. principles and criteria) for the production of a commodity and/or attributes of a product or process. Hence, they are operational-level institutions as they aim to affect environmental management decisions of commodity producers. Here, we focus on third-party certification standards, i.e. the process in which the compliance with these standards is assessed, evaluated and certified by third parties.

Transnational environmental governance through standards and certification has been coined 'multi-level' and 'decentralized' with a view to its organizational dimension (Abbott, 2011). Some also speak of 'hybrid', 'collaborative' and 'experimentalist' governance (Ponte, 2014; Gunningham, 2009; Overdevest and Zeitlin, 2014), emphasizing the interrelational aspects of complex governance arrangements. Notwithstanding the epistemic and conceptual differences behind these terms, they all originate from attempts by various scholars to understand not only why and on what grounds these forms of governance emerge, but also how and to what effects interactions occur (Eberlein et al., 2014). In this section we examine certification standards as examples of polycentric governance: characterizing the problems they seek to address as well as the joint production approach; mapping generic organizational and institutional arrangements as they have become institutionalized in the field; and discussing their implications.

Environmental standards as 'entrepreneurial authorities' in global environmental governance

Environmental certification standards come to bear on a variety of different sectors, such as agrifood industries, extractive industries and fisheries – operating across diverse environmental policy domains, such as climate change, biodiversity and marine governance. They address environmental problems that are transnational in nature, such as emissions resulting from deforestation due to agricultural expansion. As well as their impacts, global commodity markets and their complex transboundary production chains pose collective action problems (Abbott, 2011). As a 'geographically unrestricted means of governance matched to the supply-chain-centred organization of global markets' (Auld, 2014, p. 126), certification standards transcend nation-state boundaries and directly affect environmental management at points of production. Hence, by devising and enforcing rules for environmental management, these transnational actors engage in the management of public goods, namely the conservation of natural ecosystems and their functions (including the capacity of the atmosphere to absorb emissions).

Environmental standards are often referred to as 'private' or 'voluntary' as they do not emerge from state authority. That said, a growing part of the literature questions the private–public dichotomy as many governance mechanisms showcase operational dependencies among different actors (Overdevest and Zeitlin, 2014). For example, standards' principles and criteria increasingly refer to existing public ones, such as national legislation and international norms. Conversely, state actors at all levels have used environmental standards, for example, as frameworks or in due diligence processes (Pattberg, 2012). These instances of horizontal coordination support our conceptualization of the transnational arena as polycentric governance. For the purpose of analytical clarity, however, we retain the distinction between state and non-state actors.

Private authority here can be understood as 'non-state actors [who] make rules or set standards that other relevant actors ... adopt' (Green, 2014, p. 29). This definition leaves a broad scope of targeted rule-takers: whoever legitimizes authority by adopting the rules (e.g. businesses adopting standards through certification of compliance; governments adopting standards in procurement or regulations). From the relational understanding of private authority it follows that its emergence is a function of demand. Green (2014) discerns 'delegated' from 'entrepreneurial authority', with certification standards typically being an example of the latter. The origins differ: state actors are collective principals in delegated authority; 'entrepreneurial authority exploits windows of opportunity to try to establish themselves as benefit providers to potential rule-adopters' (Green, 2014, p. 39). One is *de jure* and *ex-ante*; the other is *de facto* and *ex-post*. In both cases, consent to change behaviour results from perceived legitimacy (see also van Leeuwen, this volume).

Environmental standards attempt to align the provision of public goods with incentives of private firms along the respective commodity production chains. In the resulting 'joint production', private benefits subsidize the voluntary provision of a public good. In this vein, environmental standards have been characterized as 'green clubs' (Potoski and Prakash, 2013), which provide benefits to corporate members (e.g. reputational benefits, pre-emption of regulation) along with environmental goods to the public (e.g. climate protection; protection of local natural resources). It is exactly here that trade-offs may arise. For instance, more stringent standards benefit environmental public goods but may lower club membership due to increased costs for private beneficiaries. Consequently, it is important to examine how schemes organize governance functions to understand whether and how this tension is balanced.

Consistent with the framing of environmental standards as entrepreneurs, Reinecke et al. (2012) identify 'standard markets', i.e. issue areas in which multiple offerings of standards coexist. Although they address more or less common objectives, a dynamic of differentiation characterizes these fields – and with that, sustained contestation of interpretation of issues and solutions that resembles the competitive rivalry of polycentric governance. Given the need to mobilize private actors, however, 'competition may deepen some of the problems observed with respect to voluntary standards, such as corporate capture and short-termism, displacing more integrated approaches to systemic sustainability challenges and long-term social empowerment' (Reinecke et al., 2012, p. 28).

The multi-stakeholder approach of rule-making

Establishing entrepreneurial authority is particularly 'messy and complex' (Green, 2014) for it needs to devise rules, and – in the absence of a governmental mandate – 'sell' them to multiple targeted audiences (Black, 2008). While there is no constitutionally grounded legal order establishing legitimacy and accountability relationships, the organizational field of sustainability standards is highly institutionalized: 'decision-making procedures that follow a "multi-stakeholder approach" and guaranteed inclusiveness, [and] transparency and accountability,' (Dingwerth and Pattberg, 2009, p. 724) have become shared organizational features of sustainability standards. One term that signifies this institutionalization of the field is 'second generation' standards. It describes standard-setting initiatives that engage in 'roundtabling', i.e. standard governance is organized as a participatory process involving multiple stakeholders (Ponte, 2014). They differ from 'first generation' standards that have been mainly led by NGOs or industry actors. Getting key supply chain actors (e.g. retailers, producers) involved from the outset (i.e. in standard-formulation and governance processes) warrants a certain degree of uptake, while reducing the proliferation of competing and potentially weaker standard schemes. Participation by global and local NGOs and intergovernmental organizations establishes a voice for affected publics, and strengthens claims of legitimacy and accountability (Brassett et al., 2012).

In fact, some of these practices are manifested in the form of codes that can be referred to as collective choice institutions of an overarching framework. Their institutionalization has been driven by further organizations in the field, namely, the International Social and Environmental Accreditation and Labelling (ISEAL) Alliance, and the global environmental NGO World Wide Fund for Nature (WWF). ISEAL, the global membership association for sustainability standards, provides codes for good practices in standard formulation, implementation and monitoring. For example, the 'Standard Setting Code' sets out inclusive deliberation in rule-formulation processes; or the 'Impacts Code' that requires standards to develop monitoring and evaluation instruments. Seeking to prevent a Northern hemisphere 'club-mentality', the WWF, a member and initiator of several commodity roundtables, encourages refinement of global standards to fit local contexts, engagement with small producers, and inclusion of local communities in the certification process (Brassett et al., 2012). Some commodity standards have engrained these practices into their standards and certification procedures.

The organizational models of 'roundtabling' standard schemes thus adopt a 'complex web of institutional and governance features, developed managerial systems that are time- and resource-consuming, and enacted procedures to meet codes of good practice in standard setting and management' (Ponte, 2014, p. 9). However, there are also deficiencies with a view to inclusion of stakeholders, distribution of power, and unsystematic monitoring and accountability in standard setting and implementation (Brasset et al., 2012). These have been documented in several insightful studies but shall not be in our focus of attention here.

Implementation through third-party certification

Resulting from processes of standard-formulation in the collective choice arena are standards that function at the operational level of our three-tier structure. To become effective, standards need to be enforced. That is, businesses need to seek alignment with a standard, implement the respective criteria, and verify compliance by auditing, to obtain certification (Figure 7.2). Separation of rule-making and implementation in processes of auditing and certification is another feature of environmental standards that has become institutionalized in the field, which is achieved in third-party certification. Hence, verification of standards is yet another source of private authority, as it requires an independent third party, namely certification bodies and their auditors, to provide for this governance function.

Impartiality is a central characteristic of third-party certification, which is why it is considered more objective and effective, and hence more legitimate (Hatanaka and Busch, 2008). Certifiers' independence – from governments, assessed entities, suppliers or standard organizations – is thus of pivotal importance. To this end, certification bodies which want to contract with standard bodies to audit their standard, are themselves audited and accredited by accreditation bodies – a formal recognition of competency to carry out its tasks in specific sectors.

In this vertical division of labour along the governance chain of implementation, interactions between standard, certification and accreditation bodies are guided by formal rules, which are referred to as assurance requirements. These set out eligible accreditation bodies, criteria and processes, as well as auditor training specifications and audit processes. The rules organize interactions and attempt to safeguard transparent, independent and competent assessment of compliance with a standard's requirements. This systematization of certification has been developed in quality management, and is manifested in standards itself (e.g. ISO norms 19011, 17021 and ISO 65/ EN 45012). Complementing these norms, ISEAL has also laid out an 'Assurance Code' that stipulates the institutional and organizational design of a 'credible assurance system' for sustainability standards. Though not binding, the 'Assurance Code' grants a certain degree of 'voice' and 'entry/exit' to the affected public by defining 'best practices' such as stakeholder consultation in auditing, certification and accreditation procedures.

Notably, critics refer to this institutional design as a 'rational myth' that permeates despite deficiencies and decoupling of actual auditing practices (Boiral and Gendron, 2011). Nevertheless, the form of certification systems, i.e. how interactions are organized, is critical for the role they have come to play in transnational governance (Dingwerth and Pattberg, 2009). The rise of certification standards 'is part of the shift from government to governance, as it enables the state, retailers and NGOs to regulate relevant actors in an indirect and cost-effective way', argue Hatanaka and Busch (2008, p. 77).

In summary, it becomes clear that 'roundtabling' environmental standards not only represents additional political entrepreneurs to increasingly crowded and complex global environmental governance arenas, but multi-stakeholder certification standards in particular coordinate with further actors – jointly carrying out governance functions from crafting collective entities that formulate

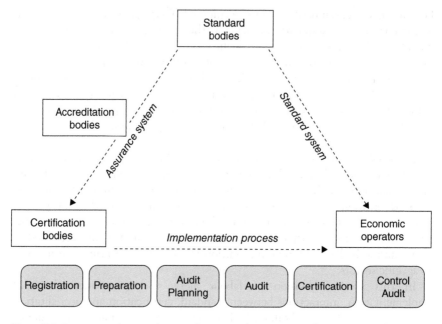

Figure 7.2 Institutional script that regularizes implementation of environmental standards through third-party certification. (Source: Adapted from van Dam et al., 2012.)

standards, to enforcing and monitoring rules through third-party certification that affect environmental management. Thereby, their horizontal and vertical interrelations are institutionalized to the extent that these patterns of ordering can be described as overarching rules – and transnational arenas of governance through standards as polycentric systems of governance. Challenges of multiple accountability relationships in polycentricity are exemplified by the tensions inherent in standards' joint production approach. Aiming at inclusiveness based on multiple institutionalized accountability relationships in various governance functions, roundtabling schemes attempt to balance these tensions by providing voice to stakeholders.

Mapping polycentric systems for sustainable biofuels

Non-state environmental standards and certification systems, to be sure, are subject to manifold contestations (Brassett et al., 2012). Besides challenges of enforcing the voluntary standards, critics refer to roundtables' risks of hijack by powerful stakeholders and institutional capture. Their proliferation has triggered concerns with regard to lack of effective coordination, increased transaction costs due to complexity, and growing competition between multi-stakeholder initiatives and business-dominated schemes that may result in a 'race to the bottom' in standards markets. Specifically relating to the EU Renewable Energy Directive, which explicitly delegates authority for certification standards for providing 'sustainability' in biofuel production chains, some have expressed hope that this hybrid approach could 'usher the process of certification – and its deliberative foundations – into commodity governance more broadly' (ibid., p. 392).

Nested polycentric governance for sustainable biofuels in the EU

In 2009, the EU adopted the Renewable Energy Directive 2009/28/EC (RED) and amended the complementary Fuel Quality Directive 98/70/EC through Directive 2009/30/EC (in the following referred to as EU-RED). The legislation stipulates that by 2020, the share of energy from renewable sources in transport shall reach a share of at least 10 per cent. For biofuels and other liquid bioenergy carriers, the EU-RED provides mandatory sustainability criteria (Moser et al., 2014): In order to be counted toward the 10 per cent target and to be eligible for funding schemes, biofuels were required to prove reduced life-cycle greenhouse gas (GHG) emission reductions of 35 per cent (increasing to 50 per cent in 2017 and to 60 per cent after 2018 for new plants). Fuels produced on land with recognized high biodiversity and carbon stocks and on peatland cannot be counted (Table 7.1). The directives do not include social or socioeconomic criteria, a point of major criticisms by NGOs and researchers.

Compliance with the RED mandatory sustainability criteria can be demonstrated in three ways: voluntary certification within several qualifying sustainability standards; Member State competent authority criteria, or bilateral agreements between the EU and third countries. Member States are to accept sustainability standards adopted by the European Commission (EC), and no bilateral agreements have been established with producer countries, making certification standards the central transnational governance mechanism. In other words, the EU is a captive market for sustainable biofuels (Ponte, 2014), and certification is *de facto* mandatory for producers, including from third countries.

Although certification programmes have long interacted with state regulation, this intervention can be considered significant as it exemplifies hybrid governance by actively blending state authority and private actors (Bailis and Baka, 2011): it is a public policy by European governmental bodies that stipulates extra-territorial enforcement and to this end employs a network of trans-territorial actors, the certification standards, opening up 'new avenues of functional authority' (Kay and Ackrill, 2014). But how exactly are these 'new avenues and functional authorities' constituted?

To enforce compliance with its minimum set of environmental criteria, the EU delegates the right to craft and enforce certification systems to further actors. The EC recognizes qualifying standards that contain at least the minimum set of criteria and provide for 'competent', 'independent', fraud-free and frequent certification of the whole supply chain (Table 7.1).

Hence, in polycentricity terms, the EC represents the central actor in the constitutional arena of this governance solution. The EU-RED policy itself then

Table 7.1 Qualifiers for recognition of standard systems under the EU-RED scheme

Type of criteria	Explication
Sustainability criteria	• Land use criteria: It is not allowed to convert land with high carbon stock or land with high biodiversity value into land used for production of biofuels, i.e. no forests, wetland or otherwise protected areas shall be destroyed to grow biofuels. • Minimum greenhouse gas savings compared to fossil fuels: It must be proven that biofuels emit at least 35 per cent less greenhouse gases then petrol (raised to at least 50 per cent from 2017, at least 60 per cent for new installations from 2018). • Chain of custody monitoring: The system needs to monitor the whole production chain, i.e. from how the crops are grown through the manufacturing process to the pump.
Assurance system criteria	• All companies in the supply chain are audited before making any claims about sustainability under the scheme. • Follow-up audits of companies in the supply chain takes place at least once a year. • The auditors are competent and independent. • The administrative system is protected against fraud.

Source: Based on European Commission, 2011.

is a collective-level institution that determines eligible decision-making units in collective choice arenas, to which it delegates the enforcement and monitoring of the operational-level rules they craft (Figure 7.3). Emerging from this overarching framework is a nested polycentric system, in which the EU-RED has a certain degree of hierarchical authority over certification standards and biofuel producers within and outside the EU.

It is a case of both delegated and entrepreneurial authority: convergence with and acceptance under the EU-RED presents a strategic advantage for standard-setters because of the strong case of legitimacy, which is why the directives have not only evoked proliferation of standards developed 'on demand'. But also, a number of standard schemes, which have been initiated or developed prior to the EU-RED have adopted standard contents and sought acceptance as well (Table 7.2).

Twelve of the seventeen schemes accepted under the EU-RED in mid-2014 operate transnationally, i.e. beyond EU borders, including a number of schemes that have been developed by corporations such as the global biofuel producer Neste Oil. Overall, initiators of standards for governing 'sustainable' conduct in biofuel production chains under EU-RED have included diverse groups of actors, partly in collaborative constellations (Table 7.2). We discern roundtable initiatives, governmental bodies in conjunction with multi-stakeholder groups or

Table 7.2 Twelve transnational sustainability schemes approved by the EU-RED (as of August 2014)

Schemes	Timing	Initiators[m]	(Multi-)Stakeholder involvement[m]	Feedstock/fuel type	Criteria
General schemes					
Roundtable for Responsible Soy – RTRS[a]	Initiated prior to RED; operational in 2011; RED-approved in 2011	WWF, Maggi Group, Unilever, Cordaid, Coop, Fetraf-Sul	Standard setting: yes Governance: yes Auditing: yes	Soy/biodiesel	RED and further environmental and social criteria
Roundtable for Sustainable Palm Oil – RSPO[b]	Initiated prior to RED; operational in 2008; RED-approved in 2012	WWF, Migros, Unilever, Malaysian Palm Oil Association, Aarhus United UK Ltd	Standard setting: yes Governance: limited Auditing: yes	Oil palm/biodiesel	RED and further environmental and social criteria
Bonsucro[c]	Initiated prior to RED; operational in 2010; RED-approved in 2011	WWF & IFC (World Bank)	Standard setting: yes Governance: yes Auditing: limited	Sugar cane/ethanol	RED and further environmental and social criteria
International Sustainability and Carbon Certification – ISCC[d]	Initiated prior to RED*; operational in 2010; approved in 2011	Initiated and facilitated by Meo Carbon Solutions Consulting and funded by the German Ministry of Agriculture (BMELV)	Standard setting: limited Governance: limited Auditing: limited	Wide range of feedstock and fuel types; non-energy outputs like bioplastics	RED and further environmental and social criteria
Roundtable on Sustainable Biomaterials – RSB[e]	Initiated prior to RED; operational in 2011; RED-approved in 2011	Multi-stakeholder forum including NGOs such as WWF, facilitated by the Swiss EPFL (École Polytechnique Fédérale de Lausanne) Energy Center	Standard setting: yes Governance: yes Auditing: yes	Wide range of feedstock and fuel types; non-energy outputs like bioplastics	RED and further environmental and social criteria
Netherlands Technical Agreement – NTA 8080/81[f]	Initiated prior to RED*; operational in 2011; RED-approved in 2012	Initiated by the Dutch government, managed by the Netherlands Standards Institute (NEN) (based on Cramer Criteria)	Standard setting: yes Governance: yes Auditing: yes	Wide range of feedstock and fuel types	RED and further environmental and social criteria

Table 7.2 continued

Schemes	Timing	Initiators[m]	(Multi-)Stakeholder involvement[m]	Feedstock/fuel type	Criteria
Biomass Biofuels voluntary scheme – 2BSvs[g]	Initiated following RED; operational in 2011; RED-approved in 2011	Associations representing the French biofuel industry and auditing firm Bureau Veritas as technical advisor	Standard setting: limited; Governance: limited; Auditing: no	Wide range of feedstock and fuel types	RED only
REDcert[h]	Initiated prior to RED*; operational in 2011 RED-approved in 2012	Twelve German farming/biofuels industry associations	Standard setting: limited; Governance: limited; Auditing: no	Wide range of feedstock and fuel types	RED only
Grain and Feed Trade Association Trade Assurance Scheme – GTAS[i]	Initiated prior to RED; operational in 2005; RED-approved in 2014	GAFTA (Grain and Feed Trade Association)	Standard setting: no; Governance: no; Auditing: no	Wide range of feedstock but certification covers only first processor	RED and quality and safety management criteria
Company-owned schemes					
Greenergy Brazilian bioethanol verification programme[j]	Initiated prior to RED*; operational in 2007; RED-approved in 2011	Greenergy Ltd, ProForest, WWF, independent consultancy	Standard setting: limited; Governance: no; Auditing: no	Sugarcane/ethanol	RED and further environmental and social criteria
Abengoa RED Bioenergy Sustainability Assurance – RBSA[k]	Initiated following RED; operational in 2011; RED-approved in 2011	Abengoa Bioenergia, S.A.	Standard setting: no; Governance: no; Auditing: no	Wide range of feedstock and fuel types	RED only
HVO Renewable Diesel Scheme for Verification of Compliance with RED[l]	Initiated following RED; operational in 2014; RED-approved in 2014	Neste Oil Oyj	Standard setting: no; Governance: no; Auditing: no	All feedstock suitable for biodiesel production	RED only

* Schemes initiated prior to RED but also following national biofuel sustainability regulation in EU member states.

Sources: a (www.responsiblesoy.org/); b (www.rspo.org/); c (www.bonsucro.com/); d (www.iscc-system.org/); e (http://rsb.org/); f (www.sustainable-biomass.org/); g (http://en.2bsvs.org/); h (www.redcert.org/index.php?lang=en&Itemid=208); i (www.gafta.com/gtas); j (www.greenergy.com); k (www.abengoabioenergy.com/web/en/rbsa/); l (www.nesteoil.com/default.asp?path=1,41,12079,20846,21127); m (WWF, 2013; Moser et al., 2014; Ponte, 2014).

industry actors, as well as single companies and industry associations. Interestingly, although the EU biofuels market significantly relies on imports and the regulation has caused contestation from producer countries (Moser et al., 2014), we count no certification scheme initiated in these countries.

Since EU-RED qualifiers do not address standard governance, institutional design varies greatly. While some EU-RED schemes are ISEAL members (Bonsucro, Roundtable for Sustainable Palm Oil [RSPO], and Roundtable for Sustainable Biomaterials [RSB] are full members; Roundtable for Responsible Soy [RTRS] is associated), the majority are not (WWF, 2013). ISEAL members (and the Dutch NTA 8080) are multi-stakeholder initiatives, although levels of stakeholder inclusion differ among these systems (Moser et al., 2014). Among these, the RSB is a remarkable example due to its unprecedented degree of consensus-based standard formulation, which saw more than 120 member organizations from over 30 developed and developing countries contribute, and its continuous efforts of inclusive and science-based governance. Among the schemes accepted under the EU-RED, the RSB is considered the most comprehensive and stringent.

In contrast, particularly the industry-dominated certification standards created to supply the RED do not adhere to ISEAL codes (WWF, 2013). Their designers, acting at the constitutional level of our three-tier structure (Figure 7.3), have established top-down governance structures that do not provide equal voice (if any) to stakeholders.

Given its success in uptake, the International Sustainability and Carbon Certification (ISCC) standard represents a noteworthy intermediate case. It was developed under the auspices of a German consultancy and financed by the German government. It involved stakeholders from NGOs and academia, though industry actors clearly dominated. The resulting standard is similar to the RSB regarding the scope of principles covered, but considered slightly less stringent and less inclusive in auditing. After its establishment, the ISCC adopted some features of a deliberative roundtable in its governance structure, which have thus been coined 'shallow and cosmetic' (Ponte, 2014, p. 8). Uptake of the ISCC standard for certification, however, by far exceeds that of the RSB (Bailis et al., 2015).

It becomes clear that the collective choice arena of EU-RED governance stages diverse and competing institutional and organizational configurations of transnational governance units. Yet, they operate in partly differing institutional settings: while the EU-RED provides for a nested structure that applies to all of the units within the polycentric system, multi-stakeholder initiatives have built additional institutional interconnections and accountability relationships. In comparison, their competitors that omit 'roundtabling' are 'leaner, quicker, and more attuned to industry interests', but also inclined 'to more easily discriminate against small players and actors in the global South' (Ponte, 2014, p. 9).

This is problematic from normative and democratic standpoints, and challenges the functional capacity of the overall governance solution. Additionally, foundations of the institutional design of third-party certification,

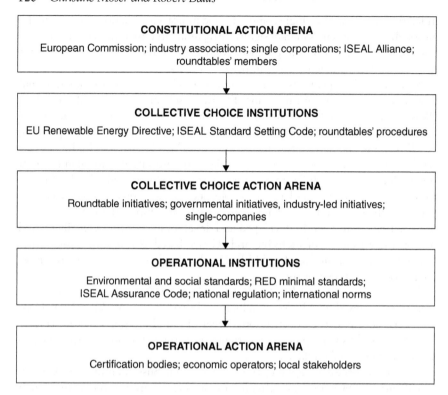

Figure 7.3 Mapping of polycentric EU-RED governance on the three-tier structure

such as functional division between standard-setters, certifiers and economic operators, are being re-shaped as the EU-RED accepts 'intermarriages' such as audit firms deploying and managing standard systems on behalf of industry (e.g. the Biofuels Biomass Sustainability Voluntary scheme [2BSvs]) and company-owned schemes by major European refiners [e.g. Neste Oil's certification system]). Here, rule-makers, rule-takers and intermediaries can hardly be discerned, challenging the very independence that EU-RED qualifiers ask for – and raising questions regarding the legitimacy and effectiveness of these schemes. Put differently, the EU-RED legitimizes avenues for functional authorities that are accountable to its corporate members primarily, and hence may prioritize realization of private over public benefits in their joint production approaches.

Does the EU promote certification over sustainability?

The effects of the EU-RED governance solution cannot be evaluated here. Nevertheless, we can identify tendencies based on figures on the regulatory share established by respective schemes (i.e. their uptake, in number of certificates issued). Despite the difficulty of comparing all RED-recognized schemes in their uptake due to differences in scope, there is some, although not conclusive evidence for an incentive to 'shop around' (Bailis et al., 2015). Comparing transnational schemes, the figures show a clear preference for the industry-led ISCC and 2BSvs standards, of which the latter contains no more than the EU-RED minimum criteria. Further, the adoption of the RSB is strikingly low; and other roundtables, too, struggle with expanding their regulatory share in the EU's biofuels certification market. Thus, the EU-RED hybrid governance solution appears to disadvantage roundtable initiatives as they have become institutionalized in the field of transnational governance.

What are the implications for standard implementation and decision structures? Clearly, the EU-RED not only embeds biofuel production to a certain, though minimal extent. It facilitates coherence among the multiple standards with a view to the environmental criteria. As a tendency, the sustainability standards developed in multi-stakeholder processes are more likely to set out stringent criteria, and to address social issues of biofuel production beyond the purely environmental EU-RED criteria such as human and labour rights, economic well-being and land rights of affected communities. In contrast, standards developed to comply with EU-RED tend to feature the minimum environmental criteria provided in the meta-standard and exhibit overall less stringency (Table 7.2).

In addition, the schemes also differ in conformance requirements that determine (at the operational level) which certification bodies are eligible, what training and expertise is required for auditing, and how auditing is conducted. Participatory standards tend to set out specific practices: auditors are to consult workers and local stakeholders for verifying compliance with certain criteria. Some RED standards include criteria that stipulate consultation with local communities, such as the free, prior and informant consensus (FPIC) method to rule out illegal or conflictive acquisition and use of land. Such requirements give voice to affected publics in and around production sites by including them in operational-level action arenas (Figure 7.3).

Furthermore, a comparison by the WWF (2013) shows that roundtables as well as the ISCC, to account for local contingencies, allow their generic criteria to be adapted (though only the RTRS and RSPO organize deliberative local stakeholder consultations). Schemes with a degree of deliberation, which exceed the EU's minimum criteria, also refer to relevant international norms (e.g. International Labour Organization [ILO]) conventions) and governmental legislation at points of production (e.g. national legislation on protected areas). Though little evidence exists, these links to international norms and conventions are assumed to have complementary 'normative and regulatory effects' by making these often weakly implemented norms more effective in practice (Pattberg, 2012).

Ironically in this context, while the RSB does not withstand the competition in material effects, its moral authority is unrivalled as is mirrored in its status as normative point of reference: for example, the Inter-American Development Bank's 'Biofuels Sustainability Scorecard' was informed by the RSB standard (Moser et al., 2014). This kind of horizontal interaction between private and public governance units has been argued to serve as a pathway of 'ratcheting-up' in the long run, as seen in the forestry sector (Overdevest and Zeitlin, 2014). Two interrelated mechanisms have been identified as helpful in this regard: benchmarking and comparison of schemes; and NGO campaigns mobilizing consumers and arm-twisting powerful industry actors. While the EU-RED carries the function of regulating industry, mobilizing social movements and consumers for 'sustainable' biofuels is more difficult for several reasons (Ponte, 2014). This leaves peer review processes of benchmarking and comparing standards relatively toothless, and refers us back to the role the EU-RED regulation could have played in safeguarding procedural qualities of its governance solution and facilitating transnational social learning towards sustainable biofuels.

Conclusion

Polycentricity, as sketched out here, describes the multi-level institutional arrangements that evolve to address complex problems. It offers a useful perspective to conceptualize the modes of environmental governance that have emerged in the Anthropocene. It refers to heterogeneity as both the beginning and end of governance solutions, and to the crucial role of institutional design for effective and legitimate governance.

Taking governance of biofuels as an example, we have explored the institutional complexity taking shape within the context of the EU's hybrid transnational governance for sustainable biofuels. The institutional landscape has been shaped, in many ways, by the urgency of problems and complex challenges associated with the massive ramp-up of biofuel production that occurred since biofuel mandates were first introduced: food price spikes, land grabs, protests and riots, as well as analyses highlighting the risk of large-scale land-use change and raising concerns that biofuels would actually increase rather than reduce emissions of climate-forcing pollutants.

To embed the interconnected risks of a market it has actively helped to create, the EU's approach orchestrates a complex governance arrangement of diverse sustainability standards and certification based on mandatory sustainability criteria prescribed by the RED. While the RED minimum criteria clearly do not serve to reduce tensions between conflicting biofuel objectives, the hope is that the directive will usher procedural practices of roundtable standards in global biofuel production chains.

The EU-RED, however, does not join up with established institutional scripts of the organizational field of standard setting and certification. As a result, not only are the differing certification standards under EU-RED in fierce rivalry but the notion of sustainability, too, is subject to a competition between different values, knowledge systems, and potentially also methods of implementation. Assessing the regulatory share of RED-accepted standards, we find that this competition indeed favours industry-led initiatives and marginalizes roundtable initiatives – thereby undermining accountability relationships that could yield effective and more legitimate governance.

To be sure, evidence on the effectiveness of roundtable governance vis-à-vis industry-led initiatives is not conclusive. More research is needed to understand how standards are translated and operationalized in the contractual line of accountability that certification systems form, and how different institutional design relates to outcomes. Spelling out such a research programme requires more substantive empirical enquiries of organizational models and interrelations in transnational governance. This would add more resolution to our understanding of polycentric systems, and reversely highlight the dimension of power in the concept of polycentricity.

We conclude by placing our findings in the context of the Anthropocene concept and the dimensions of urgency, complexity and responsibility. Arguably, the EU's hybrid governance towards sustainable biofuels – notwithstanding the adequacy of a massive deployment of biofuels in the first place – represents an approach that enabled a timely and flexible response to urgent sustainability challenges of global biofuel feedstock production. Joining up with certification standards in a polycentric arrangement, the significantly novel form of hybrid governance has enabled embedding trans-territorial biofuel production to a certain extent. In this regard, institutional complexity in our case reflects the material complexity of governing transnational supply chains. However, the EU's minimal environmental standard does not respond to the material complexity of biofuels sustainability, leaving several urgent environmental and socio-economic issues unaddressed. Furthermore, and ironically, the *de jure* re-regulation by the RED, by ways of its institutional design, *de facto* has led to a de-regulation of the organizational field of certification standards. Thereby, it has scaled the centres of decision-making away from multi-stakeholder roundtables, whose institutional design aims at addressing multi-faceted responsibilities in transnational environmental governance.

References

Abbott, K. W. (2011) The transnational regime complex for climate change. *Environment and Planning C: Government and Policy* 30(4): 571–590.

Auld, G. (2014) Confronting trade-offs and interactive effects in the choice of policy focus: Specialized versus comprehensive private governance. *Regulation & Governance* 8(1): 126–148.

Bailis, R. and Baka, J. (2011) Constructing sustainable biofuels: Governance of the emerging biofuel economy. *Annals of the Association of American Geographers* 101(4): 827–838.

Bailis, R., Solomon, B. D., Moser, C. and Hildebrandt, T. (2015) Biofuel sustainability in Latin America and the Caribbean – a review of recent experiences and future prospects. *Biofuels* 5(5) (online Sept 2015): 469–485.

Biermann, F. and Pattberg, P. (2012) Global environmental governance revisited. In Biermann F. and Pattberg, P. (eds). *Global Environmental Governance Reconsidered*. London and Cambridge: MIT Press, pp. 1–24.

Black, J. (2008) Constructing and contesting legitimacy and accountability in polycentric regulatory regimes. *Regulation & Governance* 2(2): 137–164.

Boiral, O. and Gendron, Y. (2011) Sustainable development and certification practices: Lessons learned and prospects. *Business Strategy and the Environment* 347(20): 331–347.

Brassett, J., Richardson, B. and Smith, W. (2012) Private experiments in global governance: Primary commodity roundtables and the politics of deliberation. *International Theory* 4(03): 367–399.

Considine, M. (2002) The end of the line? Accountable governance in the age of networks, partnerships, and joined-up services. *Governance* 15(1): 21–40.

Dingwerth, K. and Pattberg, P. (2009) World politics and organizational fields: The case of transnational sustainability governance. *European Journal of International Relations* 15(4): 707–743.

Eberlein, B., Abbott, K. W., Black, J., Meidinger, E. and Wood, S. (2014) Transnational business governance interactions: Conceptualization and framework for analysis. *Regulation & Governance* 8(1): 1–21.

European Commission (2011) Memo: Certification schemes for biofuels (19 July). Brussels: EC.

Galaz, V., Crona, B., Österblom, H., Olsson, P. and Folke, C. (2012) Polycentric systems and interacting planetary boundaries – Emerging governance of climate change–ocean acidification–marine biodiversity. *Ecological Economics* 81: 21–32.

Green, J. F. (2014) *Rethinking Private Authority. Agents and Entrepreneurs in Global Environmental Governance.* Princeton, NJ: Princeton University Press.

Gruby, R. L. and Basurto, X. (2013) Multi-level governance for large marine commons: Politics and polycentricity in Palau's protected area network. *Environmental Science & Policy* 33: 260–272.

Gunningham, N. (2009) The new collaborative environmental governance: The localization of regulation. *Journal of Law and Society* 36(1): 145–166.

Gupta, A. and Mason, M. (2014) A transparency turn in global environmental governance. In Gupta A. and Mason, M. (eds), *Transparency in Global Environmental Governance. A Critical Perspective.* Cambridge and London: MIT Press, pp. 3–38.

Hatanaka, M. and Busch, L. (2008) Third-party certification in the global agrifood system: An objective or socially mediated governance mechanism? *Sociologia Ruralis* 48(1): 73–91.

Huitema, D., Mostert, E. and Pahl-Wostl, C. (2009) Adaptive water governance: Assessing the institutional prescriptions of adaptive (co-)management from a governance perspective and defining a research agenda. *Ecology and Society* 14(1). http://www.ecologyandsociety.org/vol14/iss1/art26/

Kay, A. and Ackrill, R. (2014) *Challenges in Extra-Territorial Policy and Business Implementation: EU Biofuels Policy.* Paper presented at the Conference on Regulatory Governance, Barcelona, 25–27 June.

Keohane, R. O. (2006) Accountability in world politics. *Scandinavian Political Studies* 29(2): 75–87.

Keohane, R. O. and Victor, D. G. (2011) The regime complex for climate change. *Perspectives on Politics* 9(01): 7–23.

Lambin, E. F., Meyfroidt, P., Rueda, X., Blackman, A., Börner, J., Cerutti, P. O. et al. (2014) Effectiveness and synergies of policy instruments for land use governance in tropical regions. *Global Environmental Change* 28: 129–140.

Lövbrand, E., Beck, S., Chilvers, J., Forsyth, T., Hedrén, J., Hulme, M. et al. (2015) Who speaks for the future of Earth? How critical social science can extend the conversation on the Anthropocene. *Global Environmental Change* 32: 211–218.

McGinnis, M. D. and Ostrom, E. (2011) Reflections on Vincent Ostrom, public administration, and polycentricity. *Publice Administration Review* 72: 15–25.

Moser, C., Hildebrandt, T. and Bailis, R. (2014) Sustainable development of biofuels in Latin America and the Caribbean. In Solomon, B. D. and Bailis, R. (eds), Biofuel Sustainability in Latin America and the Caribbean – A Review of Recent Experiences and Future Prospects. New York, NY: Springer, pp. 27–69.

Oberthür, S. (2009) Interplay management: Enhancing environmental policy integration among international institutions. *International Environmental Agreements: Politics, Law and Economics* 9(4): 371–391.

Ostrom, E. (2005) *Understanding Institutional Diversity*. Princeton, NJ: Princeton University Press.

Ostrom, V. (1999) Polycentricity (Part 1). In McGinnis, M. D. (ed), *Polycentricity and Local Public Economies: Readings from the Workshop in Political Theory and Policy Analysis*. Ann Arbor: University of Michigan Press, pp. 52–74.

Ostrom, V., Tiebout, C. M. and Warren, R. (1961) The organization of government in metropolitan areas: A theoretical inquiry. *American Political Science Review* 55(04): 831–842.

Overdevest, C. and Zeitlin, J. (2014) Assembling an experimentalist regime: Transnational governance interactions in the forest sector. *Regulation & Governance* 8(1): 22–48.

Paavola, J. (2007) Institutions and environmental governance: A reconceptualization. *Ecological Economics* 63(1): 93–103.

Pahl-Wostl, C., Lebel, L., Knieper, C. and Nikitina, E. (2012) From applying panaceas to mastering complexity: Toward adaptive water governance in river basins. *Environmental Science & Policy* 23: 24–34. http://doi.org/10.1016/j.envsci.2012.07.014

Pattberg, P. (2012) Transnational environmental regimes. In Biermann, F. and Pattberg, P. (eds), *Global Environmental Governance Reconsidered*. London and Cambridge: MIT Press, pp. 97–122.

Ponte, S. (2014) "Roundtabling" sustainability: Lessons from the biofuel industry. *Geoforum* 54: 261–271.

Potoski, M. and Prakash, A. (2013) Green clubs: Collective action and voluntary environmental programs. *Annual Review of Political Science* 16(1): 399–419. http://doi.org/10.1146/annurev-polisci-032211-211224

Raustiala, K. and Victor, D. G. (2004) The regime complex for plant genetic resources. *International Organization* 58(02): 277–309.

Reinecke, J., Manning, S. and von Hagen, O. (2012) The emergence of a standards market: Multiplicity of sustainability standards in the global coffee industry. *Organization Studies* 33(5–6): 791–814.

Skelcher, C. (2005) Jurisdictional integrity, polycentrism, and the design of democratic governance. *Governance: An International Journal of Policy, Administration, and Institutions* 18(1): 89–110.

Van Dam, J., Ugarte, S. and van Iersel, S. (2012) *Selecting a Biomass Certification System{--} A Benchmark on Level of Assurance, Costs and Benefits*. Study Report, March 2012. Utrecht: NL Agency.

Van Zeben, J. (2013) *Research Agenda For a Polycentric European Union*. The Vincent and Elinor Ostrom Workshop in Political Theory and Policy Analysis Working Paper Series, No. W13-13. http://papers.ssrn.com/sol3/papers.cfm?abstract_id=2261006

WWF (2013) *Searching for Sustainability. Comparative Analysis of Certification Schemes for Biomass used for the Production of Biofuels*. Berlin: WWF. http://awsassets.panda.org/downloads/wwf_searching_for_sustainability_2013_2.pdf

Young, O. R. (2002) *The Institutional Dimensions of Environmental Change. Fit, Interplay, and Scale*. Cambridge, MA: MIT Press.

Zelli, F. and van Asselt, H. (2013) Introduction: The institutional fragmentation of global environmental governance: Causes, consequences, and responses. *Global Environmental Politics* (August): 1–13.

Zelli, F., Gupta, A. and van Asselt, H. (2013) Institutional interactions at the crossroads of trade and environment: The dominance of liberal environmentalism? *Global Governance* 19(1): 105–118.

8 Governing the Arctic in the era of the Anthropocene

Does corporate authority matter in Arctic shipping governance?

Judith van Leeuwen

Introduction

Global interest in the Arctic has awakened because it is increasingly accessible as a result of both climate change and technological innovation (Berkman and Young, 2009). The Anthropocene thus also affects the Arctic, as the increased economic potential of the region will incentivize an unprecedented impact of human activities on the Arctic's ecosystems. Concerns exist about the potential social and ecological effects of future economic activities, especially since there is no powerful, overarching governance system that provides and enforces environmental standards (de La Fayette, 2008; Molenaar, 2008; Berkman and Young, 2009). A key question is how to organize the co-evolution of indigenous societies and their surrounding environment given the increased economic use of the Arctic's resources, and how to develop effective and equitable governance solutions to achieve sustainable growth in the Arctic (see also Pattberg and Zelli, this volume; Walbott, this volume).

Next to offshore oil and gas production, fishing and tourism, shipping is likely to increase following better accessibility of the region and higher fuel prices which make shorter shipping routes attractive (Molenaar, 2008). Environmental risks of shipping in the Arctic come from both operational pollution as well as possible accidents. Operational pollution includes discharges of oil, chemicals, sewage, garbage and emissions to air of CO_2, NO_x, SO_x and PM. Accidental pollution can lead to large oil spills and loss of cargo.

This chapter questions whether corporate authority matters in Arctic shipping governance, given its institutional complex architecture in the emerging Anthropocene. A patchy set of (inter)national environmental standards exist for the Arctic (see for an overview PAME Working Group, 2009) as well as for commercial shipping (Van Leeuwen, 2010; Van Leeuwen and Kern, 2013). The International Maritime Organization, the Arctic Council and Port State Control share authority over the decision making and enforcement of these standards for shipping in general and for Arctic shipping in particular. These loci of authority are state-led in nature and suffer from the implementation gap that is characteristic for intergovernmental decision making (Tan, 2006; Van Leeuwen, 2010). One could therefore expect the emergence of non-state market driven (NSMD) initiatives to fill the regulatory and/or implementation gap left by states (Yliskylä-Peuralahti and Gritsenko, 2014).

This is however not the case. NSMD initiatives exist, but they have not institutionalized to such an extent that they complement the state-led institutions in Arctic shipping governance, a practice that is sometimes observed in other policy domains (see also Moser and Bailis, this volume). To seek an explanation as to why NSMD authority is of limited relevance in Arctic shipping governance, this chapter analyses the motivations of corporate actors to become engaged in the existing NSMD initiatives and why ship owners are hesitant to develop or actively participate in such initiatives. In doing so, I draw on insights from management literature and aim to contribute to the debate on private authority in global environmental governance as well as to the limited body of literature that investigates motivations for green shipping practices (Lai et al., 2011).

This chapter is structured as follows. The next section will introduce key concepts that guide the analysis, including private authority and different forms thereof, and motivations of corporate actors in participating in state-led and non-state market-driven governance. Section 3 will introduce the growth of Arctic shipping and the characteristics of state-led institutions in Arctic shipping governance. Section 4 will then discuss the limited relevance of NSMD initiatives and private authority in Arctic shipping governance as well as the motivations of shipping companies to actively participate in governance initiatives or not. The chapter will end with conclusions in section 5.

Corporate authority in polycentric global environmental governance

The growing fragmentation of institutions and policy initiatives in global environmental governance has recently been put forward by a number of scholars (Biermann et al., 2009; Zelli and Van Asselt, 2013). Many policy domains within global environmental governance are marked by a patchwork of international institutions that are different in character, their constituencies and their subject matter (Biermann et al., 2009, p. 16). Global governance is characterized by multiple interdependent loci of authority that are formally independent of each other (Ostrom, 2010).

Yet, polycentric governance not only refers to complex networks of multiple loci of authority, but also to the fact that such loci exist within, between and beyond the nation-state (see also Widerberg, this volume). As a result of political modernization processes, such as globalization, Europeanization and individualization, non-state market-driven loci of authority have emerged which are based on the exercise of corporate authority. This section will further discuss the emergence of as well as motivations for corporate authority.

Corporate authority in polycentric environmental governance

The boundary between public and private actors and their activities is blurring and consequently authority is dispersed between state, market and civil society actors. Different definitions for authority in general and for private or corporate authority in particular exist in the literature on global (environmental) governance. Rosenau refers to compliance as a key indicator for authority: authority is found 'in the readiness of those towards whom authority is directed to comply with the rules and policies promulgated by the authorities' (Rosenau, 2006, p. 174). Green (2014, p. 29) defines private authority as 'situations in which non-state actors make rules or set standards that other relevant actors in world politics adopt'. In a way, both definitions are complementary to each other, because Green emphasizes the rule and standard-setting capabilities while Rosenau emphasizes compliance-generating capabilities.

Both implicitly refer to the fact that authority is a relational concept in which consent with the authority exercised is given by those that are subject to that authority. For Green (2014) this consent takes place through the adoption of the rules and standards by other relevant actors in world politics while Rosenau (2006) sees the broader idea of compliance as a way to generate this consent. This chapter will combine both definitions: private authority is the ability of non-state actors to develop rules or standards for which readiness of compliance exists. It should be noted that this readiness of compliance can also be the result of strong enforcement of rules or standards. In addition, based on this definition of authority I see a locus of authority as *a more or less stable institutional setting of a policy domain in which actors develop rules and standards for which readiness of compliance exists* (also based on Van Leeuwen, 2010).

Following Green, I make a distinction between delegated private authority and entrepreneurial private authority. This implies a distinction between a state-led locus of authority and an NSMD locus of authority. Private actors become agents of the state when the state delegates authority to private actors for certain tasks to enhance its credibility, to facilitate collective decision making and/or to facilitate implementation (Green, 2014). This means that private authority is linked to a state-based locus of authority in which the state is still the principal governor. Processes of privatization or functional decentralization are examples of delegated private authority. According to Green (2014), delegated authority hardly takes place within global environmental governance and, if so, it is mostly for technical matters.

NSMD loci of authority are transnational private governance systems that derive their policy-making authority not from the state, but from the market, where the supply chain provides the institutional setting which grants authority and forms the basis of political struggle (Cashore, 2002). In these cases, entrepreneurial authority is exercised by private actors, not based on delegation of tasks by the state, but on 'the organization and control of economic, political and social activities by means of making, implementing, monitoring and enforcing rules' (Mattli and Woods, 2009 in Green, 2014, p. 80). Private authority in NSMD initiatives is commonly exercised through certification schemes, information-based standards, environmental management systems and industrial codes (Green, 2014).

Motivations driving corporate authority

The emergence of private authority is linked to a conscious decision by states (in situations of delegated authority) or by corporate actors to develop market-based rules and standards (in cases of entrepreneurial authority). In the following, I draw from the debate within management studies on why corporations green their business and engage in self-regulatory activities.

Stakeholder pressure is assumed to be a key driver for large corporations to go beyond the minimum requirements and to engage in self-regulatory practices (Perez-Batres et al., 2012). Customers, competitors, environmental lobby groups and the media are all possible stakeholders of a company and each company has a unique relationship with its stakeholders (Worthington, 2012). Stakeholders try to influence companies through lobbying for changes in governmental regulations, adversarial tactics such as issuing of lawsuits, extensive media exposure or boycotting, or cooperative approaches to work together in developing products, services or schemes (Hoffman and Georg, 2012).

As a consequence, companies have become aware of their social responsibility towards society in terms of the legal, ethical and philanthropic responsibilities that a company has, next to its economic ones (Carroll, 1991). In general, companies will aim to reduce negative reactions of stakeholders and build stakeholder support by becoming more ecologically responsive, but in practice the influence of stakeholders on a company differs depending on managerial perceptions of costs and benefits of action or inaction (Worthington, 2012). While stakeholder pressure is a key driver, the exact motivations of companies to actively engage in state-led and NSMD practices differ. The importance of a certain type of motivation varies between companies that are only part of state-led governance arrangements and those who engage in non-state market-driven governance.

Between the mid-1990s and early 2000s a debate on management addressed three sets of motivations. Governmental regulation is widely recognized as the first important external motivation to become more green (Hoffman and Georg, 2012; Worthington, 2012). Complying with existing regulation is important for the legitimation of a company, i.e. efforts to improve the appropriateness of corporate behaviour within established regulations, norms, values and beliefs (Bansal and Roth, 2000). Companies seek legitimation to protect their licence to operate, avoid fines and penalties, reduce risks to their long-term sustainability and to increase employee satisfaction (Bansal and Roth, 2000). The extent to which legislation drives change in corporate environmental performance can vary within a single industry. Factors that influence the effect of this driver are, for example, regulatory style, organizational culture, including organizational flexibility, role of industry associations and stakeholders, and the perception of the influence of regulation on a company's competitiveness (Worthington, 2012). The link between this driver of ensuring legitimation and state-led governance arrangements is easy to make. Companies will participate in state-led governance to both influence the development as well as the implementation of environmental regulation. Similarly, legitimation will also be important in NSMD governance but based on this motivation alone, it is not possible to explain why companies want to go beyond their legal requirements.

A second motivation refers to economic opportunities that come with improved environmental performance. Ecological responsiveness can improve a company's competitiveness and long-term profitability (Bansal and Roth, 2000). Lowering costs through reducing waste or resource input as well as creating markets for green products creates economic benefits for a company (Bansal and Roth, 2000; Worthington, 2012). In state-led loci of authority, economic motivations can be important when non-compliance means reduced access to the market. Many NSMD practices are based on certification and labelling activities that aim to create a market for sustainable products. Related to this motivation is the recent phenomenon of green consumerism. Green consumerism suggests an increased importance of environmental values in explaining consumer buying behaviour. How widespread this phenomenon is and to what extent this green consumerism is motivating companies to improve their environmental performance is unclear (Hoffman and Georg, 2012).

Ethical and social values are a third motivation for a company to invest in environmental behaviour. Companies sometimes act out of a sense of obligation, responsibility or philanthropy rather than self-interest (Bansal and Roth, 2000). This motivation is often related to powerful individuals within the company who promote ecological or social values (Bansal and Roth, 2000; Worthington, 2012). Although sometimes difficult to separate from other types of motivation, values play a minimal role in state-led governance arrangements. In NSMD governance, however, the link with ethical and social values is more relevant for explaining why a company follows or even initiates standards beyond what is required.

State-led Arctic shipping governance

The receding sea ice during the summer in the Arctic is interesting for the shipping sector as it provides a shorter route between Asia and the North American and European continents resulting in an increase in Arctic shipping. Several state-led Arctic institutions have emerged that are involved in shipping governance, but the most important institution is the International Maritime Organization. This section will show that private authority – both delegated and entrepreneurial – hardly plays a role, while global and regional intergovernmental institutions clearly carry the most weight in Arctic shipping governance.

Increase in Arctic shipping

Shipping in the Arctic takes place via the Northeast Passage or the Northwest Passage. The Northwest Passage follows the Northern Canadian and Alaskan coasts, while the Northeast Passage follows the Norwegian and Russian coasts. In both cases, shipping takes place within the territorial waters or the Exclusive

Economic Zones of these countries. The Northeast Passage offers most potential in the short term as it has a lower ice coverage and the Barents Sea of Norway remains ice-free due to currents of warm water from the Gulf Stream that feeds into the North Atlantic.[1] Current shipping rates in the Arctic are still very small, but clearly increasing: two German cargo ships used the Northeast Passage for the first time in 2009, four ships used the Passage in 2010, 46 in 2011 and 71 in 2013.

On the one hand the potential of Arctic shipping routes is widely recognized. The distance of maritime journeys between Europe and other countries is reduced by 30 to 50 per cent and/or 15 days if one takes the Northeast Passage on a journey from Shanghai to Hamburg for example. Experts believe that the North Pole will be completely ice-free in the summer months in the future, although they differ in opinion whether this will be by as early as 2030 or not before 2050 or 2080.[2] This would open a third possible route, i.e. the Transpolar Sea Route, which crosses the centre of the North Pole and therefore mostly runs through an international high sea area. Moreover, risks of piracy can be avoided.[3] Growth in shipping is further expected in the short term as a result of increased export of Arctic hydrocarbon resources, primarily from Russia.[4]

On the other hand, growth of maritime traffic in this area may run into some obstacles.[5] It is uncertain whether the receding ice cover is a long-term trend or part of a climatic cycle that only gives opportunities for shipping in the summer season. Moreover, there is a lack of transhipment hubs in the region, which is why most current journeys are destinational in nature, for example for transport from one Russian port to another (see also PAME Working Group, 2009). Safety issues are a concern as well. Weather conditions are variable and ships need to be certified to operate in the Arctic. The Northern Sea Route Administration of Russia generally requires ships to be accompanied by seasoned Arctic skippers while traversing the eastern section.[6] In addition, many ships still need an icebreaker escort in the summer. Another major concern are the effects of and response to incidents and accidents in the Arctic area. Adequate response is a challenge because the Arctic is a very large geographic area and the density of activity and response capabilities are low (PAME Working Group, 2009).

Arctic governance

To promote cooperation, coordination and interaction between the Arctic states on the sustainable development and environmental protection of the Arctic, the Arctic Council was established in 1996. It's unique feature is that it gives indigenous peoples a formal place in the decision-making procedure alongside Arctic and non-Arctic nation states. Actors can apply to become permanent observers so that they are allowed to attend all meetings of the Council (Smits et al., 2014). The work of the Arctic Council is hampered by the unwillingness of states to develop a binding agreement similar to the Antarctic Treaty (de La Fayette, 2008).

The Arctic Council does not have a programme budget, which means that substantive work under the Council depends on national financial contributions and the willingness of countries to take the lead in specific projects (Stokke, 2013). For example, the Arctic Council initiates assessment and monitoring work such as the Arctic Marine Shipping Assessment of 2009. This assessment presents future scenarios of Arctic shipping and evaluates national and international governance structures and the consequences of increased shipping for the local population and the environment (Stokke, 2013).

The Arctic Council also has an Emergency Prevention Preparedness and Response committee, which exchanges information on best practices and conducts projects to develop guidance and risk assessment methodologies, response exercises and training.[7] In addition, in 2013 a legally binding Agreement on Cooperation on Marine Oil Pollution Preparedness and Response in the Arctic was reached which includes voluntary operational guidelines for oil pollution preparedness and response. Under this agreement, the Arctic states agreed that each signatory will maintain a national system to respond to oil pollution incidents promptly and effectively. The agreement also aims at strengthening cooperation, coordination and mutual assistance between the parties.

A sub-regional institution that is part of the Arctic governance architecture is the Barents Euro-Arctic Region, which was established in 1993. It is the intergovernmental forum for cooperation for the Barents Region. One of the organs of this forum is the Steering Committee for the Barents Euro-Arctic Transport Area, which focuses on improving the integration of road, railway and port systems in the region, including development of coastal shipping and sea safety (Fauchald, 2011 in Stokke, 2013). Similar to the Arctic Council, the Barents Euro-Arctic Region uses knowledge generation and soft law as the main instruments in achieving cooperation.

Another sub-regional institution contributing to Arctic governance is the Nordic Council of Ministers. The council started the Arctic Cooperation programme in 2012 with the aim to support processes, projects and initiatives that will help promote sustainable development in the Arctic. The programme will support people of the Arctic in adapting to the effects of globalization and climate change. However, no specific mention is made of shipping activities in the Arctic.[8]

Preceding the Arctic Council's Agreement on Cooperation on Marine Oil Pollution Preparedness and Response in the Arctic, sub-regional agreements on oil pollution prevention and response were already in place. Similarly to the Council agreement, these agreements can best be seen as a way to enhance capacity under the International Convention on Oil Pollution Preparedness, Response and Co-operation (OPRC) of the International Maritime Organization.

International Maritime Organization

The shipping sector is an important contributor to international trade, as 90 per cent of all traded goods are transported by ships. Due to the global character of shipping, shipping governance has a long history of intergovernmental decision making through international agreements, most notably through the International Maritime Organization (IMO). The IMO was established in 1948 under the Geneva Convention and assumed its work in 1958. At the time of writing, it had adopted over 45 conventions related to maritime safety, environmental risks as well as liability and compensation for maritime claims. Three conventions form the core of the IMO's regulatory work: the 1973 International Convention for the Prevention of Pollution from Ships, as modified by the Protocol of 1978 (MARPOL 73/78), the 1974 International Convention for the Safety of Life at Sea (SOLAS) and the 1978 International Convention on Standards of Training, Certification and Watchkeeping for Seafarers (STCW). With regard to the Arctic, the OPRC Convention and the Guidelines for ships operating in polar waters (adopted in 2009) are relevant as well.

While more than 150 states ratified the MARPOL and SOLAS Conventions, covering about 98 per cent of global shipping tonnage,[9] a number of critiques exist about the functioning of IMO in maritime governance. The IMO has often been accused of being a 'ship owners' club' because of the dominance of flag states in IMO decision making (Tan, 2006). A flag state is the state where a ship is registered and has full jurisdiction over this ship at all times.

In the last 15 years, however, this jurisdictional scope has changed because port states, which experience environmental effects from shipping in their ports, gained more authority (Ringbom, 1999; Tan, 2006; Van Leeuwen, 2010; Van Leeuwen and Kern, 2013). The distinction between flag and port states and the jurisdiction of these states is laid down by the 1982 United Nations Convention on the Law of the Sea (UNCLOS). Port states have jurisdiction over any ship visiting their port and are allowed to set rules and standards for such ships. They are also allowed to inspect and prosecute ships while they are in port for violations under international law.

With the changing power relations between flag and port states, the ambition level of IMO standards with regard to environmental issues substantially increased as is illustrated by the adoption of a number of new Conventions with ambitious standards combined with lower thresholds for their entry into force, such as the Ballast Water Management Convention and the Anti-Fouling Convention.

The IMO has a history of long negotiation processes. It might easily take 20 years from the start of the agenda-setting process for a convention to its entry into force (Tan, 2006; Wuisan et al., 2012). In addition, many states cannot keep up with implementation and enforcement due to the sheer proliferation of international regulations adopted by the IMO (Tan, 2006). Finally, as the IMO does not have any enforcement powers (Vorbach, 2001), it is unable to take measures against states that fail to implement IMO standards (Ringbom, 1999).

Next to this challenge of transposing international agreements into national law, there is also the challenge of monitoring whether the behaviour of ships is according to the standards set. Flag states do not have much access to ships registered in their state, because a ship does not necessarily visit its flag state regularly. This especially goes for the open registries where the link between the ship and its flag state is weak. In addition, flag states lack the required expertise to inspect the technical specificities of a ship. This is why the majority of flag states have a contract with a classification society that inspects the ships and passes the certificates required by the IMO Conventions, e.g. the International Oil Pollution Prevention Certificate (Vorbach, 2001; Tan, 2006). In addition, classification societies themselves set classification rules for the design and construction of ships and issue certificates as a proof of compliance.

Besides the active quest for global, uniform shipping standards to allow an economically level playing field for a truly global sector, the IMO allows for some regional sensitivity in its regulations, also for the Arctic region (Stokke, 2013; Van Leeuwen, under review). For example, under the SOLAS Convention regulations on meteorological and ice-patrol services were included. Similarly, the STCW Convention includes the training of masters for ships operating in polar waters.

Non-mandatory guidelines for ships operating in the Arctic ice-covered waters have been adopted in 2002 and revised in 2009 (Guidelines for Ships Operating in Arctic Ice-covered Waters). These Guidelines were supplements to the SOLAS and MARPOL Conventions and include standards on construction, equipment and operational aspects, including both safety and environmental matters.

In 2014, the International Code for Ships Operating in Polar Waters (Polar Code) was adopted. The International Code is mandatory because it is linked to amendments to the SOLAS Convention (also adopted in 2014) and MARPOL Convention (adopted in 2015). The Polar Code is expected to enter into force on 1 January 2017. Similar to the Guidelines, the Code covers the full range of shipping matters relevant to navigation in waters surrounding the two poles – ship design, construction and equipment; operational and training concerns; search and rescue; and, equally important, the protection of the unique environment and eco-systems of the polar regions.[10] The Code requires ships operating in the Antarctic and Arctic to apply for a Polar Ship Certificate, which would classify the vessel as A, B or C:

- Category A: the ship is designed for operation in polar waters at least in medium first-year ice, which may contain old ice inclusions;
- Category B: the ship is not included in category A, but designed for operation in polar waters in at least thin first-year ice, which may contain old ice inclusions;
- Category C: a ship is designed to operate in open water or in ice conditions less severe than those included in Categories A and B.

Port state control

The enforcement gap of the IMO became subject to debate after the accident of the mammoth tanker Amoco Cadiz in 1978, which resulted in one of the largest oil spills in the world. Subsequently, France organized a conference on the enforcement of IMO standards by port states which led to the adoption of the

Paris Memoranda of Understanding (MoU) on Port State Control in 1982 by 14 European states. Under this MoU port states agreed to inspect 25 per cent of ships visiting their ports. After inspection a port state can request the rectification of a deficiency, detain or ban a ship. The outcomes of the inspections are registered in a database.

The Paris MoU has expanded its membership base to 27 parties, including Canada, and covers the waters of the European coastal states and the North Atlantic basin. It has also seen various amendments and upgrades, partly as a result of the 1996 EU Directive on Port State Control (Van Leeuwen, 2010; Van Leeuwen and Kern, 2013). For example, the Paris MoU developed a targeting policy using a ship's risk profile to base the scope, frequency and priority of inspections. The MoU also requires performance lists of individual ships, classification societies and flag states.

Other regions have followed the approach of the Paris MoU, resulting in eight further MoUs. While no separate MoU on Port State Control exists for the Arctic, all Arctic states except the US participate in the Paris MoU. The US does not participate in any of the MoUs, but ensures inspection of visiting ships through its Coast Guard, sharing most of the requirements of the MoUs (DeSombre, 2006).

Summary

Different loci of authority are involved in Arctic shipping governance each with their own (regional) membership base. A commonality between these loci is that they are state-led. The Arctic Council, sub-regional Arctic institutions, the IMO and the Paris MoU on Port State Control are all based on inter-state cooperation and decision making. While non-state actors undoubtedly influence this cooperation and decision making, the standard-setting authority is based on intergovernmental cooperation.

There are, however, differences between the authority of the institutions in Arctic shipping governance. The authority of the Arctic Council and sub-regional Arctic institutions is limited, because it is largely based on norm and discourse building and knowledge generation rather than developing rules and standards through mandatory international law. By exploring the current situation in terms of available knowledge of environmental risks, and by developing guidelines on how to deal with environmental risks related to shipping, the Arctic institutions provide a base for future collaboration on increased Arctic shipping. This set of institutions may offer the Arctic states a way to influence IMO standard setting through cognitive ideas as has been done in the development of the Polar Code (Stokke, 2013). At the same time, the Arctic Council offers the Arctic states a platform to discuss the regional implementation of IMO legislation. This is for example done with the Agreement on Cooperation on Marine Oil Pollution Preparedness and Response in the Arctic, which is strongly linked to the OPRC Convention (Rottem, 2015).

The IMO, in contrast, has strong standard-setting authority in Arctic shipping governance and produced a plethora of rules for safe and environmentally sound shipping. More specifically, the adoption of the Polar Code allows for dealing with concrete regional issues within the global realm of the IMO.

The IMO, however, lacks authority when it comes to generating compliance. This authority is in the hands of flag and port states. Flag states have delegated this power largely to classification societies. Port states have chosen to exercise their authority within a regional setting of MoUs on Port State Control. The IMO recognizes and supports these MoUs as an important element to ensure the effectiveness of IMO regulation. The proof in the pudding will be how the group of Arctic states use their port state inspection powers to generate compliance with the Polar Code either as a separate group or through the Paris MoU on Port State Control of which all but one Arctic state (US) are members.

As a consequence of the different types of authority exercised by the different institutions, a specialized and cooperative division of labour evolved within Arctic shipping governance, with each institution specializing on a certain niche (Stokke, 2013). This conclusion is also drawn by Humrich (2013) who argues that the architecture of Arctic governance exhibits cooperative, rather than competitive, fragmentation, because the Arctic Council explicitly builds on norm generation in other institutions.

What we can conclude at the same time is that private authority is of limited relevance to Arctic shipping governance. There is, nonetheless, an element of delegated authority through the classification societies who are tasked with the monitoring of IMO standards, especially when it comes to standards that require a certificate to show compliance. It also confirms Green's (2014) observation that delegated authority is usually concerned with technical matters.

Why private authority does not matter in Arctic shipping governance

The state-led nature of Arctic shipping governance does not mean that no relevant NSMD initiatives exist. The first part of this section will discuss the kinds of NSMD initiatives established for shipping as well as the motivations of corporate actors to initiate or participate in these initiatives. The second part will seek an explanation for the low level of authority that is exercised through these NSMD initiatives.

NSMD initiatives

At least 38 environmental performance initiatives exist with different scope, target groups and applications, some of which were established by the IMO or national governments (Svensson and Andersson, 2012).

This said, it depends on the way in which the IMO or national governments are involved in these initiatives as to whether they can indeed be considered an NSMD initiative. Cashore (2002) cautions that, if states use their sovereign authority and with that undermine the market-driven nature of the initiative, it should not be considered as NSMD governance.

With regard to NSMD initiatives by corporate actors, the most widespread example are classification societies that set rules a ship has to meet before it receives the class of the respective society. These private standards have become mainstream for the shipping sector with 90 per cent of the world's cargo-carrying tonnage being covered by the classification rules and standards as set by the 12 societies that are member of the International Association of Classification Societies.[11]

The system of classification societies emerged after marine insurers developed a way to assess the technical quality of a ship presented to them for insurance cover in the eighteenth century. Nowadays, classification is still needed in order to obtain insurance. The motivations for shipping companies to adhere to these classification rules are to legitimize their overall operating licence and to ensure market access, since a ship that is not classed might be refused to register in certain flag states or can be denied access to ports (DeSombre, 2006).

In addition, it is important to note that the requirements set by the classification societies are based on IMO Conventions and guidelines as well as technological development (Svensson and Andersson, 2012). Ships are therefore classed based on both IMO standards as well as standards set by the classification societies or their international associations (DeSombre, 2006). Classification societies also developed voluntary green class notations that exceed the demands of IMO requirements (Svensson and Andersson, 2012). These various concerns beg the question to what extent classification rules are really an NSMD locus of authority or whether they should rather be understood as an extension of the state-led IMO locus of authority.

The International Association of Independent Tanker Owners (Intertanko) provides another example of setting membership-based standards that ship owners have to meet before they can become a member of the association (Vorbach, 2001; DeSombre, 2006). One such standard (issued in 1994) is the requirement to be classed by one of the members of the International Association of Classification Societies (DeSombre, 2006). As a result of its membership-based standards, Intertanko built a good reputation within the IMO and with flag and port states (Vorbach, 2001). Intertanko's standards are followed for similar reasons as classification society rules: tanker owners seek to protect both their global licence to operate (regulatory motivation) and their market access (economic motivation). This notwithstanding, between 1994 and 2006 the membership base of Intertanko dropped from representing about 80 per cent of the independent tanker fleet to about 70 per cent (DeSombre, 2006).

Multiple forms of certification, labelling and indexing schemes have emerged as well. One of the first certification schemes in shipping was the Green Award. The award was initiated in 1994 by Rotterdam Municipal Port Management and the Dutch Ministry of Transport, but since 2000 operates as an independent entity. The Green Award is limited to crude oil tankers, product tankers and dry bulk carriers with a minimum size of 20,000 deadweight tonnage (HPTI Hamburg Port Training Institute GmbH 2007) and since 2014 to container ships with a deadweight tonnage of over 5,000 (Green Award Foundation, 2014). This certification scheme is largely based on economic incentives for tankers and bulk carriers through shorter port visits and reduced port fees. In addition, an enhanced reputation might yield the 241 ship owners who participate in the Green Award with economic advantages, since they become attractive for cargo owners that seek to green their supply chain (Green Award Foundation, 2014).

Another example is the Clean Shipping Index launched in 2010 and initiated by the Swedish Clean Shipping Project. This index is used by cargo owners during the procurement process to select shipping companies for transportation services, creating a competitive advantage for these companies (Wuisan et al., 2012). For instance, H&M and Akzo Nobel select ships with a good environmental profile in order to reduce the ecological footprint of their products. These cargo owners are specifically driven by the aim to improve their reputation, meeting customer demand for corporate social responsibility (ibid.). Also for ship owners, economic motivations play a role, i.e. they increase their market share of transport for large cargo owners. The institutionalization of the Clean Shipping Index is, however, still quite limited due to a range of factors (ibid.).

The Performance Metrics Tool from the Clean Cargo Working Group (CCWG) of Business for Social Responsibility is a similar example. The CCWG represents over 60 per cent of the container shipping market as well as some multinational cargo owners like Coca Cola, Nike and Ikea (Svensson and Andersson, 2012). The CCWG creates a dialogue between cargo and ship owners about the environmental footprint of cargo transport through container shipping. Based on performance data of ships, ship owners can track and benchmark their performance and report them to cargo owners. Cargo owners can then review and compare carriers' environmental performance in order to make informed buying decisions. Similarly to the Clean Shipping Index, ship owners participate for economic reasons, i.e. to be eligible for multinational cargo owners to transport their freight.

Corporate authority through NSMD initiatives

In general, one can observe that most of these initiatives are not created by the shipping industry itself. This is important because this means that corporate actors other than the ship owners are motivated to initiate NSMD initiatives. It is likely that these companies, e.g. cargo owners, have a broader set of motivations. Ship owners are participating in these NSMD initiatives to legitimize their participation in the sector and to protect their market access. To what extent social or environmental values do play a role for cargo or ship owners is still a major research gap.

There are some general characteristics of the shipping industry that can further explain the dominance of regulatory and economic motivations and the minor role of value-based motivations. There is a strong desire for uniform environmental standards in order to protect the economically level playing field within the sector (Tan, 2006; Van Leeuwen, 2010). For a long time, shipping enjoyed unlimited access to the oceans and did not pay any costs for causing pollution. The general belief in the shipping industry still is that it is the most environmental friendly mode of transportation (Van Leeuwen, 2010). Safety and environmental standards are generally seen as an additional financial and operational burden. Traditional imperatives within the sector still prevail: fast movement of cargo against low costs (Lai et al., 2011).

To prevent the burden of environmental standards from creating market distortions, global and uniform environmental standards are advocated. In addition, most unilateral standards set by a (group of) country would be ineffective anyway as they will lead to ships registering in open registries with more relaxed standards and lower tax levels. Such open registries do not require a genuine link between the ship and the country where the ship is registered. The majority of the world's merchant fleet tonnage is nowadays registered in such an open registry (DeSombre, 2006).

Another factor that is important in this regard is that shipping is hardly visible to citizens and consumers (Toonen and Lindeboom, 2015). Shipping is part of the value chain of consumer products, but is not evident as economic activity as such, unless a big accident occurs causing large oil spills. Otherwise, consumers are not likely to be very interested in how goods are transported. In the same vein, NGOs do not perform the 'watchdog' role on shipping to the same extent that they do in other industries (Yliskylä-Peuralahti and Gritsenko, 2014).

These obstacles notwithstanding, there is an emerging set of economic motivations for greening shipping operations. Spurred by the request of ports (Green Award) and cargo owners (Clean Shipping Index and CCWG) for more transparency on the environmental performance of specific ships, ship owners increasingly participate in certifications and indexing schemes (Lai et al., 2011; Yliskylä-Peuralahti and Gritsenko, 2014). In particular, some of the larger ship owners have become front runners in building a green profile and in conducting Corporate Social Responsibility activities, e.g. Mearsk, Wallenius Wilhelmsen and CMA CGM (Lai et al., 2011; Yliskylä-Peuralahti and Gritsenko, 2014). These front runners tend to be either container ship owners, as they are more closely connected to cargo owners (and consumers) through the transport of consumer products, or they come from risky sectors such as oil and chemical tanker companies (Yliskylä-Peuralahti and Gritsenko, 2014). Yet, altogether, environmental actions by shipping companies are still rather the exception than the rule and their reach is limited (Van Leeuwen, 2010; Lai et al., 2011; Wuisan et al., 2012; Yliskylä-Peuralahti and Gritsenko, 2014).

Conclusions

There is a lack of attention to understand motivations behind why shipping firms do or do not green their operations (Lai et al., 2011). This chapter contributes to the emerging literature on this topic by assessing the motivations of ship owners to participate in NSMD initiatives from other actors. At the same time, however, the chapter pointed to a relatively low number of such initiatives from the shipping industry itself. It can be concluded that those ship owners who participate in NSMD initiatives from classification societies, ports and cargo owners do so based on regulatory and economic motivations.

The findings also suggest that a stronger institutionalization of private governance within shipping is not likely in the short to middle term. Both the shipping industry's strong desire to protect an economically level playing field and the popular belief that shipping is environmentally friendly prevent the industry from further engaging in NSMD governance. If ship owners take such a step at all, it is likely that they use the IMO as a platform to turn their initiative into common practice – this, however, would not qualify as NSMD governance based on private authority (Cashore, 2002). I share therefore the conclusion that NSMD governance in the shipping industry can only come from cargo owners or ports (Lai et al., 2011; Yliskylä-Peuralahti and Gritsenko, 2014).

This said, private authority matters and should play a larger role, since complementary NSMD governance could be a way to combat some of the gaps in the existing governance system. For the time being, Arctic shipping governance is largely state-led in nature, with time-consuming decision making and considerable implementation gaps. Even though Port State Control increased the enforcement of IMO regulations, shipping governance suffers from structural flaws (Tan, 2006). In addition, the Arctic Council and Arctic states have limited authority to influence how shipping is regulated. Improving the environmental performance of shipping in the Arctic, thus, has to go via the IMO and would need to be backed up by a strong enforcement practice through Port State Control. The first step in this direction was taken through the adoption of a mandatory Polar Code, but the implementation of this Code is ultimately affected by the overarching structural flaws as well. For the Polar Code to be effective, the Arctic states have to exercise their port state authority, and the Paris MoU could be a platform to do so.

The urgency to scrutinize the current governance structures for the economic activity of Arctic shipping is high, because of the limited authority of the Arctic states. In the era of the Anthropocene with its multi-faceted responsibility, its increased material and institutional complexity and its urgency to act, the Arctic requires flexible, effective and equitable governance solutions to ensure sustainable growth. Shipping governance developed into a complex global governance system because of the global and complex nature of shipping itself. Regional specificities such as Arctic shipping pose a challenge to shipping governance, as the shipping industry does not feel comfortable with the differentiation in environmental standards throughout different areas. Yet, shipping governance increasingly has to deal with the complexity that results from differences in regional demands and interests when it comes to environmentally sound shipping (Van Leeuwen, 2015). In addition, as this chapter shows, one should look at ports, classification societies or cargo owners for future NSMD governance initiatives, rather than the shipping industry itself.

Notes

1 http://en.wikipedia.org/wiki/Arctic_shipping_routes, accessed 5-2-2015
2 http://www.spiegel.de/international/world/russia-moves-to-promote-northeast-passage-through-arctic-ocean-a-917824.html, accessed 5-2-2015
3 http://www.spiegel.de/international/world/russia-moves-to-promote-northeast-passage-through-arctic-ocean-a-917824.html, accessed 5-2-2015
4 http://www.thearcticinstitute.org/2014/10/NSR-Shipping-Report.html, accessed 5-2-2014
5 Rodrigue, J.-P., Comtois, C. and Slack, B. (2013) *The Geography of Transport Systems*, Hofstra University, Department of Global Studies & Geography, http://people.hofstra.edu/geotrans, accessed 5-2-2015
6 http://www.spiegel.de/international/world/russia-moves-to-promote-northeast-passage-through-arctic-ocean-a-917824.html, accessed 5-2-2015
7 http://www.arctic-council.org/eppr/, accessed 5-2-2015
8 http://www.nordregio.se/arcticprogramme , 18-8-2014
9 http://www.imo.org/About/Conventions/StatusOfConventions/Pages/Default.aspx, accessed 17-10-2014
10 http://www.imo.org/MediaCentre/HotTopics/polar/Pages/default.aspx, accessed 06-02-2015
11 http://www.iacs.org.uk/explained/default.aspx, accessed 13-03-2015

References

Bansal, P. and Roth, K. (2000) Why companies go green: A model of ecological responsiveness. *Academy of Management Journal* 43(4): 717–736.

Berkman, P. A. and Young, O. R. (2009) Governance and environmental change in the Arctic Ocean. *Science* 324(5925): 339–340.

Biermann, F., Pattberg, P., Van Asselt, H. and Zelli, F. (2009) The fragmentation of global governance architectures: A framework for analysis. *Global Environmental Politics* 9(4): 14–40.

Carroll, A. B. (1991) The pyramid of corporate social responsibility: Toward the moral management of organizational stakeholders. *Business Horizons* 34(4): 39–48.

Cashore, B. (2002) Legitimacy and the privatization of environmental governance: How non-state market-driven (NSMD) governance systems gain rule-making authority. *Governance* 15(4): 503–529.

de La Fayette, L. A. (2008) Oceans governance in the Arctic. *The International Journal of Marine and Coastal Law* 23(3): 531–566.

DeSombre, E. R. (2006) *Flagging Standard; Globalization and Environmental, Safety and Labor Regulations at Sea*. Cambridge, MA, and London: MIT Press.

Green Award Foundation (2014) *Annual Report 2013–2014*. Rotterdam: Green Award Foundation.

Green, J. F. (2014) *Rethinking Private Authority: Agents and Entrepreneurs in Global Environmental Governance*. Princeton, NJ and Oxford: Princeton University Press.

Hoffman, A. J. and Georg, S. (2012) *A History of Research on Business and the Natural Environment: Conversations from the Field*. Paper No. 1174. Michigan: Ross School of Business.

HPTI Hamburg Port Training Institute GmbH (2007) *Study on Ships Producing Reduced Quantities of Ships Generated Waste – Present Situation and Future Opportunities to Encourage the Development of Cleaner Ships*. Lisbon: European Maritime Safety Agency.

Humrich, C. (2013) Fragmented international governance of arctic offshore oil: Governance challenges and institutional improvement. *Global Environmental Politics* 13(3): 79–99.

Lai, K.-H., Lun, V. Y., Wong, C. W. and Cheng, T. (2011) Green shipping practices in the shipping industry: Conceptualization, adoption, and implications. *Resources, Conservation and Recycling* 55(6): 631–638.

Molenaar, E. J. (2008) Arctic marine shipping: Overview of the international legal framework, gaps, and options. *Journal of Transnational Law & Policy* 18: 289–326.

Ostrom, E. (2010). Beyond markets and states: Polycentric governance of complex economic systems. *The American Economic Review* 100(3): 641–672.

PAME Working Group (2009) *Arctic Council: Arctic Marine Shipping Assessment 2009 Report*. Tromsø: Arctic Council.

Perez-Batres, L. A., Doh, J. P., Miller, V. V. and Pisani, M. J. (2012) Stakeholder pressures as determinants of CSR strategic choice: Why do firms choose symbolic versus substantive self-regulatory codes of conduct? *Journal of Business Ethics* 110(2): 157–172.

Ringbom, H. (1999) Preventing pollution from ships – reflections on the 'adequacy' of existing rules. *Review of European Community & International Environmental Law* 8(1): 21–28.

Rosenau, J. N. (2006) *The Study of World Politics: Globalization and Governance*. London and New York: Routledge.

Rottem, S. V. (2015) A note on the Arctic Council agreements. *Ocean Development & International Law* 46(1): 50–59.

Smits, C. A., van Tatenhove, J. M. and van Leeuwen, J. (2014) Authority in Arctic governance: Changing spheres of authority in Greenlandic offshore oil and gas developments. *International Environmental Agreements* 14(4): 1–20.

Stokke, O. (2013). Regime interplay in Arctic shipping governance: Explaining regional niche selection. *International Environmental Agreements: Politics, Law and Economics* 13(1): 65–85.

Svensson, E. and Andersson, K. (2012) *Inventory and Evaluation of Environmental Performance Indices for Shipping*. Gothenburg: Chalmers University of Technology.

Tan, A. (2006) *Vessel-Source Marine Pollution: The Law and Politics of International Regulation*. Cambridge: Cambridge University Press.

Toonen, H. M. and Lindeboom, H. J. (2015) Dark green electricity comes from the sea: Capitalizing on ecological merits of offshore wind power? *Renewable and Sustainable Energy Reviews* 42: 1023–1033.

Van Leeuwen, J. (2010) *Who Greens the Waves? Changing Authority in the Environmental Governance of Shipping and Offshore Oil and Gas Production*. Wageningen: Wageningen Academic Publishers.

Van Leeuwen, J. (2015) The regionalisation of maritime governance: Towards a polycentric governance system for sustainable shipping in the European Union. *Ocean & Coastal Management*. Available online (http://dx.doi.org/10.1016/j.ocecoaman.2015.05.013)

Van Leeuwen, J. and Kern K. (2013) The external dimension of European Union marine governance: Institutional interplay between the EU and the International Maritime Organization. *Global Environmental Politics* 13(1): 69–87.

Vorbach, J. E. (2001) The vital role of non-flag state actors in the pursuit of safer shipping. *Ocean Development & International Law* 32(1): 27–42.

Worthington, I. (2012) *Greening Business: Research, Theory, and Practice*. New York: Oxford University Press.

Wuisan, L., van Leeuwen, J. and van Koppen, C. (2012) Greening international shipping through private governance: A case study of the Clean Shipping Project. *Marine Policy* 36(1): 165–173.

Yliskylä-Peuralahti, J. and Gritsenko, D. (2014) Binding rules or voluntary actions? A conceptual framework for CSR in shipping. *WMU Journal of Maritime Affairs* 13(2): 251–268.

Zelli, F. and Van Asselt, H. (2013) Introduction: The institutional fragmentation of global environmental governance: Causes, consequences, and responses. *Global Environmental Politics* 13(3): 1–13.

9 International river governance

Extreme events as a trigger for discursive change in the Rhine river basin

Christine Prokopf

> In Köhln, a town of monks and bones,
> And pavements fang'd with murderous stones
> And rags, and hags, and hideous wenches;
> I counted two and seventy stenches,
> All well defined, and several stinks!
> Ye Nymphs that reign o'er sewers and sinks,
> The river Rhine, it is well known,
> Doth wash your city of Cologne;
> But tell me, Nymphs, what power divine
> Shall henceforth wash the river Rhine?
>
> (Samuel Taylor Coleridge, 1912 [1828])

Introduction

Rivers and stream systems have always been at the crossroads of nature, economic use, political demarcations and the daily life of people who are in need of the water to survive and who develop their cultures along rivers. The challenge of providing effective and equitable water governance is further severed in the Anthropocene with its material and institutional complexity, multiple responsibility and enhanced urgency to act. An increasing number of scholars, therefore, caution that 'our governance skills need to make substantial progress' (Gupta et al., 2013, p. 578) and they call for a global normative water governance framework in the Anthropocene. In the same vein, this volume provides conceptual and theoretical guidance for governance in the Anthropocene, claiming that human societies must steer away from critical tipping points that might lead to rapid and irreversible change, while ensuring sustainable livelihoods for all (see Pattberg and Zelli, this volume).

River Basin Organisations (RBOs) are institutions that might contribute to this normative programme of governance in the Anthropocene by providing such effective and equitable solutions. The problem, though, is the specific context of each river basin that effectively makes it difficult to develop copy-paste model institutions that would work for any river basin. In this chapter, I will focus on the case of the Rhine river basin with its international RBO.

I locate my research in its strategic development towards a comprehensive institutional governance strategy and examine this puzzle to elucidate how this positive development was possible. I explore the ideational foundations of this development by revealing discursive shifts that were triggered by two extreme events, a fire at a chemical plant in 1986 and floods in 1995. The discourses on pollution – shifting towards an ecosystem approach – and floods – shifting towards human responsibility for and agency in these 'natural' disasters – set the groundwork for key and urgently needed institutional changes. These changes are the basis for an increased awareness of tipping points, providing an institutional fit for the high interconnectedness of river governance in the Anthropocene and addressing aspects of multiple responsibility and equity. I will conclude with some thoughts on how the role of extreme events as analysed here sets challenges to the concept of Anthropocene.

For the purpose of this chapter, I understand RBOs as 'institutionalized forms of cooperation that are based on binding international agreements covering the geographically defined area of international river or lake basins characterized by principles, norms, rules and governance mechanisms' (Schmeier et al., 2013, p. 8). They are formed as intergovernmental bodies to implement treaties or ensure the compliance of participants. Many rivers are transnational as they cross international borders or take waters from tributaries in different countries. Wolf (1998, pp. 251–252) counts 261 international watersheds affecting about 40 per cent of the world's population. Based on these demarcations, Schmeier counted 121 RBOs (Schmeier, 2013).

The institutional designs of RBOs reflect the specific problem-solving strategies for rivers: water scarcity or abundance, the need for common rules for a common interest (e.g. navigation), water pollution, protection and conservation (e.g. biodiversity or resilience), the diverse purposes that water serves (e.g. agriculture), flow pattern (e.g. dams for generating hydro-energy) or quality (e.g. through wastewater discharge from economic activities or the population's sewage). How actors decide to cooperate vis-à-vis these problems ranges from single-issue agreements to comprehensive agreements that possibly broaden RBOs' jurisdictional scopes over time due to new challenges to the river. Thus, the objects of regulation greatly vary – as may the benefits of cooperation. Given this diversity, the need for a context-sensitive assessment of cooperation concerning water was voiced early on, for example, by Elhance (2000, p. 221): 'A clear recognition of the uniqueness of hydropolitics in each basin is a prerequisite for successful negotiation and mediation efforts.'

The Rhine is an important case which I employ to scrutinise the significance of extreme events for discursive shifts in the context of river governance. The Rhine had a pre-existing pollution problem that dates back to the Romantic period, as Coleridge's rhymes that lead into this article have enshrined for posterity. And Coleridge was lucky enough to see the Rhine before the industrial revolution. As Cioc (2002, p. 143) puts it: 'the Rhine made the transition from a clean-flowing to a near-dead river so incrementally that its plight was overlooked, at least until the 1970s when the water quality had reached such a low point that only the most blinkered could fail to see'.

One of the governance strategies for the Rhine has been to install an intergovernmental body, the International Commission for the Protection of the Rhine (ICPR). Historians like Cioc (2002, pp. 177–201) and Tümmers (1994, p. 162 and pp. 401–405) interpret this process as the effort of governments to clean the Rhine up shortly before reaching a point of no return towards a dead river. The actual impact of the ICPR's work on the Rhine's water quality and biodiversity is disputed. What makes the ICPR an interesting case for political scientists is its contribution to the creation of similar institutions by serving as a model: the Rhine and the ICPR were awarded the first European Riverprize in 2013 and lauded by Bart Fokkens, Chairman of the European Riverprize Judging Panel: 'The Rhine is ... an example for other river basins in Europe and all over the world' (International River Foundation, 2013).

An emerging strand of literature that lends itself to the study of river governance is discursive institutionalism. For Schmidt (2010), this novel approach subsumes all theoretical perspectives that base their analyses of institutions on the communication of ideas and their meaning in context. She sees it as especially suitable for explaining institutional change by 'demonstrating how and when ideas in discursive interactions enable actors to overcome constraints which explanations in terms of interests, path dependence, and/or culture present as overwhelming impediments to action' (ibid., p. 4). A crucial feature of Schmidt's approach is that she does not aim to replace the 'other institutionalisms', rather she sees them as complementary. Discursive institutionalism allows for a 'more dynamic view of change in which ideas and discourse overcome obstacles that the three more equilibrium-focused and static older institutionalisms posit as insurmountable' (Schmidt, 2008, p. 304). Schmidt therefore demands analyses that 'show empirically how, when, where, and why ideas and discourse matter for institutional change, and when they do not' (Schmidt, 2010, p. 21). This analytical framework treats institutions as pre-existing, constraining structures that are, at the same time, contingent, changeable constructs (Schmidt, 2008, p. 314).

Situating myself within this discursive institutionalist programme, I will show that two extreme events strengthened alternative perspectives in the discourses on the Rhine's pollution and floods. While these perspectives had previously been established, after earlier events, they failed to achieve a majority position at that point in time. I assume that this discursive forefront made them politically relevant and was a prerequisite for any subsequent institutional development, notwithstanding (theory-based) factors that came into play later. With this approach, I follow Helen Ingram (2011). She emphasises the reciprocal relationship between ideas and opportunities for change: 'to ignite change, events must be accompanied by new issue definitions, public mobilization, and committed leadership' (ibid., p. 258). Based on this understanding, change is coupled with political opportunities that are of public concern and make different ways of knowing significant. For the governance of the Rhine in the

Anthropocene, this implies a shift towards understanding the river as an interconnected system – an understanding that includes, but surpasses a mere conceptualisation of the river as an ecosystem.

The chapter continues by presenting the case study of the Rhine river basin and the development of its RBO, the ICPR. Following this, I briefly sketch the methodological approach of my study. In a third step, the chapter presents the results of the analysis of the pollution and the flood discourses. It examines the shifts in these discourses that were triggered by the extreme events. The chapter concludes with a careful appraisal of the ICPR as a best practice institution in river governance and assesses the consequences of the results for the normative programme of the Anthropocene.

The Rhine river basin and the development of the ICPR

The Rhine river basin encompasses several countries and their subdivisions: from the catchment area of its sources in Austria, Switzerland and even some parts of Italy, flowing through Liechtenstein, France and Germany, taking in waters from Luxembourg and Belgium, the Rhine reaches the North Sea in the Netherlands. Human intervention in its flow course has been considerable including the first widely disputed massive intervention planned by the civil engineer Tulla in the early nineteenth century (Simon-Muscheid and Simon, 2005, pp. 40–41). The Rhine basin is densely populated, has been a lifeline for many people living on its banks and the banks of its tributaries, and is still employed for the generation of drinking water. Its economic importance is unwaning in the fields of transport and energy generation, as well as for chemicals and other industries located on its banks.

Consequently, the list of treaties concerning the Rhine and its tributaries is long, ranging from the 1449 Strasbourg Regulations (see Wieriks and Schulte-Wülwer-Leidig, 1997, p. 145) to the Mannheim Convention of 1815 which created the Central Commission for the Navigation of the Rhine, credited as 'the first international organisation in history' (Kiss, 1985, p. 620). Wolf counts 37 international treaties on the Rhine and its tributaries starting in 1820 (Wolf, 2002, pp. 114–117). Thus, it is not surprising that the Rhine is widely studied for its institutionalisation. Furthermore, it is located in an economically prosperous and, after World War II, democratic environment with strong integration tendencies, which situates it in a favourable environment for the development of institutions.

The development of cooperation along the Rhine is well-studied with regard to the issue of pollution although the contribution of institutions to the clean-up of the Rhine is contested (see for example Bernauer and Moser, 1996; Verweij, 2000). At an international conference on salmon fishing in the Rhine in 1948, the Netherlands, Germany, France, Luxembourg and Switzerland decided to create the ICPR and officialised their decision through an exchange of notes in 1950 (Holtrup, 1999, p. 89). In 1963, the so called Bern Convention was signed. It officially created the ICPR, which consisted of four delegates per signatory.

Three tasks were formulated: analysis of the pollution of the Rhine, propositions for protecting the Rhine against pollution, and preparation of treaties between the signatories on the protection of the Rhine.

The institutionalisation proceeded with the preparation of three agreements on different sources of pollution: chemicals, chlorides and thermal pollution. These were based on the decision making of the first (1972) conference of Rhine ministers – since then, the parties to the ICPR steer the river's governance via these now regular conferences. In the end, only two agreements were signed in 1976. In his analysis of these events, Kiss noted that '[pollution control] requires, however, not only the goodwill of the governments, but also their concrete intervention. Real progress was achieved only when, ten years after the establishment of the International Commission of Koblenz, the ministers of the riparian states took up the matter' (Kiss, 1985, p. 637). Mingst (1981) makes note of the persistent weakness of transnational decision making at that time, which in her opinion could only be tackled by the rise of a 'more critical need' (ibid., p. 173).

This need arose on 1 November 1986 with the accident at the Sandoz chemical plant in Schweizerhalle (Switzerland) where chemically contaminated firefighting water directly entered the Rhine resulting in large-scale damage to the Rhine's flora and fauna. Although this was by no means the first chemical accident along the Rhine, it was a catalyst for change, as I will demonstrate below. The ICPR member states finally agreed on a non-binding Rhine Action Programme in 1987 with the aim of reducing pollution, re-increasing the biodiversity with a special focus on salmon, enabling the continuous use of Rhine water as a source of drinking water and disburdening river sediments. This constituted a completely different approach to the problem of Rhine water quality and an increase in the ICPR's mandate. To be specific, Huisman (1995), then part of the Netherland's delegation, qualified this shift as a transformation into an integrated, ecosystem-related commitment wherein common goals were set for the states to implement autonomously with equal responsibility.

The strategic development of the ICPR towards a comprehensive understanding of the river Rhine benefited from another class of events, namely the floods before and in 1995. The floods in early 1995 were not the first great floods along the Rhine, but the culmination of a series of great floods with almost the highest gauges in the twentieth century. In their wake, the ministers for the environment of Germany, France, the Netherlands, Belgium and Luxembourg declared in the 'Arles Declaration' that the risk to the people living along the Rhine and Meuse rivers and their tributaries were no longer acceptable and needed to be mitigated. They charged the ICPR with the mandate of developing a programme similar to the Rhine Action Programme to reduce the flood problem. Interestingly, the environment ministers prescribed that besides classical water management measures (e.g. dikes), the measures would have to include spatial planning, which for them comprised land use in agriculture and forestry, environmental protection, urbanisation and recreation. In the following years, the ICPR developed a Flood Action Plan that was acknowledged by the conference of Rhine ministers in 1998.

With these two major adaptions to its mission, the ICPR developed a governance approach for the Rhine river basin that tackles major challenges in the Anthropocene: it steers the Rhine ecosystem away from critical tipping points and tries to achieve sustainable livelihood for all riparian stakeholders in a complex environment so as to enable the co-evolution of people and environment.

The analysis that follows provides an explanation of the critical link between these two extreme events and the political negotiations that lead to the Rhine Action Programme and the Arles Declaration. I will specify where the direction of change arose from, and that respective concerns were already present in earlier discourses but could only be brought into a majority position by two extreme events.

Method: Media analysis

I will now focalise on the most important extreme events along the river: the Sandoz fire in 1986 and the floods in 1995. I conducted an analysis of media content to map the public debate on pollution and floods, respectively. In doing so, I demonstrate the continuities and differences between earlier chemical accidents or floods that failed to trigger change and the extreme events in focus. By linking the debates around these events, I am able to map shifts and continuities in the understanding of the events. Working within a discursive institutionalist frame, I understand these discursive shifts as meaningful for explaining institutional change. In that sense, I am talking of a pollution and a flood discourse. My understanding of discourse and discursive in this chapter is therefore pragmatic and will not be elaborated on further as the chapter's aim is to put emphasis on the empirical results and their meaning for the concept of the Anthropocene.

Since Germany is the Rhine's biggest and geographically most affected riparian, I concentrated on the German media debate. I assessed it via two weekly, high-circulation quality newspapers, namely *Die Zeit* and *Der Spiegel* as they go beyond mere event reporting and provide more comprehensive insights

Table 9.1 Number of articles on selected events

Event(s)	Newspaper	
	Die Zeit	Der Spiegel
Chemical accident in 1969/70: Pollution of the Rhine with Thiodan	3	2
Chemical accident in 1986/87: Pollution coming from a fire at a Sandoz chemical plant	7	9
Several severe floods along the Rhine in 1983, 1988, 1993/94	4	4
Severe floods in 1995	8	2

on the distribution and change of perspectives. Though being both slightly left wing and liberal, they are both important for opinion formation in Germany. I studied articles in the two months following the respective event. In the earlier pollution case the body of texts is complemented by some later reporting when further knowledge about the incident penetrated the public debate. I provided translations for quotes from these articles.

In total, I assessed the importance of two discursive events by relating them to the debate around earlier events of similar character. The observed changes in the discourse can be attributed to new answers to a set of three questions:

- *Perception of the event:* In both cases, the character of the event is understood substantively different.
- *Responsibility and agency:* In both cases, the understanding of who is responsible for the event per se changes as does the development of coping strategies. This implies changes in the attribution of agency for involvement in the solution of the problem.
- *Approach to problem solving:* In both cases, new approaches on how to cope with the current problem and how to prevent further ones become dominant.

Obviously, the changes analysed below are specific, depending on the respective issues area. How changes could manifest themselves in the field of pollution or floods is explained in detail in the following sections.

The discourse on (chemical) pollution: Discursive events and categories for analysis

The discourse on the pollution of the Rhine is influenced by two events. These are two chemical incidents. The first one is the pollution of the Rhine with Thiodan in 1969. Although the source of the pollution continues to remain unclear, a chemical plant along the German tributary Main was suspected by the public to have disposed of the insecticide Thiodan into the river. It caused a massive death of fish that floated into the Rhine and up to the North Sea. The critical preoccupation with the chemical industry links this pollution with the fire at a Sandoz chemical plant in 1986. This incident gained more visibility due to the red tint the Rhine was given by the chemicals in the firefighting water. It also affected more riparians as the incident happened upstream in Switzerland. Therefore, it received more public attention (see for example Durth, 1996, p. 27). The media contributions after these two events fuse into one discourse on the pollution of the Rhine.

The following categories, which guided my analysis of the discourse on pollution and my comparison of the events, reflect key changes in the mission of the ICPR:

- *Perception of the event:* There is a change towards an ecosystem approach that replaces the concentration on single polluting substances. Bernauer and

Moser (1996, pp. 410–411) relate this change to a pre-existing environmental awareness – a result that, however, will be challenged by this analysis.

- *Responsibility and agency*: The Rhine Action Programme sees the ecosystem restoration of the Rhine as a collective problem for the riparians rather than interpreting pollution as a negative externality (see Lindemann, 2008, p. 126, 130). This represents a new self-positioning of riparians that contrasts with earlier positions wherein distinctions between upstream and downstream parties were prominent demarcations of responsibility. In essence, we move from a system of asymmetric agency to symmetric responsibility (see Dieperink, 1998, p. 476). Furthermore, the Rhine Action Programme allows for actors other than the convention parties to contribute to its implementation, making it more inclusive and democratic. This is especially valid for non-state actors at the local level (see Myint, 2008, pp. 142–143).
- *Approach to problem solving*: The Rhine Action Programme breaks with earlier governance approaches by defining common goals and thresholds without going into detailed prescriptions about who has to reduce which substance in what way. Verweij (1999, pp. 459–460) describes this as an individualistic approach where the choice of the best level and actors for implementation is left to the parties, keeping a hierarchical approach only in the goal setting.

The discourse on floods: Discursive events and categories for analysis

The inclusion of floods by the 1995 Arles Declaration as subjects of cooperation within the ICPR marked a shift towards comprehensiveness – a shift that does justice to the governance requirements in the Anthropocene. Whereas chemical pollution has always been, in one way or the other, attributable to humans, the issue of floods gave way to a new perspective on the relationship between humanity and nature. There have been substantive floods affecting different parts of the Rhine in 1983, 1988, 1993/94 that jointly contributed to the perception that flooding had reached irregular levels. The most important discursive event is the 1995 flood. While not significantly bigger than earlier floods, it fostered a potential for change that seems to have come from iteration of the experience by the short sequence after the floods of the winter of 1993/94. Since the earlier floods received almost no attention in the aforementioned weekly newspapers, I will include earlier reporting on all of them for tracing the change in the discourse.

I derived my categories for the analysis of the discourse on floods from the changes in the mission of the ICPR after the Arles Declaration. These mirror the centrality of the human–nature relationship.

- *Perception of the event*: The new perception of flood risks is made possible by the assumed character of the event as something not extraordinary but iterative. This change enables new responsibilities, making floods – and in consequence the human governance of nature – a political problem that has to be governed.

- *Responsibility and agency*: The change towards the acceptance of a human responsibility for the floods gives room for agency: If humans caused the floods, they can change their behaviour to prevent or mitigate future floods.
- *Approach to problem solving*: The solutions proposed also mirror the change in the relationship between humanity and nature. If floods are only caused naturally, they can only be prepared for, whereas a flood caused or aggravated by humans allows for mitigation or even prevention.

Analysis of discursive changes after extreme events along the Rhine river

The discourse on chemical pollution: The development of an ecosystem approach

To explain how the Sandoz accident provided the momentum for change, I will show how an alternative discursive position had already announced itself at an earlier occasion, around the pollution of the Rhine with Thiodan; and that the Sandoz incident was instrumental for bringing this discursive position to the forefront.

Pollution of the Rhine with Thiodan in 1969: Perception of the event

In the Thiodan case, on the one hand, the articles already put forward an ecosystem understanding of the river as they also portray the damages done in terms of an ecosystem analysis. *Der Spiegel*, for instance, wrote in its 38/1970 issue: 'many synthetic substances ... whose effects the magicians in the chemical laboratories are unaware of, transform the biology of the Rhine.' On the other hand, the articles assume a single source of pollution and are most interested in the possible combination of factors that led to the massive killing of fish.

Pollution of the Rhine with Thiodan in 1969: Responsibility and agency

The asymmetric position of the riparians is already identified as a problem, e.g. by *Der Spiegel* in its 27/1969 issue where it was noted that the Dutch authorities were informed too late. However, this asymmetric positioning of actors has yet to transform into a collective problem in the majority of the articles. *Der Spiegel* (in 27/1969) portrays the individual actions of one particular actor: a public water supply company interpreting the potential death of trouts that served as living filters in the reservoir, fed by Rhine groundwater, as an emergency signal that too many poisons had entered the reservoir. Follow-up reporting depicts such individualistic contributions to solving the pollution problem as not possible and legitimate, e.g. in *Die Zeit* in 28/1969, claiming that 'we can only sit and watch inactively what will unfold'.

Pollution of the Rhine with Thiodan in 1969: Approach to problem solving

In the reporting, the hierarchical governance approach is already very clearly characterised as problematic. Within this discourse the authorities are portrayed as accepting responsibility only within their own limits of governance and ignoring other levels or actors. For example *Die Zeit* writes in issue 27/1969: 'for the "relevant authority", the problem seemed to end at the border of their operational area and to flow out into a state one does not share friendly relations with.' The articles also explicitly criticise this hierarchical and non-cooperative mode of problem solving, e.g. *Die Zeit* issue 10/1970: 'The medical history of great-grandfather Rhine reveals the story of a patient with many doctors, each of whom accuses the other of incompetence or malpractice.'

Accident at the Sandoz chemical plant in 1986: Perception of the event

The Sandoz accident led to a changed perception of the pollution of the Rhine into a holistic problem that holds implications for the 'ecosystem' as a whole (e.g. in *Der Spiegel* 49/1986). Most of the articles referred to the notion of an ecosystem and cautioned against the long convalescence period of a damaged ecosystem. Some articles, e.g. *Der Spiegel* in issue 49/1986, go as far as to consider longstanding consequences of the accident for the North Sea. This shift of perspective also benefited from enhanced possibilities of visualisation: both newspapers relied on extended maps showing the Rhine either as a location of chemical industries or as a polluted source of drinking water in their articles.

While the reportings on the Sandoz fire cast a critical eye on the role that the chemical industry played, interestingly, they put up for question the pre-existence of strong environmental awareness. This observation increases the significance of the change represented in the perception as ecosystem. For instance, *Die Zeit* writes in issue 49/1986: 'Credulous people could toast each other with Rhine water – if only the series of environmental scandals on the Rhine would end.' The newspapers further ask if consumers would be ready to bear the costs of safeguard mechanisms, e.g. *Die Zeit* in issues 47/1986 and 49/1986. Following this line of argument, a critical chemicals expert is cited in *Der Spiegel* issue 47/1986. While hoping that the disaster might bring about a change in environmental policy, the expert holds that 'the creeping, continuous burden of chemicals is absent from consciousness and does not lead to consequences'. What is more, the environmental awareness of the conservative political elite is questioned in the media, such as in *Der Spiegel* issues 49/1986 and 50/1986: 'Can it be true: The federal government of Helmut Kohl cares for algae, water fleas, and eels in Germany's most beautiful stream? ... It cannot.'

Accident at the Sandoz chemical plant in 1986: Responsibility and agency

A more equitable perspective across riparians in terms of responsibility and vulnerability emerged in the discourse after the Sandoz fire. The potential for recognising each other not as actors with different interests, but as jointly responsible and equally affected regardless of where an event begins was high. As the accident occurred in Switzerland, it effectively turned France and Germany into downstream partners suffering from pollution while at the same time being upstreamers for the Netherlands. Thus, awareness of the transnationality of the damage intensified (the Rhine as a 'multi-ethnic river', *Der Spiegel* issue 47/1986), challenging and even placing blame on ongoing asymmetric perspectives, e.g. in *Die Zeit* issues 47/1986 and 48/1986.

At the same time, new actors are attributed agency: a lot of quotations from non-state actors can be found across the articles under study. In general, these actors are given high credibility in contrast to state actors. For example, *Die Zeit* writes about the diverse manifestations of civil society protests against pollution. It also portrays business actors' enforcement of strict actions towards polluters as implemented by, for instance, the port of Rotterdam in an article that was featured in issue 47/1986. Further actors mentioned for example by *Der Spiegel* are citizen initiatives (49/1986), environmental NGOs (49/1986) or (critical) experts (47/1986).

Accident at the Sandoz chemical plant in 1986: Approach to problem solving

In the search for a solution to the pollution, the approach taken by parties to the convention is discredited, namely to concentrate on a number of distinct pollution sources and reduce them by setting standards through single treaties. By pointing to the example of the ICPR, which is portrayed as one actor in the failing system of protection, *Der Spiegel* in 1/1987 questions the existing approach of responding to pollution. Despite the attribution of agency to new actors, the proposed solutions mostly call upon governmental and administrative entities to formulate new regulations, lower threshold values and to promote the horizontal and vertical dissemination of information about pollution and polluting incidents. Alternative solutions do not attribute agency to new actors from business or civil society or to individuals. Instead, they remind the industrialised society that, while regulations can minimise risks, it nevertheless has to endure certain risks.

This is exemplified in issue 47/1986 of *Die Zeit*. There, an author writes: 'A single fire ... has threatened the precarious balance between the environment and its use by humanity. This should make us think if we may produce all that we can, if short-term progress can be accounted for in the long-term. The freedom of the market does not free us from the preventive care for nature that we all live and benefit from – as will our children.' A similar opinion is voiced in *Der Spiegel* issue 49/1986. The proposed approaches to solve the problem of pollution, thus, go in the direction of the later policy development within the ICPR, even if the subsequent policy-making process produces outputs that surpass these proposals.

Conclusions

The comparison of the discursive events related to the Rhine's pollution represents a remarkable shift towards understanding the Rhine as an ecosystem, more equitable perspectives among riparians and the increased influence of non-state actors. It is only in the search for alternative solutions to the pollution problem that the public debate does not mirror later policy development. Instead, it challenges the awareness of the people and proposes radical alternatives. The policy changes are therefore caused by the disaster rather than by a generally increased environmental awareness. The extreme event of the Sandoz accident engendered massive public attention and, thus, an opportunity to promote alternative perceptions of the Rhine – perceptions that initially emerged, albeit as the position of a discursive minority, at an earlier pollution with Thiodan.

The discourse on floods: Bringing human responsibility for nature back in

In this section, I demonstrate how the alternative discursive position of human responsibility and agency, established during earlier floods, gained ground after the flood in 1995 to illustrate how the floods along the Rhine gave way to a new perspective on the relationship between humanity and nature.

Rhine floods in 1983, 1988 and 1993: Perception of the event

In the reporting on these floods, events were characterised as something unseen before – even though three different flood periods are covered. In the 16/1983 issue of *Der Spiegel* a director of a waterways directorate is quoted as qualifying the floods as an event happening only every 1,000 years. Coverage within these newspapers, for instance, *Die Zeit* issue 2/1994 and *Der Spiegel* issue 14/1988, further suggests that for the public, floods on the Rhine were perceived as an unusual spectacle. Observing a crowd of people gazing at the floods, a waiter from Cologne is quoted in the latter article as saying, 'I have been working here for 40 years, but I have never experienced something like this'.

Interestingly, there is scant reporting in *Die Zeit* apart from some small notes: an article in issue 17/1983 claims that floods are not politically relevant. Another one, in issue 3/1994, suggests that political actors are not interested in the floods because they are not directly affected. Or, as suggested in an article in issue 1/1994, such actors are only interested if they can use the floods for their own purposes. In this regard, the newspaper criticises the European Commission for using financial transfers to address flood damages, insinuating that it does so to 'win its citizens' hearts'.

Rhine floods in 1983, 1988 and 1993: Responsibility and agency

In 1983, *Der Spiegel* focused on the evaluation of natural causes of the flood. It first described rainfall as the flood's cause in an article in issue 16/1983, later as a trigger that cannot be held responsible in an article in 14/1988. Moreover, *Der Spiegel* deals with the effects of human intervention and responsibility by framing it as a dispute between ecologists and members of the administrative bodies. The newspaper seems to take side with the ecologists by disagreeing with the administrative actors' views. Among others the sealing of soil and the changing of its structure by agriculture and conifer monocultures are explicitly named as factors that increase the flood's effect.

Five years later, a different focus, namely a stronger ecological viewpoint, dominates the reporting of *Der Spiegel*, e.g. in issue 14/1988. The factors addressed in issue 16/1983 as 'failed policies' are now evaluated in detail vis-à-vis their effects on the floods. These policies are now denoted as intentional decisions that might only be reconsidered in the advent of a 'fairly big flood' which is predicted to happen sooner or later.

Rhine floods in 1983, 1988 and 1993: Approaches to problem solving

The approaches to problem solving proposed by *Der Spiegel* articles in 1983 include preparedness through technical systems (radar early warning), mitigation by decentralised local cisterns, and prevention in the sense of re-naturalisation of river banks and conservation of flood plains. The first two solutions are presented as innovations in contrast to the third one, which would be the most appropriate for the described problem but is not politically viable as indicated in an article in issue 23/1983: 'But instead of getting down to the root of the problem by restricting land use, the *Betonfraktion* … of water engineers advocates for a continuation of the fatal activities.' *Betonfraktion* literally translates to 'concrete faction'.

The paper uses this play on words to polemicise the water engineers' practice of placing concrete in the river beds to channel the rivers and thereby increase their flow rate. The 1988 coverage by *Der Spiegel* enlarges upon this view, pleading for solidarity across the community of riparians. The problems for the downstream riparians can only be solved by the upstream riparians; however, according to an article in issue 14/1988 this would require that a lot of people 'become reasonable and become aware of mistakes made'.

Rhine flood in 1995: Perception of the event

The 1995 floods are reported on daily with extensive use of metaphors, thus generating more attention than earlier floods. *Die Zeit* frames the 1995 floods differently than it had previous ones, namely as political problems. This change can be explained by the flood's timing and character. It made clear that the 1993 flood had not been as exceptional as originally assumed: with another great flood occurring within two years, the term 'hundred-year flood' for the 1993 flood was proven wrong and the current flood could not be framed as exceptional anymore. This perspective is strengthened by reporting on the shifts in behaviour of wine makers and re-insurers, featured in the *Die Zeit* issue 6/1995, that prepare for future floods. The loss of exceptionality was symbolised by a government building in Bonn (featuring in *Der Spiegel* issue 5/1995), which, after being damaged in 1993, risked being inundated a second time.

Rhine flood in 1995: Responsibility and agency

The reporting on this flood is dominated by the new perspectives on human responsibility for the floods and their agency in preventing it, as it had already emerged at an earlier stage of the debate. Now, instead of natural causes, human behaviour, which has rendered the Rhine a 'river without room', is charged for the damage to the river because of, for instance, the change of soil structures and straightening works. This problem definition can be found in *Die Zeit* issue 5/1995. The following issue (6/1995) refers to local authorities who, obviously not having drawn lessons from the 1993 floods, started planning a building in the affected area two months after. Issue 9/1995 features letters from citizens reaffirming the problem definition of the floods as a man-made problem.

Nevertheless, the dominant problem presentation aroused opposition, which is presented as a legitimate perspective. One example featured in *Der Spiegel* issue 5/1995 and *Die Zeit* issue 6/1995 is the NIMBY reaction of a community opposing the creation of a retention area on fields directly adjacent to their village. *Die Zeit* also impartially presents two parts of the problem definition – the contribution to soil sealing and forest declines – as an ecologist's view, contradicting the one of a state-employed water engineer. In its most important contribution on the subject in issue 3/1994, *Die Zeit* goes into further detail on the argument on human causes of the flood. The strongest opposing argument is included in an article in the same issue that focuses on the relationship between man and nature. The article portrays this relationship as antagonistic: one where nature is a forceful and indifferent constant causing catastrophes impervious to human intervention. It also depicts mankind as creating a cultural landscape 'painfully wrenched' from nature. In a relationship like this, mankind should stop contributing to catastrophes with misused technologies and instead put more efforts into mitigating and adapting to unavoidable disasters.

Both newspapers suggest that the now problematic issues have resulted from intentional political decisions and that, therefore, humans are responsible for them. For the first time, they start to question the political actors' insistence on their positions. 'Nobody really thinks about rerouting' is just one statement cited in *Der Spiegel* issue 6/1995. *Die Zeit* challenges the official positions by demanding from the federal government the development of national flood management (issue 6/1995). Moreover the newspaper proposes that the Rhine riparians are not to be blamed for the floods. In the same two issues, both newspapers stress human agency by presenting initiatives from different levels to illustrate new directions to be taken while warning that the disaster could reoccur on a larger scale or on other rivers.

Rhine flood in 1995: Approach to problem solving

The directions presented to solve the flood problem are not as diverse as in the coverage on earlier floods. Instead, they focus on the area of prevention and mitigation through two major types of measures: the re-naturalisation of riverbanks, and the creation of artificial, technically floodable retention areas. These two types are clearly distinguished from each other: unlike re-naturalised land, retention areas may be flooded or not, depending on the (political) will to do so. Thus, solidary decisions by a community of riparians would be necessary (*Die Zeit*, 6/1995). The approach to problem solving that is presented in conclusion explicitly relies on human agency to influence the flood event and is not confined to preparing for it.

Conclusions

As outlined above, the 1995 floods lacked exceptional character. The occurrence of yet another flood allowed for existing flood-related perceptions on human responsibility to become politically relevant. These perceptions are reflected in the flood policies developed by the ICPR on the environmental ministers' insistence. The 1998 ministers' conference of the ICPR saw the first agreement on a Flood Action Plan developed by the secretariat. As the ministers lauded themselves, 'with this approach, a comprehensive concept for a biotope system is realised for the first time worldwide. The measures for the ecological valorisation have to be interlocked with those for flood protection with the aim of improving the water structure and to extend and to reactivate the floodplain forests' (Ministerial Declaration, 12th Conference of Rhine Ministers, 22 January 1998, Rotterdam).

On the same occasion, they agreed on the draft for the new Rhine treaty (Convention on the Protection of the Rhine) signed in 1999 that now includes the objective of sustainable development of the Rhine ecosystem.

Looking forward: Climate change as new issue of concern

In the flood-related debates from 1995 onwards, there is only one really new argument in contrast to the floods before 1995 that should be considered particular. For the first time, the notion of climate change emerged in connection with the extreme event of a flood. As it remains today, no extreme event can be attributed directly to climate change, as *Die Zeit* expressed in issue 6/1995: 'Whether or not the greenhouse effect causes more rain is, in light of the current state of research, a matter of faith.' The lack of reliability of the argument is used for interpretations in both directions, not only for the sceptical perspective, but also for the potential mainstream perspective that climate change may play a role (*Der Spiegel*, issue 6/1995). References to climate change are used to strengthen the demand to initiate re-naturalisation measures and to create retention areas.

The notion of climate change was not included in the Flood Action Plan or the 1999 treaty. The Rhine ministers' communiqué in 2007 names dry periods and an increasing water temperature as challenges caused by climate change (next to floods, of course) and provides the ICPR with a study mandate. The results presented at the conference in 2013 confirm these priorities for the Rhine basin and task the ICPR to develop a climate change adaption strategy until 2014 with a view to assessing existing countrywide or regional management measures.

Conclusions

Coleridge would perhaps be relieved to know that humanity finally accepted its responsibility for cleaning the river Rhine although it had to stink severely before this could happen. As shown in this article, two extreme events, in particular, triggered significant progress in transboundary cooperation efforts. The fire at the Sandoz plant in 1986 and the floods in 1995 made it possible to strengthen perceptions that had originated in earlier debates on pollution and floods, but that had, up until then, not yet gained political relevance. Without these two events, the ICPR would not have its model character for an institution that accounts for the questions of urgency and responsibility in the Anthropocene.

In this paper, I used a discursive institutionalist approach (cf. Schmidt, 2010) for analysing precisely how two extreme events had a significant impact on key discourses and, subsequently, on the institutionalisation of cooperation along the Rhine. I have demonstrated that, in contrast to earlier events, the chemical accident at Sandoz enabled a discursive change towards an ecosystem focus. Additionally, the hierarchical structures were then dissolved in favour of a subsidiary cooperation culture which could only be successful through the new balanced and equitable self-positioning of riparians.

In the flood-related discourse, the iteration of disasters created an opportunity for change. There, too, a discursive shift took place, altering problem definitions and facilitating solutions which had not previously been politically relevant. The new perspective redefined the relationship between the Rhine's riparians and the Rhine itself in holding people, not nature, accountable for the floods, and, in consequence, acknowledging their agency to govern floods. Concerning the ICPR's institutional journey, these ideational changes prepared the ground for the institutionalisation processes that allowed this institution to develop new tasks and a new agenda beyond water pollution and, ultimately, a more comprehensive mandate.

In both cases, high public attention activated a public debate wherein pre-existing perspectives could gain political relevance, putting pressure onto political actors. The ICPR, as it presents itself nowadays, seems to be an institution that is in line with the normative programme of the Anthropocene. This institutional development benefited from discursive changes following two extreme events that are neither repeatable nor morally desirable in other river basin settings. This caveat should be kept in mind when referring to the ICPR as a role model for how to construct RBOs living up to the ambitions of the Anthropocene.

Nevertheless, this article also seeks to draw conclusions that go beyond its case study. We could cynically generalise that damaging technical accidents and repeated natural disasters are needed to trigger the development of institutions – in line with an increased awareness of human responsibility in the era of the Anthropocene. Specifically, institutions that transcend jurisdictional boundaries of a diverse set of upstreamers and downstreamers do justice to an increased urgency to act. They induce a common vision for the ecosystem that drives preventive and adaptive measures against floods. Such a conclusion can claim some validity, as environmental accidents have in the past often induced previously unwilling governments to initiate greener policies and more sustainable resource management – and to establish respective institutions. Yet, relying on accidents or disasters is not a viable solution.

What do these findings mean with regard to core aspects of the Anthropocene like urgency, responsibility and complexity? To begin, the story of the ICPR's development can be seen as a story of a two-step realisation of the material complexity of river governance. As a consequence of this development, today ICPR's governance mechanism puts into practice an understanding of rivers that lives up to the complexity and interconnectedness of the Anthropocene: it privileges an ecosystem approach targeting the river as a whole from source to mouth and balances the ecosystem's needs with human interests to protection and economic, social and cultural uses of the river as a resource.

If change requires that people gain awareness of this complexity, this hints at how actors can contribute to the Anthropocene's normative agenda, i.e. to an urgency to act. It must be noted, however, that in this case, awareness was a necessary, but not sufficient condition. Extreme events were still needed to trigger policy changes. A follow-up question would therefore be: which other mechanism could serve in a comparable manner as an alternative trigger?

This question might well be framed in terms of responsibility. How is political commitment across stakeholders emerging, assuming the aforementioned general awareness of complexity and interconnectedness? This question especially concerns governments that are decisive for all sorts of transboundary governance arrangements on natural resources, as, in this case, rivers.

The observations and findings that have been presented in this chapter are most relevant with regard to the aspect of urgency. In the case of the Rhine, there were actions against pollution, since pollution became more and more visible and had consequences for people's health. But the significant programmatic changes only took place when extreme events brought new perspectives to the forefront, in line with the interdependent and holistic perspective of the Anthropocene. In summary, in spite of general awareness, the challenge is how humanity can act *before* reaching critical tipping points and before disaster strikes. This means actively taking responsibility for the urgency to act without the need for extreme triggering events.

References

Bernauer, T. and Moser, P. (1996) Reducing pollution of the river Rhine: The influence of international cooperation. *The Journal of Environment & Development* 5(4): 389–415.

Cioc, M. (2002) *The Rhine. An Eco-Biography, 1815–2000*. Seattle and London: University of Washington Press.

Coleridge, S. T. (1912) [1828] Cologne. In Coleridge, E. H. (ed), *The Complete Poetical Works of Samuel Taylor Coleridge*. Oxford: Clarendon Press, p. 477. http://www. gutenberg.org/files/29091/29091-h/29091-h.htm#stcvol1_Page_477 [accessed 23 October 2015].

Dieperink, C. (1998) From open sewer to salmon run: Lessons from the Rhine water quality regime. *Water Policy* 1(5): 471–485.

Durth, R. (1996) *Grenzüberschreitende Umweltprobleme und regionale Integration. Zur politischen Ökonomie von Oberlauf-Unterlauf-Problemen an internationalen Flüssen.* Baden-Baden: Nomos.

Elhance, A. P. (2000) Hydropolitics: Grounds for despair, reasons for hope. *International Negotiation* 5(2): 201–222.

Gupta, J., Pahl-Wostl, C. and Zondervan, R. (2013) 'Glocal' water governance: A multi-level challenge in the Anthropocene. *Current Opinion in Environmental Sustainability* 5(6): 573–580.

Holtrup, P. (1999) *Der Schutz grenzüberschreitender Flüsse in Europa. Zur Effektivität internationaler Umweltregime.* Jülich: Forschungszentrum Jülich.

Huisman, P. (1995) From one-sided promotion of individual interests to integrated water management in the Rhine basin. *Water Science and Technology* 31(8): 59–66.

Ingram, H. (2011) Beyond universal remedies for good water governance. A political and contextual approach. In Garrido, A. and Ingram, H. M. (eds), *Water for Food in a Changing World*. London, New York: Routledge, pp. 241–261.

International River Foundation (2013) River Rhine wins the first IRF European Riverprize. Available from: http://www.riverfoundation.org.au/docs/2013_IRF_ European_Riverprize_Winner_Announced_FINAL [accessed 25 June 2015].

Kiss, A. (1985) The protection of the Rhine against pollution. *Natural Resources Journal* 25(3): 613–638.

Lindemann, S. (2008) Understanding water regime formation—a research framework with lessons from Europe. *Global Environmental Politics* 8(4): 117–140.

Mingst, K. (1981) The functionalist and regime perspectives: The case of Rhine river cooperation. *Journal of Common Market Studies* 20(2): 161–173.

Myint, T. (2008) Adaptability of international river basin regimes: Linkage problems in the Rhine. In Pahl-Wostl, C., Kabat, P. and Möltgen, J. (eds), *Adaptive and Integrated Water Management. Coping with Complexity and Uncertainty*. Berlin, New York: Springer, pp. 125–145.

Schmeier, S. (2013) *Governing International Watercourses. River Basin Organizations and the Sustainable Governance of Internationally Shared Rivers and Lakes*. New York: Routledge.

Schmeier, S., Gerlak, A. K. and Schulze, S. (2013) *Who Governs Internationally Shared Watercourses? Clearing the Muddy Waters of International River Basin Organizations*. Lund and Amsterdam: Earth System Governance, Working Paper No. 28. Available from: http://www.earthsystemgovernance.org/sites/default/files/publications/files/ESG-WorkingPaper-28_Schmeier%20et%20al.pdf [accessed 28 July 2014].

Schmidt, V. A. (2008) Discursive institutionalism: The explanatory power of ideas and discourse. *Annual Review of Political Science* 11: 303–326.

Schmidt, V. A. (2010) Taking ideas and discourse seriously: Explaining change through discursive institutionalism as the fourth 'new institutionalism'. *European Political Science Review* 2(01): 1–25.

Simon-Muscheid, K. and Simon, C. (2005) Umweltgeschichte des Rheins. Ökohistorische Zugriffe in der gesellschaftichen Dimension. *Jahrbuch für Regionalgeschichte* 23: 35–54.

Tümmers, H. J. (1994) *Der Rhein. Ein europäischer Fluß und seine Geschichte*. München: C. H. Beck.

Verweij, M. (1999) A watershed on the Rhine: Changing approaches to international environmental cooperation. *GeoJournal* 47(3): 453–461.

Verweij, M. (2000) Why Is the River Rhine cleaner than the Great Lakes (despite looser regulation)? *Law & Society Review* 34(4): 1007–1054.

Wieriks, K. and Schulte-Wülwer-Leidig, A. (1997) Integrated water management for the Rhine river basin, from pollution prevention to ecosystem improvement. *Natural Resources Forum* 21(2): 147–156.

Wolf, A. T. (1998) Conflict and cooperation along international waterways. *Water Policy* 1(2): 251–265.

Wolf, A. T. (2002) *Atlas of International Freshwater Agreements*. Nairobi, Kenya: UNEP.

Part III

Accountability and legitimacy in the Anthropocene

10 Democratic accountability in the Anthropocene

Toward a non-legislative model

Walter F. Baber and Robert V. Bartlett

Introduction

The primary mechanism for holding administrative agencies accountable in any democratic polity is the practice of legislative oversight, a mechanism that is severely challenged by the globalization and modernization that characterize the Anthropocene. Globalization and modernization amplify humankind's ability to disturb ecosystems in fundamental ways, creating an urgent and growing need for responses that will yield, and constitute, effective governance. Meeting the need for effective governance requires development of institutional arrangements that involve strong administrative capacities (Bauer et al., 2012). But neither globalization nor modernization, nor anything else, is moving humankind toward creation of anything resembling a global legislature that could ever effectively exert oversight over even the limited earth system administrative capacities already developed over the last century. The forces of modernization and globalization (such as the internationalization of capital and hollowing out of the nation state) that give rise to the ecological challenge of the Anthropocene also prevent effective global legislative oversight by national legislatures acting individually or in concert. And should some sort of legislative body or collection of democratic authorities ever emerge and attempt to assume responsibility for oversight of administered environmental governance (the prospects of which are vanishingly low), it would be overwhelmed by the immense and growing complexity of the fragmented, multi-level proliferation of institutions, networks, and relationships that will necessarily constitute the evolving governance system of the Anthropocene.

The complexity and interpenetration of the environmental problematique, the impact severity of some crucial environmental trajectories, and the unfathomable diversity of humans and human cultures combine to make governing the interaction with earth's natural systems the most daunting challenge humans will ever face. The challenge is doubly daunting because of its urgency: many of the most frightening and irreversible trends in the global environment are caused by deeply imbedded forces that cannot be altered, stopped, or reversed in the short term of a few years. Time is of the essence for beginning and accelerating obviously needed transformations, even as knowledge about the world remains grossly inadequate to light very many of the paths that global society must start down. The processes that must be confronted and reflexively transformed lie at the heart of modernity, notably the forces and relations of economic production, the ways that risk is managed, and the processes of knowledge generation and dissemination (Christoff and Eckersley, 2013, p. 30). If it is ever going to be possible for humans to undertake successful global environmental governance, it must be by embracing principles and adopting rules for complex institutions that can effectively and equitably exercise responsibilities for protecting the rest of nature (in all its complexity) from humans and humans (in all their diversity) from themselves.

The circumstances of the Anthropocene call for building some considerable measure of ecological rationality into processes and structures responsible for environmental governance. Moreover, deliberative democratic practice is prerequisite for the learning, local knowledge, and engagement that enlightened environmental governing requires. Effective governance institutions and rules must be grounded in widely shared understandings, created by those they address, applicable equally to all, capable of learning from (and adapting to) experience, rationally grounded, and internalized by those who adopt and experience them (Baber and Bartlett, 2015, pp. 1–11). Only democratic processes have the potential to inform and legitimate environmental governance at every level in ways that respond to the challenges of ecological rationality, popular participation, and globalization. Accountability is central to all democratic practice. But what hope can there be for the urgent task of cultivating global accountability mechanisms in the Anthropocene if global legislative oversight of administrative capacities is unlikely, if not impossible? What alternative form of democratic accountability could fit the political circumstances of global governance in the Anthropocene? A more urgent task for future theorizing, innovation, and experimentation is hard to imagine.

Prior experience may have something to teach us. A substantial source of global administrative experience has been accumulated by the United Nations system and the many other international intergovernmental agencies that have been established in the last century. Unfortunately most of these agencies suffer from overall accountability deficit issues and, in any event, none offer a model of real democratic accountability. There is, however, one real-world organization or system that does offer some promise of being a fruitful subject of investigation, namely, the world's most fully developed example of supranational government: the European Union (EU). Even with decades of treaty tinkering and the evolution of practice—on a limited continental rather than a world scale—the EU has been unable to design and authorize legislative bodies that can exercise broad and effectual legislative oversight. Given the failure to establish legislative oversight, it should not be surprising that the EU has also experimented with alternative mechanisms of accountability that do not rely on legislative oversight. The EU is a pioneer of transnational democratic oversight and administrative accountability and, as such, its incremental and trial-and-error innovations, as inadequate as they still are, offer lessons for the problem of accountability of global governance in the absence of effective legislative authority.

Analysis of the emerging administrative practices of the European Union, including review of the peculiarities of the delegation of administrative discretion, the obstacles to direct legislative oversight, and attempts to achieve oversight through the evolving "open method of coordination" (OMC), suggests opportunity for further EU reforms to create a deliberative framework capable of producing the independent norms needed to constrain the substantial administrative discretion vested in the EU Commission. A deliberative model of administrative accountability could be grafted onto these existing non-legislative accountability mechanisms to accomplish just that at each level and stage of the policy process by identifying normative principles, choosing policy models, and adopting action plans and implementation strategies. The resulting model of transnational democratic accountability is one fully transferable to the broader global transnational accountability challenges of environmental governance in the Anthropocene. It does not rely on new legislative inputs or continuous monitoring by elected officials (the fantasy of global legislative oversight), but it can accommodate augmentation of existing administrative competencies. Moreover, it can fit the continuing political circumstances of the Anthropocene—that is, it can constitute an accountability system responsive to the urgency of achieving greater democratic accountability, building on responsibilities that both nongovernmental and intergovernmental organizations already exercise well and adaptable to the complexity of (mostly non-hierarchical) future governance.

Delegation and oversight in the European Union

If one were to listen only to the sharpest of Eurocritics, one would conclude that the European Union presents a remarkable paradox. It is alleged, on the one hand, to be a feckless and fragile creation—accomplishing little or nothing and ready to fly apart at any instant. This criticism is heard especially loudly on the subject of European foreign policy (Helwig, 2013; Toje, 2008). On the other hand, the EU is often chastised for what is alleged to be its overbearing and intrusive behaviour—displacing local initiative and threatening national sovereignty (Adam and Maier, 2011). Before dismissing the sceptics (as officials of the EU Commission have sometimes been inclined to do) as inveterate complainers who want to have it both ways, we should ask ourselves whether these two strands of criticism ever converge without self-contradiction.

Were Eurosceptics to squarely face the challenge of reconciling their apparently contradictory criticisms, they could credibly say something like the following: it is entirely possible for a government (or set of governing institutions) to be simultaneously intrusive and ineffectual, to threaten national sovereignty without offering a credible replacement for it. All it need do is interrupt existing processes of democratic governance without itself being sufficiently democratic. The result would be a politics that is ineffective precisely because it is undemocratic (Baber and Bartlett, 2005). Other ways of reconciling the apparent contradictions in Euroscepticism are, undoubtedly, available. But among the various arguments sceptics might offer, this one is probably the most substantively plausible and certainly the most normatively important.

It is not for us, of course, to litigate the differences between Eurosceptics and advocates of continued European integration. We frame the problem in this way simply because doing so serves to focus attention on a central tendency of government—the inclination of legislators to leave the details of law-making to bureaucrats (or, more charitably, the inability of legislators to do otherwise). This tendency has long been recognized to be problematic, and it is one further exacerbated by legislators inevitably being overwhelmed by the complexity and urgency of the challenges of the Anthropocene. More recently, this practice has even been criticized as a threat to the existence of constitutional government itself, liberal or otherwise (Iancu, 2012). A standard defense of legislative delegation is that governmental efficiency is improved and the effectiveness of policy outcomes enhanced by the practice of leaving policy details to substantive specialists and technical experts. At its strongest, this defense amounts to an entirely plausible argument that legislative delegation is not merely prudent but (given the complexity of the modern state) a practical necessity (Shane, 2010). As a subsidiary element within this general argument, criticisms of legislative delegation grounded in democratic theory are additionally answered by reference to the practice of legislative oversight (Pelizzo and Stapenhurst, 2013). In the United States, the enterprise of legitimating legislative delegation and the administrative discretion that results from it has been a central focus of administrative law scholars. In his landmark statement on discretionary justice, Davis (1969) was careful to distinguish legislative delegation of authority (guided by principles inherent in the delegation) from areas of administrative discretion (wherein the limits of administrative powers leave the administrator free to choose among alternative courses of action). It is with these normatively unconstrained choices that the democrat must be primarily concerned. Much of the scholarship in administrative law has focused precisely on this problem. In spite of promising early efforts, scholarship by American, English, and European scholars of administrative law has not seen the embrace of comparative approaches that has been typical of other areas of legal research and practice (Boughey, 2013). As a result, scholarship addressing the problem of administrative accountability in global governance is especially deficient. But it must be addressed because accountability is a central element of the political legitimacy to which both global governance and the EU aspires. This aspiration of global governance for legitimacy may also be thwarted by factors similar to "structural factors in the EU that have made it especially difficult to devise a satisfactory solution in pragmatic and normative terms to the dilemma of legitimating secondary rules of a legislative nature" (Craig, 2012, p. 111).

It is critically important to the legitimacy of democratic government that the discretionary acts of bureaucratic officials be guided and constrained by normative principles not of their own devising (Habermas, 1996). Where unelected government officials are judged only by standards of their own creation, no genuine accountability is possible and democracy is ever at risk. The problem is exacerbated by the fact that much modern legislation, and especially that of the EU, is framed in "relatively open-textured terms, thereby necessitating greater specification through subsequent action" (Craig, 2012, p. 109). Dubious claims regarding the adequacy of so-called "outcome legitimacy" notwithstanding (Scharpf, 1999), behavioural norms that are not the result of or at least consistent with basically democratic processes are (from a democratic perspective) of deeply problematic provenance. Detailed legislative oversight, to the extent that competent authorities can exercise it, is one potential response to that problem.

In this respect, however, the European Union has a significant problem. The three institutions that share legislative power in the EU—the European Parliament, the European Council, and the Council of Ministers—are all structurally incapable of exercising much legislative oversight of European Commission actions. These bodies have three basic ways to exercise legislative power—the Community method, Comitology, and treaty reform. To put matters succinctly, each of these methods requires the cooperation of Commission administrators for elected officials to legislate, making legislative changes of administrative decisions virtually impossible. The Community method vests the power of initiating an act of legislation in the European Commission, whose administrative actions would be the subject of any legislative oversight. Comitology (to the extent that it is still a viable option) is a process carried out through rule-making committees that are chaired by Commission representatives empowered to set the committees' agendas. Treaty reform, though not subject to unilateral obstruction by the Commission, requires a unanimous vote from both an intergovernmental conference (IGC) and the member states themselves (Miller, 2011), all of which are proceedings in which the Commission can involve itself politically. It would be remarkable indeed if a decision could ever be reached over significant Commission objections. In short, the EU legislative process is fundamentally flawed in terms of administrative accountability—"they, the actors who make the Union legitimate, cannot overrule the EU's regulators, the actors who make it functional" (ibid., p. 325).

The independent norms needed to constrain the administrative discretion of EU Commission decision making are unlikely to be provided by elected EU officials (at least, as the Union is now constituted). It is important, however, that this situation be viewed against the backdrop of the EU's overall policy objectives. In 2000, pursuant to its general goals of becoming the world's most competitive and dynamic knowledge-based economy (European Council, 2000a), the EU Council adopted the "open method of coordination" (OMC). The Council described the OMC as a decentralized process in which member states, regional and local governments, and social partners and civil society would be actively involved (European Council, 2000b). The general components of the OMC included the establishment of guidelines for the Union (including specific timelines for achieving short-, medium-, and long-term policy goals), qualitative as well as quantitative benchmarks based upon global best practices but tailored to the needs of the various member states, translation of these European guidelines into national and regional policy objectives (including specific performance targets and adopting measures), and periodic monitoring, evaluation, and peer review (conceived of and organized as a mutual learning process).

The OMC process was reaffirmed in 2005. A new three-year planning cycle was introduced, the starting point of which is an EU Commission synoptic document—the strategic report. Based upon its consideration of this report, the European Council adopts integrated guidelines. Acting on the basis of these guidelines, member states then draw up national reform programs, after consultation with all stakeholders (European Council, 2005). Whether or not this "re-launched" version of the OMC will achieve the economic and social objectives of the EU remains to be seen. This much, however, is clear: the Commission still plays its historic role as the initiator of the process of establishing the general goals and policy objectives of the EU. Member states are charged with tailoring these policies to their needs, and sub-national governments continue to be imagined as an important part of the implementation process. Fundamental normative values are still established at the level of the Union and on the basis of an agenda devised by unelected officials of the EU Commission and other EU agencies. By any measure, this represents a massive delegation of legislative authority, creating an expansive zone of administrative discretion within which the future direction of the EU is charted. Elected officials of the EU can then exercise some (conventionally understood) limited oversight of how this discretion is exercised, but are still poorly situated to do so.

The central objective of legislative oversight is to ensure that "administration does not have access to the normative premises underlying its decisions" and that administrative power "may not be used to intervene in, or substitute for, processes of legislation and adjudication" (Habermas, 1996, p. 173). By this standard, the situation of the European Commission as we have here described it is clearly problematic. Circumstances are further complicated by the fact that "democratic self-control and self-realization has until now been credibly realized only in the context of the nation-state" (Habermas, 1998, p. 61). How these advantages of self-government can be replicated in a polity that extends beyond national boundaries is unclear. Even the capacity for "democratic self-steering within the national society" is being seriously degraded by the "disempowerment of the nation-state" that results from globalization's impact on national regulatory and fiscal independence of action (ibid., p. 67). If this degradation of the nation-state conspires with the transnational character of environmental risks to make it necessary to address environmental protection at the global level, it becomes all the more imperative that the democratic deficit of international politics be addressed.

In search of policy norms: A deliberative model of administrative accountability

Changes in the EU's legislative process have so far done nothing to alter the fact that it is "an elite project above the heads of the people concerned" and continues to operate with democratic deficits resulting from its "essentially intergovernmental and bureaucratic" characteristics (Habermas, 2009, p. 80). Adoption of a deliberative model of administrative accountability, summarized in Table 10.1, suggests several additional accountability mechanisms that could be added to what the EU already does, such that it could better address the problem of providing governing norms to constrain the exercise of administrative discretion by the Commission, and do so in a way that satisfies the requirement that those norms not be the creation of the Commission itself (the table and portions of the accompanying discussion are adapted from Baber (2010) and Baber and Bartlett (2015)). If such a model were adopted, instead of generating the normative principles that guide its own use of administrative discretion, the European Commission would serve as the convener of deliberative conferences to perform that task. To put it most simply, the Commission (either directly or through other EU agencies) would commission rather than create the principles needed to constrain its use of administrative discretion.

In the context of environmental governance, deliberative democratic practice has generally focused either on choices between competing policy models (such as direct command-and-control regulation versus market-based regulatory strategies) or on the development of local implementation agreements within the context of an existing national regulatory scheme. But widely supported normative principles and general propositions of law (a stage of policy development that is logically prior to the choice of policy models or implementation plans) could be identified through the technique of juristic deliberation—the adjudication by citizen juries of hypothetical cases involving disputes (Baber and Bartlett, 2009). This could be done across a wide range of factual circumstances without directly engaging the perceived interests of the citizens who participate in such deliberations.

In juristic deliberation, participants are presented with a richly detailed set of circumstances involving the loss of an environmental good caused by one actor and imposed upon a different actor or actors. The simulation is, if fact, a hypothetical legal case—complete with parties to be heard, pleadings to be weighed, and philosophical problems to be resolved. This approach, employing

Table 10.1 Adoption of a deliberative model of administrative accountability

Governance challenges	Deliberative technique	Deliberative problem	Deliberative product	Regulative standard
Distributional justice	Juristic deliberation	Hypothetical cases	General legal principles	Normative consensus
Institutions and policy integration	Deliberative polling/policy juries	Alternative policy paradigms	Policy goals and objectives	Political consensus
Social causes/ consequences of change	Stakeholder partnerships	Contending local discourses	Implementation plans/regulatory co-production	Social consensus

hypothetical cases in the development of administrative law, was first suggested by the work of Kenneth Culp Davis (1969). The factual circumstances of the cases, however, require participants to choose between hypothetical outcomes that represent some of the underlying normative principles of environmental protection.

As an example, we have developed a series of scenarios in which neighbouring states lodge disputes against one another in a "court" over the use of a river that makes up their shared border (Baber and Bartlett, 2015, pp. 207–222). One of the disputes asks "jurors" whether the existing pattern of resource utilization (which significantly favors one state) should be respected or whether that pattern should be altered to allow both states to exploit the river's resources more equally (based on factors like their size and population). The level of consensus achieved in early trials (ibid., pp. 197–205) has been quite high, and it has shown considerable durability in the face of subsequent discussions about how the normative principles that had been agreed to could be concretized in policy models and, eventually, plans of administrative action. The advantages of this approach are clear. When environmental governance issues implicate basic normative questions (as they generally do), a preliminary deliberative experience with consensual norm building offers a foundation of mutuality that has the potential to expedite agreement at later stages of the policy process. Moreover, a sufficiently rigorous and representative collection of these deliberative trials (commissioned, say, by the European Commission and conducted in and with the cooperation of the member states) would provide the raw material necessary for the European Law Institute to restate the results in a form suitable as a point of departure for the process of EU legislation as it currently exists within the Community Method. This process of juristic deliberation, using hypothetical legal cases to identify basic normative principles as a basis for the exercise of the Commission's responsibility to initiate a legislative proceeding, is represented by the entries in the first row of Table 10.1.

Deliberative democratic techniques are more commonly used at the next stage of the policy process—the choice among competing policy models. Within the deliberative democratic experience is a planning technique that seems generally well suited to selecting from among competing environmental policy paradigms, a technique usually referred to in the U.S. as deliberative polling (Fishkin, 1995) and in Europe as the policy (or citizen) jury (Huitema et al., 2007). It involves convening deliberative assemblies of up to several hundred individuals who are presented with information regarding an existing public policy and the leading alternative approaches. These assemblies are then divided into groups of 12–15 persons, each of which deliberates the choices presented to it (Fishkin and Laslett, 2003; Gastil and Levine, 2005). In some cases, the jury is asked to come to the most inclusive consensus that it can. In other cases, no conclusion is asked of the jury. Rather, the participants are surveyed after their deliberations to determine their considered opinion as opposed to their initial preferences.

In the context of watershed policy, for example, a policy jury might be presented with the choice between, on the one hand, a piecemeal approach to the constituent problems of soil conservation, species protection, and so forth or, on the other hand, a policy model that emphasizes the development of a comprehensive resource utilization plan encompassing within it the entire scope of the watershed. Or deliberative assemblies might be asked to choose from alternative biodiversity policies, such as those exemplified by the US and Italy. Biodiversity policy in the US has long been dominated by the Endangered Species Act (ESA), which imposes strict (some would say draconian) restrictions on the killing of living beings once their species has been determined to be endangered. Another paradigm is the biodiversity policy of Italy, which emphasizes a comprehensive planning approach in which both the direct and the indirect effects of government decisions across a wide range of policy areas are to be evaluated for their impacts on plants and animals. The ESA has often been criticized for its narrow and belated focus on species that may have already become "terminally ill." The Italian approach, on the other hand, has been faulted for a lack of focus and for not having sufficient enforcement capacity to actually protect anything. It should be unsurprising that a broader bio-habitat perspective has developed recently in the US and that Italy has taken steps to put more teeth in its biodiversity policy. Our own deliberative experiments in both countries suggest that this convergence is due, at least in part, to the existence of an underlying consensus (among Americans and Italians, at least) on the general contours of what an effective biodiversity policy requires.

Observers of deliberative democratic practice see both promise and peril in experience with deliberative polling. On the one hand, policy juries have been lauded for offering us the best glimpse into the preferences of a more informed and engaged electorate—preferences that differ markedly from those expressed in conventional polls, in the voting booth, and in legislation engineered by self-interested lobbying groups (Ackerman and Fishkin, 2003). On the other hand, it has also been argued that deliberating groups are prone to error as a consequence of group polarization (Sunstein, 2006). Even these critics, however, concede that their concerns apply largely to deliberative groups that are homogeneous. There is little to suggest that politically diverse policy juries are less able than elite decision makers to achieve ecologically rational results, and the advantages of such broadly democratic approaches in terms of political rationality should be evident. When methods of selection are used that provide demographically and ideologically heterogeneous deliberative groups, there is no reason to doubt the authenticity of any political consensus that emerges. Ultimately, a deliberative democratic approach is preferable to other approaches because it contains within itself the means of revising both its procedures and its products at the initiative of either organizers or participants (Gutmann and Thompson, 2004). Prior to ratification of the Lisbon Treaty in 2009, the democratic theorist in search of an accountability mechanism at this stage of the EU policy process would have encountered significant frustration. But two innovations adopted in the Lisbon Treaty suggest new institutional opportunities for this kind of deliberative uptake.

A new category of administrative law, the delegated act, was created at Lisbon. This form of law is best thought of as an amendment (often technical in nature) to a pre-existing piece of EU legislation. Given the general, often aspirational, nature of EU law, even so significant a choice as that between command-and-control regulations and market-based incentive systems could well fall within the ambit of this new process. In the alternative, the Lisbon Treaty has also authorized a process of citizen initiative, designed to allow what amounts to a petition drive to place a legislative proposal before the European Parliament (Miller, 2011). Given the ongoing experimentation with deliberative polling conducted online, the use of that technique to both craft legislative proposals and secure the citizen support necessary to place them before the European Parliament should be obvious. Although it is still too early to say with any certainty what these innovations will yield, clearly they offer at least the possibility for the European Commission to secure external normative standards for the exercise of its discretionary authority. These potential applications of the process of deliberative polling at the stage of the choice between contending policy paradigms in order to identify basic policy objectives and models is represented in the second row of Table 10.1.

Finally, deliberative democracy is already a familiar feature of action plans and policy implementation, particularly in the realm of watershed policy by watershed partnerships (Sabatier et al., 2005; Hardy, 2010; Hauser et al., 2012). Subnational stakeholder groups of this sort have already engaged the interests of deliberative democratic theorists (Baber and Bartlett, 2005). These structures of governance can best be understood as arrangements for organizing and reconciling competing local discourses about the implications of general legal requirements when applied to local questions. The objective is to develop implementation plans at the subnational level that will achieve national (or international) objectives through the coproduction of regulatory management. One concrete example of this approach has been described as "collaborative learning" (Cheng and Fiero, 2005), an approach to policy development that is strongly reminiscent of the European Commission's mission to promote mutual learning at the level of local implementation decisions.

Collaborative learning, which is a recent innovation in public participation that departs from the traditional focus on issues and interests, is an approach designed specifically to address the complexity and rancorous conflict that often characterizes the management of public lands. Collaborative learning is characterized by a systems approach to understanding natural resource issues, the promotion (instead of avoidance) of dialogue about differences among stakeholders, and a focus on feasible improvements in concrete circumstances rather than ideal outcomes over the longer term. Unlike deliberative polling, which seeks stratified random samples of the population, collaborative learning employs landscape-based working groups that represent key stakeholder groups, of which the watershed partnership is an outstanding example (Clark, 1997). These voluntary groups convene at the local or regional level to discuss issues of watershed management. Possessing no formal authority, watershed partnerships are open to anyone wishing to participate. They generally attract large landowners and corporations whose behaviour substantially affects watershed outcomes, environmentalists who can take up or forgo their right to sue under a variety of statutory schemes, and government officials who want to find safe ground in between. Collaborative learning on the model of stakeholder partnerships offers an opportunity for the European Commission to sponsor and sustain the kind of transgovernmental networks that research has already shown to be effective in improving compliance effectiveness within the EU (Hobolth and Martinsen, 2013).

Experience with the role of watershed partnerships in developing action plans is particularly illuminating from the accountability perspective. It suggests that effective partnerships must be full partnerships. Regardless of the provenance of the watershed group (citizen based, agency based, or mixed), appropriate matching of partnership structure and operation to their roles is key (Moore and Koontz, 2003). This can be accomplished only by involving the local community in the underlying research that defines the policy problem at hand, because the watershed partnership fills the gap between what public institutions can achieve on their own and what the community itself needs (Arnold and Fernandez-Gimenez, 2007; Shandas and Messer, 2008). To achieve this level of autonomous input, community members of resource management partnerships need to be full partners. The regulatory environment within which they operate must be characterized by a low level of command-and-control enforcement by central authorities (Lubell et al., 2002), and they must enjoy the political clout and legal standing necessary to engage agency representatives as equals and to insist on the development of consensual (or nearly consensual) resolutions of regulatory problems (Cronin and Ostergren, 2007). It is this peculiarly social sort of consensus that sustains the development, implementation, evaluation, and redesign of regulatory action plans during the numerous iterations through which they must pass. The potential for this sort of participatory planning to improve the accountability of the European Commission's use of its long-standing authority to promulgate implementing rules (Craig, 2012) is unmistakable. This process of using stakeholder partnerships to sort through contending discourse among local contributors to policy implementation is represented in the third row of Table 10.1.

Deliberative practice and administrative accountability in global environmental governance

Analysis of an extension of the deliberative model of administrative accountability to the EU's embryonic non-legislative accountability mechanisms yields four main observations about the problems of governance accountability in the political circumstances of the Anthropocene. Briefly: (1) deliberative techniques are readily deployable and offer significant advantages with respect to administrative accountability; (2) in part because of what deliberative democratic techniques make possible in the way of accountability, they can contribute much to political legitimacy as well; (3) deliberative democracy can increase social capital for institution building and maintenance, such that loss of organizational effectiveness does not have to be an unavoidable cost of gains in legitimacy and accountability; and (4) properly designed deliberative mechanisms can produce normative premises independent of the bureaucratic institutions of governance and can in turn hold bureaucratic institutions accountable to those premises.

To elaborate, first, there is nothing so unique about the issues of environmental governance that it puts them out of the reach of democratic deliberation. New deliberative techniques like juristic deliberation can easily be imagined as tools for exploring the contours and limitations of normative consensus about both the exploitation and conservation of natural resources and the avoidance or amelioration of the results of that exploitation. Well-tested techniques like deliberative polling can readily be used to elicit a more reflective public opinion on contending models of environmental policy. Watershed partnerships are merely a preeminent example of stakeholder planning and the coproduction of regulatory implementation. At each successive step of the process of developing policies of environmental governance, deliberative techniques are readily deployable and offer significant advantages over less fully participatory approaches, particularly in terms of the political durability of the solutions that they produce and the administrative accountability being sought.

The fact that democratic deliberation is deployable at each stage of the process of environmental policy development leads to a second observation—that deliberative democracy has the potential to add significantly to the political legitimacy of global environmental governance. This is significant because issues of both natural resource management and environmental protection are likely to involve both issues of distributive justice and significant levels of political conflict. This characteristic of environmental governance makes broadening involvement in the policy process to include representatives of historically underrepresented groups more difficult, and more essential. The experience of Native American tribes, for example, indicates that their political and economic disadvantages mean that they are not often involved in watershed decision-making. But their involvement in watershed partnerships (when it occurs) leads public officials to deploy financial and human resources in ways that better manage watersheds across a full range of social values, resulting in more equitable and more defensible regulatory outcomes (Cronin and Ostergren, 2007). Thus, the realization that every step in the process of environmental governance can include significant citizen participation means that a virtuous circle of public confidence and public involvement can be created that can legitimize outcomes that are ecologically sound but that may disappoint some stakeholders and might otherwise have been rejected for that reason.

Third, recognizing that democratic deliberation has a role to play at every stage of the policy process is just a short step from realizing that the linear assumption inherent in the very concept of the policy process, and the role of administrative agencies in it, needs to be overcome. In any broadly participatory political process, arriving at consensus is a recursive proposition. Yesterday's normative agreement can always be unwound by today's political dissent or tomorrow's social discord. To a greater degree than political theorists, the skilled policy analysts and experienced public managers who populate administrative agencies are aware that all conclusions are tentative and no victory is final. That is why the leaders of collaborative watershed partnerships so often find themselves grappling with challenges of organization development and maintenance rather than the environmental issues that originally brought them to the table (Bonnell and Koontz, 2007). Collaborative environmental governance is at least as much a matter of organization building as it is environmental protection.

A long recognized strength of deliberative democracy is its tendency to increase the social capital necessary for institution building and maintenance (Shandas and Messer, 2008). It does so in at least two ways. In the first instance, well-implemented democratic deliberation makes it possible to achieve an "economy of moral disagreement." Democratic deliberation requires citizens to justify their political positions to one another by seeking a rationale that is fully public, a rationale that all deliberators could (at least in principle) accept. This requirement minimizes the outright rejection by deliberators of positions that they oppose by discouraging reliance upon comprehensive moral or religious doctrines in favour of more limited rationales that allow for the eventual convergence of their views with those of others (Gutmann and Thompson, 2004). Second, democratic deliberation has the tendency to turn a collection of separate individuals into a self-identified group whose members see one another as cooperators in a shared project rather than as opponents in a zero-sum contest. Among the norms that deliberation promotes is a norm of cooperation within the group that is often strong enough to discourage members from clinging to their positions for transient or entirely personal reasons (Miller, 2003). This effect is so marked that our own use of juristic deliberation has revealed a serious "repeat player" bias, for which we have had to account in our research protocol. We have found that when the same group of individuals is asked to resolve a series of hypothetical disputes, their ability to achieve consensus increases with every round of deliberation. For research purposes, this is obviously a significant problem. But for the environmental governance practitioner it means that deliberative exercises conducted iteratively in any given community are likely to increase that community's ability to resolve problems in a collaborative way.

Together, these two features of democratic deliberation (its tendency to reduce moral disputes and to promote consensus) can reduce the costs of organization maintenance in a stakeholder community by narrowing the grounds of disagreement among participants, thereby reducing the range of possible policy outcomes with which any final decision procedure must deal. When this result is achieved, more of the resources of environmental professionals can be turned to solving environmental problems as less time is spent overcoming the forces of organizational entropy. Ultimately, a tipping point is reached where gains in democratic legitimacy are no longer paid for with losses in organizational effectiveness. In the process, administrative agencies involved in global environmental governance become the subjects of externally generated normative constraints that impose new patterns of accountability upon their use of the administrative discretion with which they are unavoidably invested. This leads us to our fourth, and final, observation.

It might well be objected that even if the European Commission pursued some or all of the deliberative initiatives we have suggested, the results would still fall short of promoting accountability by enforcing external normative standards on its use of administrative discretion. After all, might not the Commission ignore any results that failed to advance its own agenda? Were no other EU entities concerned with assuring accountability in the continuing process of Union integration, this objection would be quite a serious one. But the existence of democratically generated external normative standards could be expected at least to marginally strengthen the ability, if not the resolve, of institutions such as the European Council, the European Parliament, and the Council of Ministers to hold the Commission to account. As well, European courts exercise significant powers of judicial review over actions of the Commission and are clearly motivated to advance the cause of uniformity in the application of EU legislative rules—something it is unlikely that they can do on their own, simply by applying general principles of law to legislative enactments (Schwarze, 2012). In reviewing any administrative action the Commission might take in response to deliberatively generated norms, courts are quite capable of comparing the reasons given by the Commission for its actions to the normative principles that it claims to be pursuing. And lest we conclude that, in relying on European courts to hold the European Commission and other EU agencies accountable, we have merely substituted one unelected form of decision-making for another, we should remember this. Normative principles generated by properly designed deliberative mechanisms are both heterologous to the appointed institutions of governance and directly democratic in their provenance. So, here we have a means of addressing both the problem of administrative accountability in the EU and the broader democratic deficit in the legislative institutions of global environmental governance generally.

Conclusion

Earlier chapters in this book suggest that making sense of the Anthropocene involves using that concept to capture many ideas in one word. Part of the appeal of "Anthropocene" is that, among other things, it provides a way of making sense of, and appreciating reflexively: (1) the immense complexity of the physical and cultural worlds and the minimal but growing human understanding of it; (2) the unthinking and often inadvertent human assumption of responsibility for directing the ill-understood relationship with this environment and even for controlling the environment itself; and (3) the inkling, barely dawning, of just how complex and urgent various transformations need to be if humans are to govern themselves onto trajectories that promise environmental richness and equitable prosperity for future generations. For many reasons, including knowledge generation, dissemination, and incorporation, necessary ubiquity of action, implementation effectiveness, openness to learning and adaptation, and the need for nearly universal normative buy-in, among others, this governance must evolve quickly, in a matter of a few decades rather than a few centuries, and it must be democratic. Much of the needed action—regulative, allocative, distributive—cannot be accomplished in a timely way and on an adequate scale other than by delegating considerable discretion to administrative agencies. If such governance is to be at all democratic, these agencies must be seen as democratically legitimate and they must be held accountable by mechanisms that are clearly democratic in their provenance.

Legislative oversight, the primary accountability responsibility within nation states, provides no prospective answer to the immense and complex accountability needs of global governance in the Anthropocene. But democratically responsible accountability is still possible in a governance world of diffused power and complex relationships. In struggling forward with this transnational accountability challenge, the EU has laid a foundation for employing a set of deliberative democratic practices that can achieve significant democratic oversight in the absence of an effectively empowered and engaged legislature. Deliberative democratic techniques can contribute to norm mapping and building, to choosing among policy models, and in developing and implementing policy action plans. By establishing new democratic responsibilities and the expectation that policies and actions must be consistent with democratically embraced normative principles, appropriately institutionalized deliberative democracy in the Anthropocene has the potential to add significantly to the accountability, and therefore political legitimacy, of global environmental governance.

References

Ackerman, B. and Fishkin, J. S. (2003) Deliberation day. In Fishkin, J. S. and Laslett, P. (eds.), *Debating Deliberative Democracy*. Malden, MA: Blackwell.

Adam, S. and Maier, M. (2011) National parties as politicizers of EU integration? Party campaign communication in the run-up to the 2009 European Parliament election. *European Union Politics* 12(3): 431–453.

Arnold, J. S. and Fernandez-Gimenez, M. (2007) Building participatory capital through participatory research: An analysis of collaboration on Tohono O'odham Tribal Rangelands in Arizona. *Society and Natural Resources* 20(6): 481–495.

Baber, W. F. (2010) Democratic deliberation and environmental practice: The case of natural resource management. *Environmental Practice* 12: 195–201.

Baber, W. F. and Bartlett, R. V. (2005) *Deliberative Environmental Politics: Democracy and Ecological Rationality*. Cambridge, MA: MIT Press.

Baber, W. F. and Bartlett, R. V. (2009) *Global Democracy and Sustainable Jurisprudence: Deliberative Environmental Law*. Cambridge, MA: MIT Press.

Baber, W. F. and Bartlett, R. V. (2015) *Consensus and Global Environmental Governance: Deliberative Democracy in Nature's Regime*. Cambridge, MA: MIT Press.

Bauer, S., Andresen, S. and Biermann, F. (2012) International bureaucracies. In Biermann, F. and Pattberg, P. (eds.), *Global Environmental Governance Reconsidered*. Cambridge, MA: MIT Press.

Bonnell, J. E. and Koontz, T. (2007) Stumbling forward: The organizational challenges of building and sustaining collaborative watershed management. *Society and Natural Resources* 20(2): 153–167.

Boughey, J. (2013) Administrative law: The next frontier for comparative law. *The International and Comparative Law Quarterly* 62(1): 55–95.

Cheng, A. S. and Fiero, J. D. (2005) *The Deliberative Democracy Handbook: Strategies for Effective Civic Engagement in the 21st Century*. San Francisco: John Wiley & Sons.

Christoff, P. and Eckersley, R. (2013) *Globalization and the Environment*. Lanham, MD: Rowman & Littlefield.

Clark, J. (1997) *Strategic Partnerships: A Strategic Guide for Local Conservation Efforts in the West*. Denver, CO: Western Governors' Association.

Craig, P. (2012) *EU Administrative Law*, 2nd ed. New York: Oxford University Press.

Cronin, A. E. and Ostergren, D. M. (2007) Democracy, participation, and Native American tribes in collaborative watershed management. *Society and Natural Resources* 20(6): 527–542.

Davis, K. C. (1969) *Discretionary Justice: A Preliminary Inquiry*. Baton Rouge, LA: Louisiana State University Press.

European Council (2000a) Presidency Conclusions, Lisbon European Council, 23–24 March. Brussels, Belgium: European Council.

European Council (2000b) Presidency Conclusions, Nice European Council Meeting, 7–9 December. Brussels, Belgium: European Council.

European Council (2005) Presidency Conclusions, European Council Brussels, 22–23 March. Brussels, Belgium: European Council.

Fishkin, J. (1995) *The Voice of the People: Public Opinion and Democracy*. New Haven, CT: Yale University Press.

Fishkin, J. S. and Laslett, P. (eds.) (2003) *Debating Deliberative Democracy*. New York: Wiley-Blackwell.

Gastil, J. and Levine, P. (eds.) (2005) *The Deliberative Democracy Handbook: Strategies for Effective Civic Engagement in the Twenty-First Century*. San Francisco, CA: Jossey-Bass.

Gutmann, A. and Thompson, D. (2004) *Why Deliberative Democracy?* Princeton, NJ: Princeton University Press.

Habermas, J. (1996) *Between Facts and Norms: Contributions to a Discourse Theory of Law and Democracy*. Cambridge, MA: MIT Press.

Habermas, J. (1998) *The Inclusion of the Other*. Cambridge, MA: MIT Press.

Habermas, J. (2009) *Europe: The Faltering Project*. Malden, MA: Polity Press.

Hardy, S. D. (2010) Governments, group membership, and watershed partnerships. *Society and Natural Resources* 23(7): 587–603.

Hauser, B. K., Koontz, T. M. and Bruskotter, J. T. (2012) Volunteer participation in collaborative watershed partnerships: Insights from the theory of planned behaviour. *Journal of Environmental Planning and Management* 55(1): 77–94.

Helwig, N. (2013) EU foreign policy and the high representative's capacity-expectations gap: A question of political will. *European Foreign Affairs Review* 18(2): 235–253.

Hobolth, M. and Martinsen, D. S. (2013) Transgovernmental networks in the European Union: Improving compliance effectively? *Journal of European Public Policy* 20(10): 1406–1424.

Huitema, D., van De Kerkhof, M. and Pesch, U. (2007) The nature of the beast: Are citizens' juries deliberative or pluralist? *Policy Sciences* 40(4): 287–311.

Iancu, B. (2012) *Legislative Delegation: The Erosion of Normative Limits in Modern Constitutionalism*. New York: Springer.

Lubell, M., Schneider, M. Scholz, J. T. and Mete, M. (2002) Watershed partnerships and the emergence of collective action institutions. *American Journal of Political Science* 46(1): 148–163.

Miller, D. (2003) Deliberative democracy and social choice. In Fishkin, J. S. and Laslett, P. (eds.), *Debating Deliberative Democracy*. Malden, MA: Blackwell Publishing.

Miller, J. L. (2011) A new 'democratic life' for the European Union? Administrative lawmaking, democratic legitimacy, and the Lisbon Treaty. *Contemporary Politics* 17(3): 321–334.

Moore, E. A. and Koontz, T. M. (2003) A typology of collaborative watershed groups: Citizen-based, agency-based, and mixed partnerships. *Society and Natural Resources* 16(5): 451–460.

Pelizzo, R. and Stapenhurst, F. (2013) *Government Accountability and Legislative Oversight*. New York: Routledge.

Sabatier, P. A., Focht, W., Lubell, M., Trachtenberg, Z., Vedlitz, A. and Matlock, M. (2005) *Swimming Upstream: Collaborative Approaches to Watershed Management*. Cambridge, MA: MIT Press.

Scharpf, F. (1999) *Governing in Europe: Effective and Democratic?* New York: Oxford University Press.

Schwarze, J. (2012) European public law in the light of the Treaty of Lisbon. *European Public Law* 18(2): 285–304.

Shandas, V. and Messer, W. B. (2008) Fostering green communities through civic engagement: Community-based environmental stewardship in the Portland area. *Journal of the American Planning Association* 74(4): 408–418.

Shane, P. M. (2010) Legislative delegation, the unitary executive, and the legitimacy of the administrative state. *Harvard Journal of Law & Public Policy* 33(1): 103–110.

Sunstein, C. R. (2006) *Infotopia: How Many Minds Produce Knowledge*. New York: Oxford University Press.

Toje, A. (2008) The consensus-expectations gap: Explaining Europe's ineffective foreign policy. *Security Dialogue* 39(1): 121–141.

11 Monitoring commitments made under the Kyoto Protocol

An effective tool for accountability in the Anthropocene?

Martina Kühner

Introduction

Calls for ambitious global and national commitments in the field of environmental protection, and in particular climate change mitigation, are numerous and have become increasingly urgent. While agreeing on such global targets has never been an easy task, compliance with them has proven even more difficult. Specifically the lack of accountability and implementation has been a common phenomenon of many Multilateral Environmental Agreements (MEAs). Reasons for non-compliance are plentiful, ranging from lack of capacity or knowledge to reluctance to implement agreements that are costly and not in line with governments' domestic priorities.

At a time when there is widespread recognition that the global community faces a new stage in planetary history, the so-called Anthropocene, the world is in need of novel, more effective ways of mitigating climate change. This includes addressing the questions inherent to the Anthropocene, in particular, how to achieve and monitor compliance through new kinds of mechanisms that take into account the complexity of institutions and actors, the diffusion of responsibility and the urgency to act. Against this backdrop, it is striking that the compliance literature has only taken modest steps towards addressing this need. There is, in fact, not even agreement on the general importance and time pressure to achieve compliance with climate commitments.

Seeking to address the dearth of research in existing innovative compliance models, this chapter focuses on the functioning of the compliance system of the Kyoto Protocol (KP), the only legally binding agreement under the United Nations Framework Convention on Climate Change (UNFCCC), and investigates the role 'soft' instruments play therein. My interest in soft instruments is, among others, based on the claim that they are arguably particularly suitable for governance in the Anthropocene. They can do justice to the inherent characteristics of the Anthropocene (see Pattberg and Zelli, this volume) in several ways: (1) they are able to assist parties to comply with their commitments, thus addressing issues of urgency by avoiding lengthy non-compliance procedures; (2) they can ease the responsibility concerns of different stakeholders through soft instruments that facilitate the accountability of parties without straitjacketing them; and (3) they provide for (in-country) expert reviews, in which the reviewing teams can take into account the complex national and international contexts in which parties have to fulfil their climate change mitigation targets.

Scholars broadly divide measures to ensure compliance with MEAs into two camps: management and enforcement (Chayes and Handler Chayes, 1993; Tallberg, 2002; Brunnée, 2012; Oberthür, 2014). While one school argues that compliance can only be achieved through coercive means, the other shows the capacity of soft managerial or facilitative approaches to enhance compliance. Additionally, in order to enable the accountability of states towards both their citizens and peer states, transparent and valid data on emissions and related information are needed (see Bartlett and Baber, this volume). Identifying such governance mechanisms that are most useful in increasing compliance has been a concern for practitioners, lawyers and scholars alike (Brunnée, 2012).

As it has developed in practice, a critical amount of states seem to lack the political will to commit to any future climate change agreement with 'strong teeth'. There are certainly some proponents for a compliance system with effective sanctioning mechanisms, both on the side of practitioners and academics. Such a governance model can address situations where trust is lacking, as it promises the ability to hold states accountable and to avoid uncertainty about the actions of peers. Yet, on the other hand, many governments are rather critical towards the 'sovereignty costs' of an ambitious model with binding and effective monitoring and enforcement procedures. They fear that this would severely compromise their national leverage over climate policy implementation (Oberthür, 2014, p. 34). As a consequence, states tend to be less likely to agree on legally binding international goals in the first place, fearing the potential 'sticks' in cases of non-compliance.

In light of this scepticism towards 'hard' or binding mechanisms, it is highly relevant to understand the value of soft instruments, which tend to be favoured by the international community in recent climate negotiations. The compliance system for the first commitment period of the KP is an interesting case to study, as it combines soft/facilitative with hard/enforcement approaches to compliance monitoring. The attribute hard refers in this context to measures that have legal force and can entail binding consequences for parties. For this reason they are also sometimes referred to as 'hard-law' instruments. Soft, on the other hand, denominates measures or mechanisms that do not have a binding character. This is why they are often named 'soft-law' instruments. However, this does not mean that these instruments are lacking any power, as they may exert influence through other, non-legalized ways. For instance, they may create transparency, enable ways of showing and demanding accountability and allow for peer or public pressure to develop.

This chapter looks at both the interaction between these two kinds of instruments and the value of the soft instruments regarding the compliance of parties with their agreed emission targets. In other words, this chapter assesses what role soft monitoring mechanisms play in achieving compliance with the commitments made under the KP.

While research on soft instruments in this field has been rather limited so far, the existing literature indicates that soft mechanisms have proven, at least to some extent, successful in providing transparency of information and, in turn, increasing the effectiveness of international regimes (Mitchell, 1998, 2011). Compliance mechanisms with soft instruments generally seem to 'enhance trust among parties, support effective implementation, and protect against the danger of free riding' (Oberthür, 2014, p. 49). More particularly, it is likely that monitoring data gained from soft compliance instruments can at least help to encourage states to be accountable through being forced to be transparent about, for instance, their progress in meeting their emission reduction targets (Mitchell, 2011).

Altogether, finding out what role soft mechanisms can play in promoting compliance can provide crucial insights for future negotiations and decisions on how to organize new compliance mechanisms in the Anthropocene. The chapter explores this potential in several steps. First of all, it introduces different instruments within the compliance system established by the KP. A second part briefly establishes the theoretical context and methodological approach of the study. The chapter then moves on to the interplay between soft and hard instruments. The role of soft mechanisms in this interplay is assessed with the help of empirical data resulting from interviews, primary documents and previous studies. Finally, the main findings of the study are summarized and put into the broader perspective of the ongoing debate on compliance monitoring.

Combining soft and hard instruments: Institutional design and the functioning of compliance monitoring in the Kyoto Protocol

While the KP itself was already adopted in 1997, arrangements to monitor and ensure compliance only emerged much later. In order to address the risk of non-compliance and to increase transparency and accountability among its parties, the KP compliance mechanism was established at the end of 2005. The main aim of this compliance system is to ensure compliance with the agreed national targets under the KP. Since these targets do not apply to developing countries, this mechanism is *de facto* focused only on developed countries (Oberthür, 2014, p. 41). All Annex I parties to the UNFCCC, thus including those countries who committed to binding emission reduction targets under the KP, are required to submit annual greenhouse gas (GHG) inventories, as well as regular national communications on their mitigation actions to the Climate Secretariat (UNFCCC, 2015a).

One important and particularly interesting feature of the compliance system of the KP is its mix of both hard and soft instruments. According to the assessment of one of the legal officers at the Climate Secretariat, the adoption of this system has been 'one of the most sophisticated responses to compliance issues' so far (Bulmer, 2012, p. 55). In the following, the different instruments of the compliance system will be outlined, including a justification of why they can be considered either hard or soft mechanisms, or a combination of both, based on the definitions provided above.

Measurement and Reporting elements constitute the 'M' and 'R' components of the MRV-system, which also entails a verification element (outlined below). They provide a framework within which parties have to measure and report on their emission-related data. Annex I parties have the obligation to report on their emissions every year, as well as to produce more extensive national communications on a regular basis. The yearly emission inventories require the provision of information on GHG emissions and removals thereof, including details on methodologies used (UNFCCC, 2015a). The national communications are only required every four to five years. States are expected to submit quantitative and qualitative 'information on emissions and removals of greenhouse gases (GHGs)' as well as information on 'national circumstances; policies and measures; vulnerability assessment; financial resources and transfer of technology; education, training and public awareness; and any other details of the activities a Party has undertaken to implement the Convention' (ibid.)

Thus, these first two elements within the compliance system, if seen in isolation from the rest of the mechanisms, can be regarded as purely soft, in the sense that they are meant to provide transparency.

It is the International Expert Review Teams (ERTs) that provide the *verification* component within the MRV system, being tasked to verify the validity of the data provided by the parties. For each review of an annual inventory submission or the periodic national communication, a team is selected from a roster of experts compiled by the KP member countries. Within one to two years after the submission of each national communication, they are expected to deliver an independent assessment of the reliability of the information provided by states, as well as a technical judgement on their level of compliance. While most of the time these experts do their work in the form of a desk review, there is also the possibility of an in-country review. In case the ERTs find an issue with compliance, they can submit a question of implementation to the Board of the Compliance Committee, which will then be passed on to the appropriate branch of the committee itself and thus trigger compliance proceedings (Herold, 2012). As the expert reviews are part of the MRV process, they formally belong to the soft part of the compliance system. However, the fact that these experts have the power to trigger a compliance procedure gives them a somewhat extended, or rather, harder mandate.

The *Compliance Committee* (CC) is the core governance tool to facilitate, but also enforce, compliance with the commitments under the KP. In line with its mandate, it builds a sort of umbrella for its two branches: the Enforcement Branch (EB) and the Facilitation Branch (FB). In case of compliance issues, parties can be referred to either branch of the CC. There are three different ways to trigger a compliance procedure. Through governments: either via the self-trigger by a concerned government and the other-trigger by another government that is party to the KP. There is also the possibility for the expert review teams to trigger a compliance proceeding (Oberthür, 2014, p. 37).

As will be described in more detail below, the two branches have different tools at hand, carrots as well as sticks, to address compliance issues. As Oberthür and Lefeber (2010, p. 148) put it, 'the FB has more discretion in applying consequences that are "softer" in nature than the EB has in applying consequences that are "stronger" in nature'.

The *Enforcement Branch* (EB) represents the stick within the compliance system. It is the only hard instrument within this governance framework through its powers to impose different kinds of sanctions. Its mandate and the possible sanction mechanisms are laid out in Article 5.1, 5.2, 7.1 and 7.4 of the protocol and focus on assessing 'compliance with the methodological and reporting requirements' (Herold, 2012, p. 124). The ten members (or respective alternate members) convene in case a question of implementation is tabled via one of the triggers of the compliance procedure described above.

If a country is considered non-compliant by the EB, then clearly defined and quasi-automatic sanctions follow. Depending on the kind of non-compliance, different sanctions apply (Oberthür and Lefeber, 2010, p. 148). For instance, when found in non-compliance with eligibility requirements, a state loses its right to participate in the carbon market mechanism. Such a hard economic penalty of being suspended from emission trading is only lifted once the party restores its compliance.

The task of the *Facilitative Branch* (FB) is to provide facilitation in order to enhance compliance in instances where a case is referred to this branch. This branch consists of ten members (plus an equal amount of alternates) and can be considered as a linking element between the soft MRV-system and the hard EB. While its tools are soft – ranging from general advice to active support – the fact that it is organized alongside the EB makes it appear less soft. The actual effect this can have on its role in fostering compliance will be discussed in the next section.

Assessing the value of soft instruments for monitoring and fostering compliance: Conceptual approach and methodological challenges

At the core of this chapter lies the question of how compliance monitoring works within the KP and the extent to which soft instruments play an important role therein. The key underlying academic debate here is on the sources of non-compliance and 'the most effective means of addressing non-compliance in international cooperation' (Tallberg, 2002, p. 609). As several observers outline, there are two major competing perspectives (Oberthür, 2014; Brunnée, 2012). On the one hand, some scholars argue in favour of an enforcement strategy towards compliance and 'stress a coercive strategy of monitoring and sanctions' (Tallberg, 2002, p. 609). On the other hand, the value of managerial approaches to compliance is highlighted by the so-called 'management theorists', with a focus on soft measures such as transparency and capacity-building (ibid.). Tallberg argues that 'enforcement and management mechanisms are most effective when combined' (2002, p. 610; also compare Oberthür, 2014). On the basis of his case study research, he concludes that 'the two strategies are complementary and mutually reinforcing, not discrete alternatives' (ibid.).

The case investigated in this chapter also consists of a compliance system that combines both management (soft) and enforcement (hard) instruments. Therefore, this research is based on a claim similar to Tallberg's in his analysis of the EU and other international compliance systems. The chapter argues that both managerial and enforcement elements have a role to play in the KP compliance system and that it is the combination of both soft and hard instruments that leads to its (relative) success in ensuring compliance.

This study is interested in assessing the value of soft instruments, which are based on a managerial logic towards compliance. Here, the main argument is that, while it is difficult to isolate the independent effect of soft instruments, such instruments play an important role in fostering compliance in international (environmental) regimes. First empirical results on this role of soft instruments and their linkage with hard instruments will be laid out in the following section.

Next to this central debate, this study also provides a link to the accountability literature (e.g. Bovens, 2007; Karlsson-Vinkhuyzen and McGee, 2013; Mashaw, 2006; Grant and Keohane, 2005). The establishment and use of the compliance monitoring system is clearly based on the needs and demands of different actors. It provides accountability between states bound under the KP, while allowing non-governmental actors to hold the parties to account for their (lack of) actions. This refers to classical accountability demands between a government and its citizens (see Bartlett and Barber, this volume), but also to an accountability relationship among parties themselves and the UNFCCC framework. Thus, the findings of this study will also offer some insights into what role soft instruments can play for accountability in different contexts. This particularly relates to actors outside the KP, for whom the data of the compliance system's MRV process are also available. They can use this monitoring data to hold the parties to the KP accountable.

Based on this theoretical and conceptual context, the following two-step methodological approach is taken. First, one needs to understand how the compliance system actually works both on paper and in practice. Therefore, I shortly discuss the interplay between soft and hard instruments within the compliance system, which are outlined in the previous section. Parallels will be drawn to what Tallberg (2002) calls 'twinning of cooperative and coercive instruments in a "management-enforcement ladder"' (p. 610). While this paper uses a slightly different language, referring to managerial tools as soft and enforcement mechanisms as hard instruments, this way of structuring the working of the compliance system will be helpful to, in a second step, analyse the added value of the soft instruments therein. This will be done by looking at the actual, practical working of the system and its components through document analysis and the consultation of previous studies, as well as by analysing interview material.

The time period for which the analysis is conducted is the first commitment period of the KP from 2008 to 2012. Due to the still ongoing review process of more recent MRV data, it is not yet possible to assess the years from 2013 onwards.

One limitation of this approach is that the effects of soft instruments can hardly be isolated from the presence and effect of the hard EB. This would require a more intensive study of this and similar cases that could check for possible independent effects of soft approaches in the absence of a stick. Such a focus on further cases would, however, go beyond the scope of this chapter. Thus, this study will focus on the interplay between the two sets of instruments and some tentative direction on how to assess the specific role of soft instruments therein. I will present first ideas on how to address this challenge of assessing the value of soft instruments independent from the interplay with other instruments at the end of the chapter.

Soft or hard at play? An empirical analysis of the value of soft instruments within the compliance system

This section scrutinizes the role of soft instruments within the compliance system by first outlining the interplay between soft and hard instruments and, second, attempting to disentangle – to the extent possible – the contribution of soft instruments for fostering compliance within the system described in section 2 above. I will show, however, that isolating the effect of soft instruments is in many instances not possible, as the interplay between soft and hard results is central to explain the (relative) success of the compliance system.

During the observation period, the CC was used in several instances, with eight countries[1] being brought in front of the EB for issues of non-compliance. All of them, except for Canada who withdrew at the end of 2011 and effectively left the KP in December 2012, got back on track by means of the compliance procedures. Some other countries managed to restore compliance without having to go through the EB, as the facilitation provided by the soft instruments, in particular the ERTs, was seemingly enough to return to compliance before a question of implementation was raised (Oberthür and Lefeber, 2010; Doelle, 2012).

Although both the EB and the FB started operating in 2006, the EB was far more active in terms of the cases it dealt with. In total it had seven questions of implementation on the table, while the FB effectively did not tackle any. All of these compliance procedures were filed by the ERTs, with states being 'reluctant to point the finger at each other (or at themselves)' (Oberthür, 2014, p. 37).

In general, the FB was rather slow in taking off, showing difficulties in interpreting its rather vague mandate and translating it into concrete room for action for the branch.[2] It took several years until the FB became more proactive, specifying an indicative working arrangement and using its early warning function to offer parties its facilitation support (ibid.). The actual role of the branch can be clearly labelled as soft, as the only action it has pursued so far was offering advice and facilitation to parties with obligations under Annex B to the Kyoto Protocol who were at risk of missing their quantitative targets or reporting obligations.[3] There is also the option for a country to call for advice from the FB as a 'pre-emptive' or 'defensive' measure to avoid being brought before the EB. However, up to now, attempts to use the FB in that way have not been accepted by the Bureau of the CC. Looking only at the performance of the FB, one could argue that the soft elements within the compliance system have not been very significant up to now. It seems as if governments and ERTs did not perceive it as useful or were not able to activate facilitation by the FB.

However, one also needs to take into account the other soft monitoring instruments within the system in order to get a full picture. Besides the procedures of the CC, the MRV process as a whole also constitutes an important element, with the reports by the parties constituting the basis of the entire compliance procedure. In particular, the 'V-part' of the process, namely the verification of national submissions by the ERTs, deserves closer scrutiny. Next to being the only effective trigger of the compliance procedure so far, the ERTs conduct a sort of expert peer review. It is on the basis of the outcomes of these reviews that the international experts decide on whether it is necessary to activate the trigger by sending a question of implementation to the CC. One interviewee highlighted that the fact that as reporting is based on established methodologies derived from the Intergovernmental Panel on Climate Change (IPCC), it increases the respect parties have for the soft MRV process.[4]

Interestingly, several disagreements, for instance regarding the correctness of amounts in the GHG-emission inventories, were solved by the ERTs and the concerned party themselves. As a consequence, no question of implementation had to be raised, avoiding a procedure in the CC (Oberthür and Lefeber, 2010, p. 147). This means that the ERTs are not purely there to verify the data and to do the technical preparation work for possible cases dealt with by the CC. The fact that they actually have the power to prevent questions of implementation in the first place shows that they can have an effect on the compliance of a party regardless of the availability of hard instruments. According to an expert, 'the in-depth review process and the opportunity that it contains to provide reactions adds, I think, credibility to the process'.[5] What is more, as evidence suggests, ERTs actively offer facilitation and advice to reviewed parties, a task that is formally located at the FB. The members of the CC themselves discussed the division of tasks between the ERTs and themselves regarding the facilitation of compliance on several occasions and 'suggested that ERT experts are perhaps in the best position to provide technical expert advice' (Doelle, 2012, p. 104). There seems to be agreement on the fact that the ERTs play a significant role in facilitating compliance.[6]

Thus, ERT actions overlap partly with the mandate of the FB, for several possible reasons. On the one hand, it is plausible that the ERTs were filling the gap left by the slow start of the FB. On the other hand, 'ERT members have been trained to be cautious about referring matters to the FB' (Doelle, 2012, p. 104). Also, it is plausible that the ERT experts found it attractive to exert their technical expertise and ability to facilitate compliance themselves in a more informal way.[7]

Another reason for the effective role of this soft element within the system can be found in the set-up of the review itself. The fact that ERTs are mostly representatives of the peer countries within the KP implies that they know their countries will be subject to review too. In addition, the reviewing process is done to a large extent by experts who are also involved in the preparation of the reports for their home countries.[8] Thus, they have an interest in a constructive review in which facilitation and learning is possible.

The evidence presented here indicates that the soft instruments within the compliance system played an important role in fostering compliance. However, the importance of the actual threat perceived by a party to be brought in front of the EB cannot be neglected in this context. This threat can incentivize parties to resolve compliance issues already at the technical level of the soft instruments. The threat can develop from the fear of a party to lose face in front of other parties and the domestic constituency when receiving a question of non-compliance. When the EB concludes that a country is in non-compliance, this can lead to reputational damage.[9] As one UNFCCC official has framed it:

> Even by the fact … of an Expert Review Team report being published – saying there is a question of implementation – there is already a naming and shaming component there. And perhaps there is of course more 'shame' in actually being legally found in non-compliance because the Expert Review Team report contains a technical finding.[10]

It seems, therefore, that the compliance system can develop soft forms of pressure. But this system can also exert influence that clearly goes beyond facilitation, peer pressure and naming and shaming. After all, the EB has hard consequences in the form of economic sanctions at its disposal. The possibility of being suspended from participation in the market-based mechanism seemed to be perceived by parties as a real threat, a stick whose impact can be quantified in Euros.[11]

Summarizing these examples and expert views, it is 'reasonable to assume that the very existence of a formal, high-level, compliance system contributes to the parties' resolve to settle their differences with the ERTs' (Oberthür and Lefeber, 2010, p. 148).

Referring to Tallberg's conceptualization, the 'management-enforcement ladder' seems to be reflected within this system. I showed how the MRV-part largely refers to managerial approaches to compliance, while the EB is at the top of this escalation ladder. The FB can in theory also be subsumed to the management-side of the system, while in practice this service has not yet been used. Finally, I found that the ERTs, while officially being part of the facilitation side of the ladder, *de facto* formed a stepping stone towards the enforcement side as they were the only effective trigger for compliance procedures. At the same time, they showed their potential to function on the managerial side by focusing on problem-solving approaches with parties to avoid compliance procedures. Altogether, the case at hand seems to be a good example of Tallberg's model, with the combination of soft and hard instruments leading to a (relatively) well-functioning mechanism.

Conclusions

Summary of findings

The compliance system as a whole has shown to be rather successful in its design for the first commitment period both in the cases of non-compliance it has dealt with so far and in the possible motivating or even deterring impact it had on other parties. However, a final assessment of its effectiveness is not yet possible. Questions of implementation have up to now only dealt with issues related to eligibility for the market-based mechanism, as well as methodological and reporting requirements. A considerable part of possible non-compliance cases could not be revealed thus far, as 'questions of implementation regarding emission targets will not reach the EB from ERTs before the second half of 2015' (Oberthür and Lefeber, 2010, p. 149). The reason for this is that the GHG inventories of 2012 will need sufficient time for review.

Nevertheless, some important lessons from the working of the soft elements within the compliance system and, in particular, its interrelation with the EB can be drawn already. Regarding the interplay between hard and soft elements within the CS, the chapter shows that both types of instruments played an important complementary or even mutually reinforcing role. In fact, the empirical insights collected for this study suggest that the soft instruments are not at all powerless and also not simply helping tools to make the EB functional. On the contrary, the MRV process seems to ensure that most parties are complying with their commitments. In the end, there were rather few questions of implementation raised compared to the overall number of parties. The structuring of the implementation exercise through different measuring and reporting tasks might already help many states, in particular the ones who are committed and have the necessary capacities to keep up with meeting their targets. Also, for those countries struggling with compliance, but willing to cooperate with the ERTs, hard measures could be avoided by the facilitation provided by the experts. Thus, one could argue that the soft instruments have the capacity to prevent actions from the enforcement side of the mechanism by effectively using their role within the MRV mandate. One could even go one step further and argue that the potential of soft instruments has still not been fully realized as the FB has not really been utilized so far. Facilitation nevertheless was an important component of fostering compliance 'the soft way'. It was, at least partly, taken over by the ERTs.

This analysis presented the interesting dynamics between soft and hard instruments within the compliance system of the KP. It has shown a compelling case where soft components bring an added value to the compliance system. On the other hand, several experts[12] indicated that soft instruments alone would not be sufficient to achieve the same result. Therefore, it is this *combination* of instruments that seems to account for the relative success of the compliance system.

Avenues for further research

This study provided initial and preliminary evidence on the value of soft instruments in achieving compliance irrespective of the availability of hard instruments. Future research should focus on collecting more evidence on this issue, for instance by means of collecting and analysing experts' and other stakeholders' insights and perceptions on both the practical interplay between soft and hard compliance instruments, as well as the usefulness of the soft instruments.

Several ways of addressing this shortcoming exist: (1) interviewing experts within the KP on their perceptions regarding the role of the soft instruments; (2) looking in more detail at the actual use of soft instruments by actors within the KP; (3) moving the analysis beyond the KP to a venue where no EB conflicts with soft instruments; and (4) look at how other stakeholders, such as non-governmental actors, perceive and use the data provided by the soft MRV-system of the KP.

With regard to other empirical cases, similar distinctions would be useful. On the one hand, future studies could investigate cases where the enforcement approach is central. On the other hand, monitoring systems that only rely on managerial approaches to achieving compliance would need to be assessed. Interesting cases in the field of sustainable development that lend themselves to such studies are: (1) the OECD Environmental Performance Review, which uses a peer review system to incentivize peer states to comply with commonly agreed standards; (2) the former UN Commission on Sustainable Development (CSD) which was mandated to monitor progress on the commitments agreed upon under Agenda 21 and which only relied on managerial instruments such as transparency, knowledge exchange and capacity building in order to achieve this mandate; (3) the newly established voluntary monitoring system for the Sustainable Development Goals (SDGs). Finally, other cases where soft and hard components are combined, such as the Convention on Biological Diversity, could complement this research. Looking at cases with different combinations of carrots and sticks will provide more solid conclusions on this matter.

Outlook: Compliance monitoring in the Anthropocene

Any future international climate agreement will have to consider the way in which signatory parties will promote compliance. What such a compliance system will look like depends on several factors. As Oberthür argues, 'there may be a trade-off between (the stringency of) any compliance mechanism and the willingness of countries to participate in an international agreement and to commit to ambitious action' (2014, p. 34). In other words, a political compromise needs to be struck between a climate deal with a (nearly) global reach, thus covering many more worldwide emissions than under the KP, or to have an agreement with a strong compliance system that has the power to sanction parties deemed non-compliant, at the cost of a smaller membership or more differentiated obligations.

This will not be an easy trade-off, as both a broad membership and a high level of compliance have their advantages. While the former widens the scope of the potential impact on global emission reductions, the latter is crucial to build trust among the parties and, consequently, to motivate other parties to comply. A weak compliance mechanism might lead to a lack of confidence among parties, something that can undermine the whole agreement, in particular due to the considerable economic interests linked to the policy field at hand (ibid.).

More specifically, as parties themselves have been reluctant to trigger a procedure, it would be important that there are other triggers in a new agreement. Next to the ERTs, which have initiated all procedures so far, other actors outside the binding framework (beyond parties) should be able to trigger a compliance procedure. This could incentivize NGOs to better use MRV-data to hold parties to account. In other MEAs there is already the possibility of such an external trigger. In addition, the possibilities to use the FB should be improved, for instance by better clarifying its role and differentiating it more clearly from those of the ERTs.

In light of the new climate arrangement starting from 2020, the insights this chapter provided lead to the conclusion that soft instruments certainly matter for compliance. However, opting solely for a soft managerial approach to compliance could imply a great risk that states will in the end not hold to what they agreed upon in the 2015 climate talks in Paris.

Therefore, to strike a balance between core features of the Anthropocene – complexity, urgency, responsibility – a combination between soft and hard instruments seems to be the most suitable middle way, combining the values stemming from both worlds: facilitation and enforcement. This chapter has provided evidence of how such an approach can adequately address such challenges. First, the combination of soft and hard instruments does justice to the complexity of the climate change topic, since it provides a flexible set of mechanisms which can address different challenges ranging from the lack of capacity and knowledge to missing political will. Second, urgency is addressed through a pragmatic combination of feasibility and coerciveness. On the one hand, the system provides soft reporting guidelines and facilitation to meet them, while, on the other hand, it sets hard deadlines, reviews with key timelines and the possibility of enforcing deliverables using the stick of the EB. Third and finally, such a compliance structure offers incentives and mechanisms for parties to take on responsibility and be accountable for their climate actions. It also provides transparency, allowing for other actors outside the KP to hold parties to account and to remind them of their commitments and responsibility to mitigate climate change.

Altogether, there is not only an urgent need for the international community to commit to ambitious climate mitigation targets, but in addition there is the imperative to agree and act upon an effective compliance system that can actually provide a framework to facilitate and, if necessary, enforce the action that is desperately needed to safeguard our environment and human well-being within these planetary boundaries.

Acknowledgements

I would like to express my gratitude to all interviewees. A first round of interviews was conducted at the UNFCCC during the exploratory research phase in 2014. In spring 2015, a second round of interviews was carried out. The interpretation of the interview data remains my own responsibility. I would also like to thank the editors of this book, as well as Professor Thomas Conzelmann and Dr Ron Cörvers for their support and valuable comments on earlier drafts of this chapter.

Notes

1 Greece, Canada, Croatia, Bulgaria, Romania, Ukraine, Lithuania and Slovakia (UNFCCC, 2015b).
2 Interview#2 with two UNFCCC officials, 17 February 2014; Interview#1 with a member of the Compliance Committee, 1 April 2015; Interview#1 with a former member of the Compliance Committee, 15 April 2015.
3 Interview#1 with a UNFCCC official on 14 February 2014; Interview#2 with two UNFCCC officials on 17 February 2014.
4 Interview#1 with a UNFCCC official, 17 February 2014.
5 Interview#1 with an expert, 21 February 2014.
6 Ibid.; Interview#2 with two UNFCCC officials, 17 February 2014; Interviews#1, 2, 3 and 4 with members of the Compliance Committee, 5 March 2015.
7 Interview#1 with a member of the Compliance Committee, 1 April 2015. Interview#1 with a member of the Compliance Committee, 5 March 2015.
8 Interview#1 with a UNFCCC official, 14 February 2014.
9 Interview#2 with a member of the Compliance Committee, 5 May 2015; Interview#1 with a former member of the Compliance Committee, 15 April 2015.
10 Interview#1 with a UNFCCC official, 14 February 2014.
11 Interview#1 with a former member of the Compliance Committee, 15 April 2015; Interview#1 with a UNFCCC official, 14 February 2014.
12 Interview#1 with a member of the Compliance Committee, 5 March 2015; Interview#1 with a former member of the Compliance Committee, 15 April 2015.

References

Bovens, M. A. (2007) Analysing and assessing accountability: A conceptual framework. *European Law Journal* 13(4): 447–468.
Brunnée, J. (2012) Promoting compliance with multilateral environmental agreements. In Brunnée, J., Doelle, M. and Rajamani, L. (eds), *Promoting Compliance in an Evolving Climate Regime*. New York: Cambridge University Press, pp. 38–54.
Bulmer, J. (2012) Compliance regimes in multilateral environmental agreements. In Brunnée, J., Doelle, M. and Rajamani, L. (eds), *Promoting Compliance in an Evolving Climate Regime*. New York: Cambridge University Press, pp. 55–73.
Chayes, A. and Handler Chayes, A. (1993) On compliance. *International Organization* 47(2): 175–205.
Doelle, M. (2012). Experience with the facilitative and enforcement branches of the Kyoto compliance system. In Brunnée, J., Doelle, M. and Rajamani, L. (eds), *Promoting Compliance in an Evolving Climate Regime*. New York: Cambridge University Press, pp. 102–121.

Grant, R. W. and Keohane, R. O. (2005) Accountability and abuses of power in world politics. *American Political Science Review* 99(1): 29–43.

Herold, A. (2012) Experiences with Articles 5, 7, and 8 defining the monitoring, reporting and verification system under the Kyoto Protocol. In Brunnée, J., Doelle, M. and Rajamani, L. (eds), *Promoting Compliance in an Evolving Climate Regime*. New York: Cambridge University Press, pp. 122–146.

Karlsson-Vinkhuyzen, S. I. and McGee, J. (2013) Legitimacy in an era of fragmentation: The case of global climate governance. *Global Environmental Politics* 13(3): 56–78.

Mashaw, J. L. (2006) Accountability and institutional design: Some thoughts on the grammar of governance. In Dowdle, M. (ed), *Public Accountability: Designs, Dilemmas and Experiences*. Cambridge: Cambridge University Press, pp. 115–156.

Mitchell, R. B. (1998) Sources of transparency: Information systems in international regimes. *International Studies Quarterly* (42): 109–130.

Mitchell, R. B. (2011) Transparency for governance: The mechanisms and effectiveness of disclosure-based and education-based transparency policies. *Ecological Economics* 70: 1882–2890.

Oberthür, S. (2014) Options for a compliance mechanism in a 2015 climate agreement. *Climate Law* 4: 30–49.

Oberthür, S. and Lefeber, R. (2010) Holding countries to account: The Kyoto Protocol's compliance system revisited after four years of experience. *Climate Law* 1: 133–158.

Tallberg, J. (2002) Paths to compliance: Enforcement, management, and the European Union. *International Organization* 56: 609–643.

UNFCCC (2015a) National Reports. Available from: http://unfccc.int/national_reports/items/1408.php [accessed 11 June 2015].

UNFCCC (2015b) Compliance under the Kyoto Protocol. Available from: http://unfcc.int/kyoto_protocol/compliance/items/2875.php [accessed 11 June 2015].

12 The legitimacy and transformation of global climate governance in the Anthropocene

Implications for the global South

Marija Isailovic

Introduction

Following the lead of Nobel Laureate Paul Crutzen in his short piece 'The geology of mankind' in *Nature* in 2002, scientists have quickly adopted the term Anthropocene to denote a new human-dominated geological epoch resulting from dramatic, and partly human-made changes, the planet has gone through (see Pattberg and Zelli, this volume). These changes can be traced back to the second part of the eighteenth century when global atmospheric concentrations of carbon dioxide and methane began to rise due to human fossil fuel use and continued to increase rapidly ever since the early phase of industrialization (Crutzen, 2002). The Anthropocene discourse emphasizes the coupling of human society and earth systems through the concept of 'planetary boundaries' which investigates effects of human actions on various planetary systems, in order to identify 'a safe operating space for humanity' (Rockström et al., 2009). Such narrative provides understanding of the urgency of human dominance on the planet through the concepts such as 'the great acceleration', 'thresholds' and 'tipping points'.

However, while natural scientists have developed different methodologies and approaches for tackling global environmental change, social and political scientists still have to catch up when it comes to understanding the fundamental challenges of politics and governance in the Anthropocene. Such a social science perspective is much needed, for instance, to address argumentative flaws in narratives produced by natural scientists that coined the term Anthropocene – and to address the need to develop a new understanding of politics behind the concept (Wissenburg, this volume). In its current form, the concept does not sufficiently reflect on the fundamental problems permeating human–nature relations in general and the major transitions of global environmental governance architectures in particular (Maldonado, this volume; Widerberg, this volume). In turn, a social science perspective raises new questions with regard to the effectiveness and legitimacy of global policy-making as well as new opportunities for rethinking core concepts of environmental governance scholarship (see Pattberg and Zelli, this volume).

One such question regards the global equity dimension. Currently, the Anthropocene concept does not fully do justice to the specific position of the global South and its actors. Research and practice of negotiations and agenda setting in global environmental governance have shown that differences in opinions, interests and norms as well as access to resources between the global North and global South are still considerable. They take a central position in shaping future sustainable governance in many issue areas of world politics (Biermann, 2007).

The perception of a North–South divide has been questioned by some scholars, since it obscures intra-state variations as well as the increasing fragmentation within the global South, illustrated by the tensions between emerging economies on the one hand and less developed and small island developing states on the other. However, although such variations do exist, other scholars argue that developing countries or the global South often represent a collective actor in global environmental negotiations and cannot be entirely neglected (Najam, 2005; Okereke, 2008). In this chapter, I follow this argument, using the term global South to invoke 'a set of shared histories of many countries in the geographic south – colonialism, a struggle to address widespread poverty, and a predominant policy concern with the process of "development" over the past few decades' (Dubash and Morgan, 2012, p. 263).

Such a shared context of the global South requires a reconceptualization of some of the theoretical assumptions underpinning the literature on the legitimacy and transformation of global climate governance in the context of the Anthropocene. In their introductory chapter the editors of this volume present three key aspects of the Anthropocene that are likely to be reflected in political and social science scholarly debates, namely complexity, responsibility and urgency to act (see Pattberg and Zelli, this volume). First, the perspective that the Anthropocene concept puts on the human species, viewing humankind as the new geological agent, masks the complexity and diversity of human agents and resources – and in particular the political nature of societal relations and structures. The way homo sapiens is conceptualized as an isolated driver of global environmental change does not consider a diverse network of technological, cultural or political aspects that contributed to environmental change (Palsson et al., 2013). Second, the Anthropocene concept strongly emphasizes the interdependence of the community of all nations, which requires a much stronger effective and especially equitable and legitimate institutional framework for global cooperation and responsibility of its actors (Biermann, 2014). Finally, social sciences should not barely identify the drivers, barriers and incentives for 'successful' negotiations and behavioural change, but also have a normative task in light of the urgency to act in the Anthropocene. With regard to sustainable development, this means to explore policy options, in collaboration with stakeholders from the global South, which ensure that humanities can live within natural limits while addressing a set of structural and historical global inequalities (Palsson et al., 2013). This normative call implies that, in the end, the Anthropocene is intrinsically political and has to be understood as a global political phenomenon (Biermann, 2014).

Against this backdrop, this chapter seeks to contribute to the Anthropocene debate by offering a legitimacy-based understanding of ongoing transformations of world politics from a global South perspective. Rather than providing empirical evidence-based research, the question is how such legitimacy concerns can be situated and assessed against three key aspects of the Anthropocene debate as identified in this volume, namely complexity, responsibility and urgency to act.

In this chapter I first introduce changing patterns of authority in global climate governance and new legitimation processes that arise in such a transforming landscape. Based on the insight into these general developments, I secondly identify two specific legitimacy debates from the perspective of the global South. These include, on the one hand, debates on the blurring of North–South boundaries and the responsibility of Southern actors, and, on the other hand, debates on the blurring of the public-private divide. Finally, I discuss these debates in the context of the three key aspects of the Anthropocene. I conclude with an outlook towards further legitimacy issues that have to be taken into consideration in future debates on the Anthropocene.

Legitimacy and transformation of global climate governance

Global climate governance rests as a site of considerable legitimacy concerns, as numerous studies indicated its ineffectiveness and lack of authority to solve environmental problems and advocated for the need for reform (Abbott et al., 2012; Biermann and Bauer, 2005). The legitimacy of the international climate regime was largely questioned not only due to the gridlock surrounding the negotiation process between countries on reaching emission reduction targets, but also due to its expert-based policies and decision-making procedures (Buchanan and Keohane, 2006).

Besides the international climate system, a large set of governance arrangements have emerged that are built on non-hierarchical steering. They are characterized by decentralized, voluntary, market-oriented interaction between public and private actors, as opposed to 'old governance' that builds on hierarchical top-down modes of steering and traditional regulation (Bäckstrand, 2008; see also Widerberg, this volume). They are understood as transnational climate governance arrangements that cut across borders and involve sub- and non-state actors (Hale and Held, 2011). Such arrangements include a variety of initiatives such as: club-like forums; regulated (e.g. EU ETS) and voluntary markets (e.g. Voluntary Carbon Standard and the Gold Standard); initiatives that keep corporations accountable for their carbon footprints either through self-regulations (e.g. Carbon Disclosure Project) or through scrutiny by civil society organizations (CSOs); public–private governance networks that implement internationally agreed outcomes (e.g. the Renewable Energy and Energy Efficiency Partnership); and transnational municipal networks such as C40 global cities partnerships.

The institutionalization of such forms of governance has increasingly become the focal point of debates on the legitimacy of global climate governance as it creates new global governing patterns beyond the state by an ever increasing inclusion of non-state actors. On the other hand, this might also amount to a total privatization of governance paired with loss of democratic oversight and parliamentary control of power and accountability (Scholte, 2011; Biermann and Pattberg, 2008). In summary, the fragmented global climate governance architecture is a site of considerable legitimacy problems – not only due to the crisis of international UN climate system and unsuccessful reform efforts, but also due to the proliferation of different forms of governance arrangements beyond the state that create new patterns of authority.

These emerging patterns of authority have implications for how legitimacy is understood and evaluated. In the following, I first sketch some of the major changing patterns of authority in global climate governance before presenting implications of this change for legitimacy and legitimation processes.

Changing patterns of authority in global climate governance

Regulatory standards institutions

As Cashore (2002) noted, one of the major trends that has implications on how authority and legitimacy are understood is the increasing use of procedures in which state authority is shared with or transferred to businesses, environmental NGOs and other actors, variously labelled 'non-state market-driven' (NSMD) governance systems (ibid.), and 'regulatory standards institutions' (Abbott and Snidal, 2009; see also van Leeuwen, this volume). Such transnational private governance arrangements do not derive their governing authority from states, but rather rely on compliance results from market incentives, customer preferences and support from environmental groups (Bernstein, 2004; Cashore, 2002).

The literature on 'private authority' stresses that non-state actors are increasingly engaged in authoritative decision-making that used to rest with states. However, there is a range of voluntary programmes that have either been sponsored by state regulators or created with little or no involvements from governments. For example, Gulbrandsen (2014) showed that governments can both restrict or enhance the rule-making authority of non-state regulatory schemes by either creating competing programmes or by enforcing existing rules and regulations, that is, either through direct regulations or in 'the shadow of hierarchy'.

Markets

A second major form of changing authority patterns are governance systems operating through markets. This is most prominent in the case of climate governance where market-based arrangements are created by states, such as the emissions trading system (ETS) of the European Union (EU) or the Clean Development Mechanism (CDM) of the Kyoto Protocol, followed by a number of 'voluntary' carbon markets established to help mitigate climate change. Voluntary carbon offsets, for instance, are usually traded by extractive industries (oil and gas and mining), but also by other sectors such as water and urban development with the support of conservation organizations, consulting firms or through partnerships. Other types of private governance arrangements such as the Carbon Disclosure Project aim to stimulate investment in a range of markets, which might limit carbon emissions.

Such market-led climate governance represents a case in point for the reconfiguration of authority and blurring of public and private boundaries. For example, Verified Carbon Standard (VCR), a private carbon offset standard, has contributed to innovations in the governance of the mechanism on Reducing Emissions from Deforestation and Forest Degradation (REDD). The VCR secretariat launched first accounting standards to help states and other sub-national actors undertake activities that had been missing in the implementation of REDD (Green, 2013).

Networked governance arrangements

Finally, transnational networked-based governance, or what is conceptualized as hybrid modes of governance, involves voluntary agreements between states and a variety of non-state actors with cross-border activities such as NGOs, foundations, companies, research institutions, or transnational associations, on specific governance objectives and on means to advance them. Unlike intergovernmental organizations – that pool their authority from governmental delegation and operate through bureaucratic structures – and unlike private regulations – that often operate in the shadow of state or market mechanisms – partnerships pool governance authority across the public and private spheres (Andonova, 2013). They embody a more direct re-articulation of roles of state and society as they operate through decentralized networks (ibid.).

Besides, transnational municipal networks (TMN) are another example of a networked form of governance among cities whose main functions include information sharing, building capacities and representing the voices of cities in the international arena, such as the World Association of Major Metropolises (Metropolis) and the C40 Cities Climate Leadership Group (C40). The role of cities as emerging actors in global climate governance not only challenged research and policy communities to reconsider at which scale the problem of climate change is to be addressed, but also the very reconfiguration of the state that takes place through the way in which they mobilize private actors alongside the (local) state (Bulkeley, 2010).

Legitimation in a transforming global climate governance landscape – processes and limits

The emerging forms of governance and their interaction with interstate governance have implications for the way formal sources of authority and their legitimacy are understood and articulated. Such new legitimation processes, their prospects and limits, are presented in this section in order to provide a contextual basis within which legitimacy concerns from the global South perspective have to be considered and reconceptualized.

Scholars have come up with very different sets of approaches for studying legitimacy, ranging from the concepts of normative legitimacy, including democratic or deliberative forms, to legal and political legitimacy. However, as Bernstein argues 'the new legitimacy concerns need to be placed in the context of an ongoing debate over the reconfiguration of global authority' (Bernstein, 2004, p. 142). In that sense, normative standards of legitimacy that have been developed in the context of relatively stable authority cannot be applied in the same manner. Traditional pillars of legitimacy, such as democracy, procedural fairness or substantive effectiveness operate significantly different in this new context (Steffek, 2009; Bernstein, 2004). Moreover, the concept of legal legitimacy and its basis of state consent and constitutionalism can no longer be applied in a political landscape where for example transnational voluntary regulatory arrangements are often quite informal, since they would otherwise be considered as illegitimate. Finally, in order to explain the interplay between legitimacy and effectiveness and their trade-off, many scholars used what Scharpf (1998) labelled input (process) and output (performance and efficiency) legitimacy. However, it has been shown that it is difficult to make a strict distinction of what constitutes legitimacy and performance in practice. Rather, the focus should lie on the connections and interplay among them (Mügge, 2011).

Some argue that transnational rule-making organizations benefit from the current legitimacy crisis of intergovernmental organizations by putting a strong emphasis on normative ideals and values of global governance such as inclusiveness, transparency, accountability and deliberativeness (Dingwerth and Pattberg, 2009). In many cases the rhetoric of such organizations translates into participatory elements such as public commenting periods for policy documents, regional stakeholder consultations and expert deliberations on particular policy issues. The fact that transnational regulatory organizations focus on regulating firms and supply chains, and not states per se, has created a high demand for their publicity.

In other words the need for political legitimacy beyond the state has increased as the regulatory authority shifted from states to private or networked governance (Bernstein, 2011). One example is the legitimacy requirements in the case of the International Social and Environmental Accreditation and Labelling (ISEAL) (see also Moser and Bailis, this volume). ISEAL members are completely autonomous from state authority and not delegated. Authority granted to ISEAL members stems from the market's supply chain in interaction with civil society, which is central for their political legitimacy. They have to promote a motivational response from those whose behaviour they seek to change, but often without the infrastructure of the state to fall back on (Black, 2008; Schouten and Glasbergen, 2011). In the same manner, the Forest Stewardship Council draws its legitimacy from NGOs in exchange for the potential behavioural change of wood retailers (Dingwerth and Pattberg, 2009).

Moreover, it is argued that the authority of the standard-setting and certification schemes stems from their attempt to combine elements of stakeholder democracy by including representation of various groups of actors.

Such attempts range from including corporations, civil society and affected local communities to capitalizing on the power shifts in markets to legitimize authority independently from states. For example, legitimacy claims by the International Organization for Standardization (ISO) purely based on technical expertise were no longer sufficient. In addition, ISO decided to move closely to a multi-stakeholder model for their Corporate Social Responsibility Standard, ISO 26000. Likewise, the Voluntary Carbon Credit Standard (VCS) contains representatives from key market players, NGOs and business lobbies. Thus, in response to the legitimacy crisis of 'privatized' governance both initiatives aimed at branching out to a broader range of interests. In the same vein, the Gold Standard, a certification system for carbon offsets to ensure credibility and adherence to broader sustainable development goals, incorporated standards that go beyond the fulfilment of internal market functions and instead focus on the pursuit of broader social and environmental aims.

When it comes to markets, the legitimation of carbon reporting and disclosure rested on the claims to be embedded in or be part of a market-based system in parallel to regulatory financial reporting – as well as on the broader corporate social responsibility frame (Kolk et al., 2008). In turn these claims all contributed to the institutionalization of carbon disclosure as a routine practice of the firms and to its alliance with environmental groups, firms and investors (ibid.).

Finally, during the 2002 World Summit on Sustainable Development (WSSD) partnerships were incorporated for the first time as an official outcome in an international environmental agreement. The UN legitimized them as an instrument to support the implementation of international agreements in the area of sustainable development, such as negotiations of the WSSD, Agenda 21 and the Millennium Development Goals. Another core legitimation strategy was that the Johannesburg partnerships are participatory and deliberative multi-stakeholder instruments that engage actors from civil society, business and academia, when business became an important constituency for UN collaboration. Therefore, the legitimation of partnerships was ultimately based on strengthening implementation while qualities such as deliberation, participation and inclusion were secondary (Bäckstrand and Kylsäter, 2014).

Moreover, in the case of Reducing Emissions from Deforestation and Forest Degradation (REDD), marketization entails the commodification of carbon stored in forested land which can be traded. Firms with obligations to reduce their emissions under an emissions trading scheme, or those wishing to engage in corporate social responsibility activities, may buy credits generated by REDD activities to compensate for continued emissions in their operations. Marketized REDD is conceived in three ways by economists and policymakers: as a financial incentive for forest conservation, a least-cost measure for climate change mitigation, and a source of alternative livelihood for forest communities (Stern, 2007).

At the same time, the legitimacy of marketization as a means of addressing environmental problems has been widely questioned. The widespread critique refers to the privatization or commodification of nature that underpins such arrangements—and to their possibility to increase global inequalities by enabling some actors to meet their obligations by investing in projects elsewhere (Boyd et al., 2012; Paterson, 2010).

New legitimacy concerns from the global South perspective

Beyond the North–South divide

Interpretations of the Anthropocene take different directions when it comes to the responsibility of developing countries for global warming. Developing countries account for only about 20 per cent of total greenhouse gas emissions since 1751, but contain about 80 per cent of the world's population. Least developed countries contributed less than 1 per cent with their population amounting to about 800 million people. Still, emissions from developing countries grew to over 40 per cent of the world's total in the last decade – with key emerging economies like China and India at the forefront. However, about 25 per cent of this rise in emissions was owning to the increase of international trade in goods and services produced in developing countries but consumed in the developed world (Steffen et al., 2011).

Moreover, the impact of climate change provides another equity concern in the North–South debate: wealthy countries are the most responsible for additional greenhouse gases in the atmosphere while developing countries will experience the greatest impact. The notions of ecological debt and climate debt have been used to capture how the global North's excessive historic use of the atmosphere's absorptive capacity has closed off similar development routes for the global South.

Accordingly, the nature and ethical basis of the international climate regime is largely put into question. Perceptions of inequality and contestation over justice have probably driven various countries to seek alternative means and arenas for dealing with climate change (Okereke, 2010). Given the current deadlocks of intergovernmental climate negotiations processes and efforts to create a new institutional framework for the post-2012 treaty, a number of scholars thus turned to the potential of transnational initiatives (Bäckstrand, 2008; Bexell et al., 2010). As a great deal of the future climate governance architecture is likely to be organized around these transnational governance arrangements, their success or failure indeed depends on the reasonable participation and engagement of developing country actors (Dingwerth, 2011).

Therefore, special attention has been given to their potential for democratizing global climate governance and closing the participatory governance gap of the international governance system. Some scholars argue that these arrangements offer new negotiation venues that may facilitate engagement of a larger number of actors beyond the state, especially from developing countries (Haas, 2004; Nanz and Steffek, 2004). However, this view remains highly contested. Others warn that such initiatives may further weaken the representation of Southern interests. Moreover, they could further facilitate the privatization of environmental governance where decision making would rest with those actors with considerable power that are primarily based in the industrialized countries (Nanz and Steffek, 2004; Pattberg, 2010).

Moreover, it is argued that a fundamental problem in climate change negotiations has been disagreement about the principles used to allocate responsibility between developed and developing countries. This disagreement has emerged in spite of equity concerns that had been institutionalized in the principles of the Kyoto Protocol, such as common but differentiated responsibility, sustainable development or technology transfer (Najam et al., 2003). For example, developing countries seek a tight long-term emission reduction goal from developed countries, while they themselves reject taking on binding commitments in the first post-2012 commitment period, which is expected to last until 2020. Moreover, developing countries disagree with what may constitute sufficient emission reductions by developed countries. It was stated that developed countries should reduce their emissions by at least 40 per cent below 1990 levels in 2020.

Other disagreements lie in Brazil, China and India's opposition to proposals to reclassify developing countries with higher emissions and higher capacity into a separate group or into what many characterize as BRICSAM countries comprising Brazil, India, China, South Africa, and Mexico (Von der Goltz, 2009). Furthermore, while the aim of developed countries is to reduce their greenhouse gas emissions in a most cost-efficient way, developing countries uniformly stress the primacy of development and poverty reduction as well as the need for new and additional funding for adaptation over mitigation action and ecological concerns (Najam, 2005).

Beyond the public–private boundary

The changing institutional landscape has also blurred the traditional role of governmental sovereignty to develop rules to which society adheres. The state consent to international treaties is no longer the sole basis for practising authority. Moreover, these changes question traditional notions of international institutions because they increasingly involve or affect non-state actors or communities (Bernstein, 2011).

On the other hand, the sole emphasis on the privatization of governance may mask the fact that many of the transnational climate governance arrangements operate in the 'shadow of hierarchy' as states and international organizations attempt to delegate some of their primary functions to non-state actors (Pattberg, 2010). Therefore, many have argued that the emerging political landscape should not be interpreted as a 'zero-sum' game whereby power is shifted from state to non-state actors indicating a replacement and decline of sovereign authority (Bäckstrand, 2008; Bulkeley and Schroeder, 2012). Instead, fragmented governance rests on multiple foci of authority where different governance forms derive their authority from different sources. It is in this context that the legitimacy of the global climate governance architecture should be examined.

There are various ways in which the blurring of public and private governance boundaries manifests itself. For example in her work on examining the role of non-state actors in global environmental politics, Green (2013) shows that the reconfigured private authority is diffused through and among a diverse set of actors resulting in their forms, namely delegated and entrepreneurial (see also van Leeuwen, this volume; Moser and Bailis, this volume). In the case of the latter, private actors simply create rules that others choose to adopt. Exclusive private forms of governance are those that involve self-regulation or coordination within industry, club goods, or services for a defined membership such as business associations. They are not public as their goal is to provide a rule, good, or service for the private benefit of their members or a target group.

On the other hand, public authority includes the pursuit of common concerns that must be publicly recognized as containing political legitimacy. Bernstein (2011) argues that the 'publicness' of private governance initiatives arises as they pursue common concerns. However, this is not sufficient as such initiatives also need to be recognized for their political legitimacy. Accordingly, disaggregating the public–private boundary means asking whether there is political authority and where it is located.

Moreover, as Vogel (2008) argues, these sharp dichotomies may be better viewed as ends on a continuum since they otherwise risk obscuring changing relations of power and authority. For example, it has been shown that many of the climate transnational governance arrangements, such as the WSSD public–private partnerships, operate in the 'shadow of hierarchy', since states and international organizations attempt to delegate some of their primary functions to non-state actors (Pattberg, 2010). Others, such as in the case of carbon markets, became highly institutionalized in world politics where the normative frameworks, rules and subsequent implementation can be traced back to an influential agency beyond the state (Pattberg and Stripple, 2008).

Voluntary, non-binding standard-setting initiatives like the Forest Stewardship Council (FSC) exert a significant impact on Southern actors as they shape new normative frameworks and induce discursive shifts in the issue area of sustainability politics where the participation of Southern actors may be direct, but also indirect (Dingwerth, 2011).

What is more, the recent rise of a transnational timber legality regime operating through forest legality verifications reconfigures the boundaries between the public and the private. The regime draws upon sustainable forest certifications, but at the same time emphasizes adherence to national laws and regulations (Cashore and Stone, 2012). Therefore, legality certification challenges the private–public distinction and the dominance of a neoliberal discourse of a marketization of governance.

Finally, the role of cities as emerging actors in global climate governance not only challenged research and policy communities to reconsider at which scale the problem of climate change is to be addressed, but in addition cities challenged the very reconfiguration of the state that takes place through the way in which they mobilize private actors alongside the (local) state (Bulkeley, 2010).

In summary, the dichotomy between public and private arrangements as well as state and non-state actors did not prove helpful for understanding how authority has been articulated and shaped through complex interactions among international and transnational governance arrangements, normative frameworks and discourses (Bäckstrand, 2008; Pattberg and Stripple, 2008). The rise of transnational climate governance initiatives does not signify a crisis of multilateralism. Instead, it indicates a transformation of multilateralism, the blurring of public and private governance spheres as well as 're-articulation' of the state and its practices (Bernstein et al., 2010). This transformation also affects the classical notion of a North–South divide, since it rearticulates the relation between state and non-state actors within and beyond the global South. It is within this context that legitimacy in the Anthropocene has to be understood and evaluated.

Conclusions

This contribution investigated new legitimacy concerns in the Anthropocene, emerging from transforming world politics in the issue area of climate change and situated the role of the global South in these perspectives. First, the chapter provided a baseline assessment of global climate governance by extracting changing patterns of global climate governance. I found that regulatory standards institutions, markets and networked governance arrangements – which emerged as informal, non-hierarchical and hybrid governance arrangements parallel with the international UN system – have high implications for the way governing authority and legitimacy is understood and performed.

The institutionalization of such forms of governance has increasingly become the focal point of debates on the legitimacy of global climate governance as it creates new global governing patterns beyond the state. Or, as others argue, it may even lead to a total privatization of governance and loss of democratic oversight and parliamentary control of power and accountability (Scholte, 2011; Biermann and Pattberg, 2008). Therefore, such fragmented global climate governance is a site of considerable legitimacy problems not only due to the crisis of the international UN climate system and efforts to reform current climate architecture, but also due to the proliferation of different forms of governance whose legitimacy has come under great scrutiny.

These developments affect the role of the global South and alter traditional legitimacy concerns. The chapter therefore concludes that thinking about the future of global climate governance and its legitimacy from the global South perspective needs to start with the political dynamics among different processes and practices of governance that connect transnational governance systems and intergovernmental negotiations. First, thinking exclusively in terms of the emergence of private governance beyond the state and the crisis of multilateralism on the one hand, and emphasizing retrenched sovereignty on the other, may obscure key aspects of the ongoing transformation of world politics. Rather, scholars increasingly point to the blurring of state/non-state divides by drawing attention to networked, hybrid or shared authority (Bulkeley and Schroeder, 2012).

Second, the view of a North–South divide has been questioned by some scholars, as it does not do justice to intra-state variations and the increasing fragmentation of the global South. This fragmentation is illustrated by tensions between emerging economies on the one hand and less developed and small island developing states on the other.

Finally, equity issues are of great concern as wealthy countries are the most responsible for the additional greenhouse gases in the atmosphere while developing countries will experience the greatest impact. The notions of ecological debt and climate debt capture how the global South is denied a similar development path to the global North due to the latter's excessive use of the planet's resources and absorptive capacity. Yet again, changing patterns of authority also mean that new faultlines of responsibility and exposure are developing within the global South, raising new questions of legitimacy, participatory and distributive justice.

These conclusions directly relate to the three key aspects of the Anthropocene highlighted in this volume: complexity, responsibility and urgency to act. The changing patterns of authority that I sketched in section 2 are institutional mirror images of an increasing material complexity of global sustainable development aspects. The sheer number of concerns could not be handled by just a few institutions, but instead informed a considerable proliferation of governance arrangements – both intergovernmental and transnational – over the last years. The resulting authority shifts, however, also imply shifts in responsibility. The erosion of traditional North–South and public–private divides has empowered certain actors. This increase in capacities and influence may also imply an increase of responsibility for acting against dangerous climate change. Thus, it is for further research to analyse whether human responsibility is adequately reflected in the emerging new governance landscape and which roles actors in the global South will play or should play. Finally, with regard to the growing urgency to act, we have to ask whether the shifting patterns of authority will deliver. Also here, crucial new questions are raised for future research: Does the involvement of new actors and new arrangements help in addressing dangerous climate change? And is the new governance landscape more adequate for the needs of the global South with regard to low-carbon development and adaptation to climate change?

References

Abbott, K. and Snidal, D. (2009) The governance triangle: Regulatory standards institutions and the shadow of the state. In Mattli, W. and Woods, N. (eds), *The Politics of Global Regulation*. Princeton, NJ: Princeton University Press.

Abbott, K., Genschel, P., Snidal, D. and Zangl, B. (2012) Orchestration: Global governance through intermediaries. Available from: http://papers.ssrn.com/sol3/papers.cfm?abstract_id=2125452 [accessed 25 June 2015].

Andonova, L. B. (2013) Boomerangs to partnerships? Explaining state participation in transnational partnerships for sustainability. *Comparative Political Studies* 47(3): 481–515.

Bäckstrand, K. (2008) Accountability of networked climate governance: The rise of transnational climate partnerships. *Global Environmental Politics* 8(3): 74–102.

Bäckstrand, K. and Kylsäter, M. (2014) Old wine in new bottles? The legitimation and delegitimation of un public–private partnerships for sustainable development from the Johannesburg Summit to the Rio+20 Summit. *Globalizations* 11(3): 331–347.

Bernstein, S. (2004) Legitimacy in global environmental governance. *Journal of International Law and International Relations* 1(1–2): 139–166.

Bernstein, S. (2011) Legitimacy in intergovernmental and non-state global governance. *Review of International Political Economy* 18(1): 17–51.

Bernstein, S., Betsill, M., Hoffmann, M. and Paterson, M. (2010) A tale of two Copenhagens: Carbon markets and climate governance. *Millennium: Journal of International Studies* 39(1): 161–173.

Bexell, M., Tallberg, J. and Uhlin, A. (2010) Democracy in global governance: The promises and pitfalls of transnational actors. *Global Governance: A Review of Multilateralism and International Organizations* 16(1): 81–101.

Biermann, F. (2007) 'Earth System governance' as a crosscutting theme of global change research. *Global Environmental Change* 17(3): 326–337.

Biermann, F. (2014) The Anthropocene: A governance perspective. *The Anthropocene Review* 1(1): 57–61.

Biermann, F. and Bauer, S. (2005) *A World Environment Organization: Solution Or Threat For Effective International Environmental Governance?* Aldershot: Ashgate Publishing.

Biermann, F. and Pattberg, P. (2008) Global environmental governance: Taking stock, moving forward. *Annual Review of Environment and Resources* 33: 277–294.

Black, J. (2008) Constructing and contesting legitimacy and accountability in polycentric regulatory regimes. *Regulation & Governance* 2(2): 137–164.

Boyd, E., Boykoff, M. and Newell, P. (2012) The 'new' carbon economy: What's new? In Newell, P., Boykoff, M. and Boyd, E. (eds), *The New Carbon Economy*. Chichester, UK: John Wiley & Sons Ltd, pp. 1–11.

Buchanan, A. and Keohane, R. O. (2006) The legitimacy of global governance institutions. *Ethics & International Affairs* 20(4): 405–437.

Bulkeley, H. (2010) Cities and the governing of climate change. *Annual Review of Environment and Resources* 35: 229–253.

Bulkeley, H. and Schroeder, H. (2012) Beyond state/non-state divides: Global cities and the governing of climate change. *European Journal of International Relations* 18(4): 743–766.

Cashore, B. (2002) Legitimacy and the privatization of environmental governance: How non-state market-driven (NSMD) governance systems gain rule-making authority. *Governance* 15(4): 503–529.

Cashore, B. and Stone, M. W. (2012) Can legality verification rescue global forest governance? Analyzing the potential of public and private policy intersection to ameliorate forest challenges in Southeast Asia. *Forest Policy and Economics* 18 (May): 13–22.

Crutzen, P. J. (2002) Geology of mankind. *Nature* 415(6867): 23–23.

Dingwerth, K. (2011) North–South parity in global governance: The affirmative procedures of the Forest Stewardship Council. Research article. Lynne Rienner Publishers. 8 March. Available from: http://journals.rienner.com/doi/abs/10.5555/ggov.2008.14.1.53 [accessed 25 June 2015].

Dingwerth, K. and Pattberg, P. (2009) World politics and organizational fields: The case of transnational sustainability governance. *European Journal of International Relations* 15(4): 707–743.

Dubash, N. K. and Morgan, B. (2012) Understanding the rise of the regulatory state of the South. *Regulation and Governance* 6(3): 261–281.

Green, J. F. (2013) *Rethinking Private Authority: Agents and Entrepreneurs in Global Environmental Governance*. Princeton, NJ: Princeton University Press.

Gulbrandsen, L. H. (2014) Dynamic governance interactions: Evolutionary effects of state responses to non-state certification programs. *Regulation & Governance* 8(1): 74–92.

Haas, P. M. (2004) Addressing the global governance deficit. *Global Environmental Politics* 4(4): 1–15.

Hale, T. and Held, D. (2011) *Handbook of Transnational Governance*. Cambridge, UK and Malden, USA: Polity Press.

Kolk, A., Levy, D. and Pinkse, J. (2008) Corporate responses in an emerging climate regime: The institutionalization and commensuration of carbon disclosure. *European Accounting Review* 17(4): 719–745.

Mügge, D. (2011) Limits of legitimacy and the primacy of politics in financial governance. *Review of International Political Economy* 18(1): 52–74.

Najam, A. (2005) Developing countries and global environmental governance: From contestation to participation to engagement. *International Environmental Agreements: Politics, Law and Economics* 5(3): 303–321.

Najam, A., Huq, S. and Sokona, Y. (2003) Climate negotiations beyond Kyoto: Developing countries' concerns and interests. *Climate Policy* 3(3): 221–231.

Nanz, P. and Steffek, J. (2004) Global governance, participation and the public sphere. *Government and Opposition* 39(2): 314–335.

Okereke, C. (2008) Equity norms in global environmental governance. *Global Environmental Politics* 8(3): 25–50.

Okereke, C. (2010) Climate justice and the international regime. *Wiley Interdisciplinary Reviews: Climate Change* 1(3): 462–474.

Palsson, G., Szerszynski, B., Sörlin, S., Marks, J., Avril, B., Crumley, C., Hackmann, H. et al. (2013) Reconceptualizing the 'anthropos' in the Anthropocene: Integrating the social sciences and humanities in global environmental change research. *Environmental Science & Policy* 28: 3–13.

Paterson, M. (2010) Legitimation and accumulation in climate change governance. *New Political Economy* 15(3): 345–368.

Pattberg, P. (2010) Public–private partnerships in global climate governance. *Wiley Interdisciplinary Reviews: Climate Change* 1(2): 279–287.

Pattberg, P. and Stripple, J. (2008) Beyond the public and private divide: Remapping transnational climate governance in the 21st century. *International Environmental Agreements: Politics, Law and Economics* 8(4): 367–388.

Rockström, J., Steffen, W., Noone, K., Persson, A., Chapin, F. S., Lambin, E. F., Lenton, T. M. et al. (2009) A safe operating space for humanity. *Nature* 461(7263): 472–475.

Scharpf, F. W. (1998) *Interdependence and Democratic Legitimation*. MPIfG working paper. Available from: http://www.econstor.eu/handle/10419/41689 [accessed 25 June 2015].

Scholte, J. A. (2011) Towards greater legitimacy in global governance. *Review of International Political Economy* 18(1): 110–120.

Schouten, G. and Glasbergen, P. (2011) Creating legitimacy in global private governance: The case of the roundtable on sustainable palm oil. *Ecological Economics* 70(11): 1891–1899.

Steffek, J. (2009) Discursive legitimation in environmental governance. *Forest Policy and Economics* 11(5–6): 313–318.

Steffen, W., Grinevald, J., Crutzen, P. and McNeill, J. (2011) The Anthropocene: Conceptual and historical perspectives. *Philosophical Transactions of the Royal Society A: Mathematical, Physical and Engineering Sciences* 369(1938): 842–867.

Stern, N. (2007) *The Economics of Climate Change: The Stern Review*. Cambridge: Cambridge University Press.

Vogel, D. (2008) Private global business regulation. *Annual Review of Political Science* 11: 261–282.

Von der Goltz, J. (2009) High stakes in a complex game: A snapshot of the climate change negotiating positions of major developing country emitters. *Centre for Global Development*, Working Paper, no. 177. Available from: http://environmentportal.in/files/GCD-Aug-09-nego.pdf [accessed 25 June 2015].

13 The practices of lobbying for rights in the Anthropocene era

Local communities, indigenous peoples and international climate negotiations

Linda Wallbott

Introduction

Not seeing the forest for the trees – this popular proverb describes a situation in which you look at things and perceive them as unconnected even though they form a bigger structure in which the single elements relate to each other in a 'logical' way. Yet, when you take a step back, the broader picture becomes visible. The fundamental message that is captured by this saying is that what we (assume to) see and what we perceive as true is inherently relative and contingent on our position in relation to the other. In the same line, we can change our positioning and the assumptions that we project, thereby altering societal relations. This consideration is also applicable to scrutinizing the conditions and effects of environmental governance in the Anthropocene.

As clarified in the introductory chapter to this edited volume, the term 'Anthropocene' denotes a new geological epoch in planetary history, one that is characterized by the unprecedented impact of human activities on the Earth's ecosystems. It could be argued though that this is a rather functionalist understanding that does not necessarily capture the political and social dimensions that shape contemporary human impacts on natural resources, including power divisions and differentiated recognition that different social groups receive in global environmental governance. Hence, I suggest a complementary threefold conceptualization of the term 'Anthropocene'.

First, it indeed describes the empirical reality of those – mostly destructive – phenomena or changes of ecosystems that are the result of human activity like accelerated climate change or the loss of biodiversity. However, and second, the term also reflects a specific normativity that puts Western industrial activities as the main point of reference for framing the history of the Earth. Similarly, it could be argued that it was possible for such a concept to surface only against the background of some prior delineation of industrial societies from their natural resource basis (see also Maldonado, this volume); yet, that it holds the promise of making up for the blind spots that come with such dualism. Third, and finally, the term may be used as an analytical device to diagnose the potentials and pitfalls of different human activities and forms of knowledge (see also Prokopf, this volume), to prescribe possible solutions and maybe even to motivate new paths in the course of organizing (more) sustainable global politics and national societies. For example, if one acknowledges the validity of such a broader understanding of the Anthropocene, then also the discourses and implementation of traditional knowledge and natural resource practices of indigenous peoples and local communities come into sight. Thus, broadening the Anthropocene perspective can be a starting point for capturing the debate around traditional, and possibly stereotypical, livelihood images of indigenous peoples residing 'in harmony with nature' and of their long-time standing as stewards of the Earth's resources. This narrative – even though it was not explicitly linked to the Anthropocene concept – has been one of the crucial assets of indigenous peoples in working their way into the space of international environmental negotiations and in lobbying successfully for formal recognition of their rights therein. Thus, a broader understanding of the Anthropocene might support demands for more inclusive governance arrangements.

In light of these considerations, this chapter will analyze the strategies of indigenous peoples in negotiations of a forest-related mitigation instrument (REDD+) under the United Nations Framework Convention on Climate Change (UNFCCC), which was agreed in 2010. For this purpose the chapter builds on a review of primary and secondary literature, as well as interviews with negotiators, indigenous peoples' representatives and observers at UNFCCC meetings and other occasions between 2010 and 2014. Theoretically, the chapter is embedded in a sociology of space approach, which contributes to enhancing our understanding of environmental governance and international negotiations in the Anthropocene by, inter alia, emphasizing the duality of structure and action, as well as of the material (natural resources) and the ideational (images, traditions etc.). Thereby it is helpful for assessing the relational qualities and dynamics of international negotiations and challenges functionalist and statist accounts of the Anthropocene. The chapter is organized as follows: in section 2 the space sociological analytical framework will be developed. Section 3 will review the standing of indigenous peoples in global politics with a special focus on how the relation with nature has been central for their self-identification and for the indigenous movement. Section 4 will then apply these conceptualizations to the empirical analysis of indigenous peoples' lobbying practices in the REDD+ negotiations. The chapter will conclude by drawing conclusions for inclusive global environmental governance in the Anthropocene era.

The dual spatiality of global environmental governance: Conceptual approaches

From container to web

Governance arrangements of natural resources are characterized by a specific dual spatiality. On the one hand, geographic territories, landscapes, biomass, and the ecosystem services – the basis for human development – are defined by physical boundaries. For a long time, these places have been regarded as static containers, the immobile scenery for action. But clear quantitative boundaries for the possible depletion of natural resources exist – the shrinking scope of the available atmospheric space (as measured against the scientifically mandated amount of how much more greenhouse gas emissions should be allowed without running into climate collapse) is a case in point. However, for a social scientist it seems self-evident 'that space can only inadequately be conceptualized as a material or earth-bound base for social processes' (Löw, 2008, p. 25). Consequently, and on the other hand, the social spaces that govern these seeming naturalities are defined through political institutions, social and economic dynamics, asymmetries and normative imprints. Thus, socio-ecological spaces are shaped through action. In addition, and in line with a recent turn in regime analysis (Oberthür and Stokke, 2011), it should be taken into account that different institutional spaces influence each other (see also Widerberg, this volume). Such interaction can be assessed in functional terms and with a view toward its impact on the performance and effectiveness of the institutions. Furthermore, it is also possible to focus on the different types of practices that actors employ to shape and take advantage of this complex setting. These dynamics might result in contestation, as actors who demand changes in one institutional setting deliberately draw on argumentative resources from another.

Here, institutionalist accounts can benefit from work that has been conducted in the area of a sociology of space. To my knowledge, this linkage has not been drawn in the context of the Anthropocene so far, even though it holds various benefits. The defining feature of this approach is that it is not interested in what space actually is – for example immobile context or locale – but how it is socially constructed and what role it takes in social processes (Lefèbvre, 2006 [1974]). The latest seminal contribution on the sociology of space has been put forward by Martina Löw who bridges the gap between a structure and action-theoretical perspectives on space. For the purpose of this chapter it is sufficient to state that she aims at moving beyond a dualism of structure and action – which would presuppose a dichotomy of the two – and to instead emphasize their duality (Löw, 2008, p. 33). For example, as shown by Harvey – still embedded in the dialectical tradition – space has become a commodity in capitalist economies: 'The incentive to create the world market, to reduce spatial barriers, and to annihilate space through time is omnipresent, as is the incentive to rationalize spatial organization into efficient configurations of production' (Harvey, 1990, p. 232). Yet, as Löw points out, Harvey's conclusion of 'time-space-compression' (ibid., p. 240), which impacts on cultural life and which changes the perception of distance and proximity, still hinges on 'a notion of "space" as a material substratum' (Löw, 2008, p. 30).

The practices of space-making

Löw subsequently elaborates on how space is constituted through actors' practices of: (1) positioning/building/movement practices (spacing); and (2) the attribution of meaning through perception/ideation/recall/imagination (synthesis). These simultaneous processes emerge through concrete, everyday practices and the concomitant 'experience of the emotional qualities of space' (ibid., p. 30). This results in a specific – yet always contingent – relationality and atmosphere. The latter aspect, the structuring power of space, depends on how material and living things are perceived in their 'situated spatial order/ing' (ibid., p. 25). The understanding goes beyond a structuralist notion of an independent spatial dynamic of materialization. Rather, it perceives of space as being 'relevant as place relatedness in action' (ibid., p. 32). Finally, Löw pays due attention to the potentials of performing subjects as they tie in with the ordering of material goods (e.g. natural resources but also bodily things like walls, tables, chairs), symbolic and intangible goods (e.g. songs, signs, knowledge, cultural values), institutional frameworks and their repercussions. In this, people (both as individuals and social groups) are also put into specific orders, depending on their social relationships which, in turn, are influenced through specific hierarchies including the attribution of authority and credibility. Equally, selective processes of inclusion and exclusion in symbolic and material terms result from these simultaneous processes of ordering and cognition, with institutional spaces being defined as 'formations permanently reproduced in routines' (ibid., p. 32). Positioning thus takes place under pre-structured conditions and always goes along with the production of new boundaries. Overall, then, spaces 'can be seen as a relational ordering of living entities and social goods' (ibid., p. 35). They are the basis as well as the field of action, and are thereby per se political. This understanding is inherently dynamic and process-oriented, assuming the existence not of a singular contained social space, but of a plurality and concomitance of potentially 'overlapping and reciprocal relations' that are 'always open and indefinite with respect to future formations' (ibid., p. 26).

Furthermore, I assume that language plays a crucial role in these processes; it is not sufficient to perceive of a relational space as the topology of its material elements or subjective (bodily) experiences. Rather, it is about assuming the existence of a relational field in which actors position themselves and others by means of particular speech acts as carriers of specific attributes, images and symbolic resources, within and also across organizational boundaries. Speaking (or being silent) and action are two sides of the same coin. Hence, the preconditions for spacing and synthesizing practices are also structured along the lines of language and by what can be said from an actor's specific position. This, in turn, also depends to a large extent on the individual actor's professional background and/or institutional affiliation. These factors – and also, when applying these considerations to political negotiations e.g. the character of ministerial office that sends a delegation to the negotiations – have usually given rise to dominance of a particular rationality and principles that guide this person's behaviour and the selection of arguments that he will acknowledge as valid. Thus, for example, research on the sociology of organizations indicates that somebody with a background in law or development studies perceives of a problem-structure, possible solutions, fundamental norms and relevant policy measures differently than somebody who was trained in physics or biology (see Pache and Santos, 2013). Similarly, what has come to be known as 'Traditional Knowledge' as the property of indigenous peoples is not easily available and accessible to actors who have been brought up in other contexts and exposed to 'Western' traditions of knowing that are dominated by natural sciences and formalized rationalities.

These outlines can inform the empirical analysis of global governance and international negotiations. Thus, it can be expected that actors who lobby for a particular cause – like indigenous peoples who struggle for their rights in climate governance – will strategically engage in constructing and reshaping political spaces by building capacities within their own peer group, and by (re-)positioning themselves rhetorically towards other interest groups inside and outside formal arenas. Material and intangible goods and performances will be used to display specific characteristics. Also, advocates will evoke a specific meaning of the matter at hand. Yet, not only will this be open to reinterpretation on side of the addressees (including, here, party delegates) of these demands, but also, given the inconclusive nature of discourse, this framing may change over time.

Similarly, one can formulate implications of the ideas about space for the Anthropocene concept. This approach is helpful because of its emphasis on the duality of structure and action, of the material (natural resources) and the ideational (images, traditions etc.) that challenge functionalist and statist appreciations (or: boundaries) of the Anthropocene concept. Second, and related to the previous paragraph, it sheds light on the mutual positioning of actors in a specific yet always contingent manner through linguistic and non-linguistic practices, thereby distinguishing those who are recognized as relevant 'anthropogenic' agents and knowledge-holders in the governing – with positive or negative impact – of the Earth's resources. In such an approach, one is able to broaden the analytical lens to capture those relational instances of mutual positioning and attribution of subjectivity – reserved for agents who are considered to hold issue-specific knowledge, credibility and authority – from which legitimated political decisions follow. Hence, a sociology of space approach holds particular value for analyzing the specific standing of indigenous peoples in global environmental governance in the era of the Anthropocene. In the next section it will be shown that the relation with the environment has also in the past been a constitutive element of indigenous peoples' identity and their mobilization at (trans)national scales.

Indigenous peoples in global politics

The contested meaning of indigeneity

The concept of indigeneity – or what it actually means to be indigenous – is contested (Banerjee, 2004, p. 224; Mende, 2015). The institutions of the United Nations have refrained from coming up with a conclusive definition, leaving it up to the self-identification of people to assume membership of the indigenous community. Thus, it has been argued that indigeneity is 'necessarily relational and historical – and therefore provisional and context related' (Cadena and Starn, 2007, p. 12). The very ambiguity of the term has facilitated its adaptability to different circumstances, including in global environmental politics. What can be asserted anyhow is that being indigenous has become a 'validated subject position' (Veber, 2004, p. 232) for those native groups that share common characteristics and challenges (in most cases vis-à-vis majority or dominant populations) in different contexts. The understanding of the term oscillates between identity-based justifications, including culturalist arguments that depict it as a static asset (Brown, 1998, p. 197; Coombe, 1998), and its instrumentalization as a resource for political action.

For a long time, indigeneity was equated with some aboriginal attribute, often normatively loaded with a notion of backwardness or the romantic stereotypical image of the primordial, uncorrupted and 'noble savage', and his intangible cultural properties or naturalized relation to territory. Thus, one main image of indigenous peoples has been that they have acted as the 'stewards' of ecosystem services, contributing tremendously to the conservation of biodiversity, including forests. This has also been referred to as the 'environmentalization of indigeneity', assuming a distinct relationship between indigenous peoples and nature/landscapes due to cultural patterns, that belongs to a 'multicultural rhetoric', opening the door for performative and symbolic strategies that would display indigenous peoples' own 'ecological disposition' when seeking access to new formal rights in domestic contexts (Silva, 2012). Even, '[c]alls for return of land and resources have a way of intertwining themselves with demands for religious freedom and other basic rights to such an extent that it is sometimes difficult to distinguish culture from its material expression' (Brown, 1998, p. 197).

It seems widely accepted that indigenous peoples have a special relation with their lands and territories, in terms of their customary laws and traditions and through the notion of collective land ownership/stewardship. These traditions link the importance of land and natural resources to questions of indigenous self-determination both culturally and economically (means of subsistence), so that a lot of resistance and critique from indigenous movements and supportive actors has focused on questions of (involuntary) displacement and resettlement. Thus, indigenous communities are often portrayed as very concrete places, residing outside the more abstract capitalist logics, as 'bearer of the gift, home to barter, shared values, and embedded relations' (Hayden, 2003, p. 360).

Additionally, as a focal point for mobilizing action, the term indigenous has served as 'a social and political category that repositions groups … into a position of transnational solidarities, rights, and participation in a dynamic social movement' (Hathaway, 2010, p. 303). Hence, indigenous political and economic activity has been characterized to increasingly feature cultural property claims targeted at both material (artefacts, sites) and intangible (sacred symbols, music, traditional knowledge) resources and even surpassing 'in importance the concerns over territory and land rights that have historically been central to indigenous mobilization' (Greene, 2004, p. 212; see also Muehlebach, 2001; Comaroff and Comaroff, 2009). Identity-based strategies serve as basic tools or strategic entry points for indigenous peoples' political claims, both in domestic and international arenas.

Land and history: Bonds of the transnational indigenous movement

The coming together of indigenous peoples and their recognition as a (potential) subject of rights in global politics is intrinsically linked to a transnational momentum (see also Anaya, 2004). The indigenous peoples' movement has been characterized as 'a powerful site of political protest and mobilization for historically marginalized groups' with a particularly strong history of activism and organization in former settler colonies (with their status as 'first peoples') (Hodgson, 2011, p. 2). On the basis of increasingly perceiving the commonalities of their respective historical experiences and structural positionings within their nation states, these groups have come together into a transnational social movement that has sought to work through the international level to influence domestic politics.

In their lobbying activities, indigenous peoples' organizations have often allied with environmental advocacy groups, thereby gaining further access and assets 'to global audiences and powerful international funding and development institutions' (Greene, 2004, p. 212). It has been argued that it was exactly this mediation, particularly by non-indigenous interlocutors, and the application of Western categories to non-Western sites that has accompanied both the politicization of indigenous culture and its treatment as property (Greene, 2004; Banerjee, 2004). The fundamental assumption that indigenous peoples share a particular concern for land and territories as well as a sense of common historicity across national borders – stemming from the shared experiences of domination and suppression during colonial times – has strongly shaped their position at the global level. Thus, the seminal UN study on the problem of discrimination against indigenous populations has found that indigenous communities, peoples and nations have 'a historical continuity with pre-invasion and pre-colonial societies that developed on their territories' and they 'are determined to preserve, develop and transmit to future generations their ancestral territories, and their ethnic identity, as the basis of their continued existence as peoples, in accordance with their own cultural patterns, social institutions and legal systems' (UN ECOSOC, 1983, para. 379).

Hence, whereas the contemporary concept of the Anthropocene assumes a particular influence of human activity *on* the natural resources of the Earth and is thereby inclined to give in to a sustained dualism of structure and action, the inherent relationship of indigenous peoples and their culture *with* their environment has always been a crucial factor for the group's identity but also for its standing as a political actor. On the other hand, it could be argued, that the repetitive invocation of this specific relationship comes at the price of continued stereotyping of indigenous agency.

Indigenous peoples and natural resource governance in the Anthropocene: Reshaping spaces

Negotiating forests in the UNFCCC: The REDD+ story

These processes have also played out in negotiations of the forest-related mitigation instrument 'Reducing Emissions from Deforestation and Forest Degradation' in UN climate negotiations. The forests of the world, and especially those located in the Amazon region but also in Asia, contain most of the planet's biodiversity (according to the Intergovernmental Panel on Climate Change (IPCC)). Forest ecosystems absorb more than 4,200 billion tons of CO_2, of which 70 per cent is bound in the forest floor (see Gulbrandsen, 2012, p. 26) and contribute to regulating the climate at a global scale. Anthropogenic impacts on the state of the world's forests have been massively destructive. For example, the IPCC estimates that emissions from land-use change – mostly tropical deforestation – in the 1990s amounted to 1.6 billion tons of global carbon emissions per year and even an estimated annual 5.8 billion tons in recent years, equal to double figure percentages (see Okereke and Dooley, 2010; Gulbrandsen, 2012; Levin et al., 2008). The main drivers of deforestation are the conversion of forests to agricultural land for commercial and subsistence use, commercial and illegal logging, and the conversion of land into plantations to grow biofuels.

Hence, due to scientific reports on forest degradation and an environmental movement that continuously gained strength, forests have been on the international agenda since the 1980s. Both the UNFCCC and the Kyoto Protocol acknowledge the ability of a forest to capture and sequester CO_2. Parties may carry out their mitigation obligations under the flexible mechanisms Joint Implementation (in Annex I countries) and Clean Development Mechanism (CDM; in non-Annex I countries) with recourse to afforestation, reforestation and deforestation, but these do not include sustainable management of existing forests, reduction of deforestation and forest degradation (Gulbrandsen, 2012, pp. 39–40; Levin et al., 2008, p. 544). These aspects entered the UNFCCC debate (again) in 2005 through a submission of Papua New Guinea and Costa Rica on reducing emissions from deforestation in developing countries (RED). The submission framed deforestation as a technical issue of land-use change emissions. Over the next years, the scope of the agenda item was expanded to also include reduction of emissions from forest degradation (REDD) and subsequently also the role of conservation, sustainable management of forests and enhancement of forest carbon stocks in developing countries (REDD+). The basic idea of REDD+ is to compensate developing countries financially for income they may lose by preserving their forests. Still, at the time of the REDD+ agreement in 2010 questions like the source of funding, the definition of forests and addressing the drivers of deforestation remained largely unresolved.

Simultaneous to the expansion of the policy, its potential impacts on biodiversity and indigenous peoples were increasingly debated. Indigenous peoples were concerned that their rights could be violated, that their traditional relationship to territories and their forest-dependence in terms of subsistence could be negatively affected through REDD+. For example, in the case of India alone, estimates concerning the number of people who depend on forests for at least parts of their livelihood range from 200 million (Sud et al., n.d.) to 275 million rural people, constituting more than one-quarter of the country's population (Aggarwal et al., 2009). Therefore indigenous peoples promoted strong rights language for the agreement and rights-based approaches to policy formulation and implementation. Particularly, the inclusion of a reference to the 2007 UN Declaration on the Rights of Indigenous Peoples would strengthen their substantive rights claims, including collective rights to lands, territories and resources, and cultural rights, and their procedural rights and the provision of 'Free Prior and Informed Consent' (FPIC). But the debate went back and forth, with parties excluding rights-based language (and the plural-s of the term peoples) repeatedly and using it as a bargaining chip to achieve gains in other areas of the negotiation process (for a detailed review of this development see Wallbott, 2014). Under the conceptual label 'safeguards', which can be interpreted either as doing no harm or as providing for additional benefits, Appendix I of the Cancun Agreements of 2010, which contains the decision on REDD+, finally mandates,

> Respect for the knowledge and rights of indigenous peoples and members of local communities, by taking into account relevant international obligations, national circumstances and laws, and noting that the United Nations General Assembly has adopted the United Nations Declaration on the Rights of Indigenous Peoples;

and

> The full and effective participation of relevant stakeholders, in particular, indigenous peoples and local communities.
>
> (UNFCCC, 2010, p. 26).

Furthermore, a footnote calls for '[t]aking into account the need for sustainable livelihoods of indigenous peoples and local communities and their interdependence on forests in most countries, reflected in the United Nations Declaration on the Rights of Indigenous Peoples' (UNFCCC, 2010, p. 27).

However, various caveats apply. To begin, the safeguards are not part of the operational text of the Cancun Agreements but are relegated to the Annex. Second, UNDRIP is merely noted, which is rather weak language in international law, and is qualified with reference to its conditionality upon national circumstances and laws. At that point, they were neither legally binding for parties nor operational. Instead, parties have been requested to promote and to support the safeguards and to develop an information system to track their implementation. For that matter, institutional questions regarding the monitoring, reporting and verification (MRV) of information have dominated the negotiations since 2010. However, despite these constraints, indigenous peoples deemed the Cancun decision a big success and also a result of their continuous lobbying efforts (interview with indigenous peoples' representative to the UNFCCC, 25 May 2012, Bonn). In the next section I will analyze these strategies in more detail, paying particular attention to the (re)shaping of relational space and indigenous peoples' self-positioning vis-à-vis other actors in the negotiation process.

The space-building practices of indigenous peoples in relation to REDD+

Self-positioning

To start with, indigenous peoples have considerably engaged in building capacities within their own transnational social movement and in argumentatively positioning themselves in relation to REDD+. On the basis of a strong strategic self-consciousness they aimed to create supportive structures that involved – necessarily – movements across institutional and geographical borders as well as the expansion of argumentative spaces:

> We were really concerned that nothing is moving and climate change is not related to indigenous peoples, like we always complained the CDM is bad, but we did not really manage to influence the process. But now we managed to influence the global process. It was a conscious decision of us to be more active.
>
> (Interview with indigenous peoples' representative
> in the UNFCCC, 25 May 2012, Bonn)

Within their community, a number of workshops and conferences were organized in different regions from which the representatives in the negotiations took relatively broad mandates in the form of documents and submissions to the UN negotiations (for a more detailed overview of these events see Wallbott, 2014). Over time, the content of these mandates changed, from relatively broad normative demands to more specific and numerical/technocratic proposals (ibid.). Further support for arriving at a confident position was facilitated through debates in the UN Permanent Forum on Indigenous Issues (UNPFII), which has been characterized as the 'most significant and internationally visible forum in which indigenous spokespeople come together' (Greene, 2004, p. 211) and as part of a strategically built institutional network through which indigenous peoples formalize their political struggles and representation.

The position was introduced to the broader debate through release of the final report of UNPFII's 2008 session on climate change mitigation measures including critical views on carbon trading and REDD+. Also, the UNPFII recommended that the UNFCCC and relevant parties should develop mechanisms to foster indigenous peoples' participation, including the establishment of a working group on local adaptation measures and traditional knowledge. Notably, the concluding session in May 2008 was chaired by Victoria Tauli-Corpuz, the founder of the indigenous organization TEBTEBBA who would later become co-chair in one of the REDD+ negotiation streams of the UNFCCC and who had been involved in the climate negotiations as party delegate before. The positioning of indigenous representatives and supportive non-indigenous individuals as co-chairs in the relevant negotiations was an asset for those who supported the inclusion of rights language in the texts. Formally, co-chairs are supposed to be neutral, but by guiding the negotiations, drafting text, giving the floor to parties etc. they have big influence on the course of negotiations (interview with party delegate/co-chair to the UNFCCC, December 2013, Oslo). For indigenous peoples this was particularly relevant, given that – in the absence of any tradable assets that they could bring to the negotiations ('They are not controlling the situation … they don't come with anything': interview with observer to the UNFCCC, 26 March 2012, Oxford) – the handling of their cause was highly dependent on individuals who could translate broad demands into arguments that were framed in a way accessible to climate negotiators.

Inside the UNFCCC, the International Indigenous Peoples Forum on Climate Change (IIPFCC) assembles representatives from Africa, Asia and Latin America, and serves as the official indigenous caucus to the Convention. From this organizational platform a main part of indigenous advocacy work that targets the negotiations has been coordinated and prepared. Additional spaces were also created, for example the Accra Caucus of 2008 which combined the import of Southern experts' knowledge and experiences on implementation from the ground with Northern experts' legal terminology and language. Through these institutional access point and against the backdrop of the formally established norm of indigenous peoples' rights (as having emerged gradually through ILO Convention No. 169 and UNDRIP) its supporters could build knowledge within their own peer group, and sustain and expand their norm-promoting activities like information dispersion, discussion and articulation of proposed texts and more general observations as well as the reporting of domestic experiences. Ultimately it was about clarifying the objective and impact of anthropogenic governing of forests through REDD+:

> [W]hat are the opportunities for the work we have been doing in terms of community rights and in terms of forest integrity? And what are the threats? What threat is REDD[+] going to be? For the forest itself. Will natural forest be converted as plantations? Will more protected areas be created where indigenous people now don't have rights to get into their own ancestral lands? … We became a very big platform of majority Southern organizations, who understand the problems, who live the problems with the communities on the ground. And then the Northern organizations who understand the issues that have been discussed, they can analyze the texts. I think that the strength of the Accra Caucus is that it has these two complementary groups.
> (Interview with indigenous peoples' representative to the UNFCCC, 25 May 2012, Bonn)

Also, indigenous peoples repositioned themselves towards parties and negotiators. They deliberately constructed new spaces, side events at UNFCCC meetings but also through national-level processes (Wallbott, 2014). In this, they positioned themselves as educators and knowledgeable counterparts for state parties that would contest UNFCCC politics by constructing argumentative linkages across different institutional spaces:

> There has been a lot of work done on biodiversity in the CBD ... The CBD has been very open to indigenous peoples. You just need to inform the UNFCCC on that. And that is what we kept telling them ... It is a UN convention, it is not different than other conventions.
>
> (Interview with indigenous peoples' representative to the UNFCCC, 25 May 2012, Bonn)

Indigenous peoples' outreach and the formation of alliances were then realized with environmental non-governmental organizations that have not only been far more established in the climate negotiations but that have also come to challenge the negative impacts of human action on the state of the Earth's resources. Thereby indigenous experiences could be aligned with more familiar anthropogenic stories of environmental change:

> I guess ... for the first time indigenous peoples were seen as a potential ally in the international level by environmental organizations for their own objectives, either the climate justice movement or the kind of REDD[+] and carbon offsetting movement. I think that is another reason why indigenous peoples issues have kind of been championed, because of REDD as well.
>
> (Interview with observer to the UNFCCC, 26 March 2012, Oxford)

The attribution of meaning

At the same time, these positioning practices of indigenous peoples were driven to a large extent by a specific synthesizing, the attribution of meaning through perception/ideation/recall/imagination. Thus, their motivation resulted from the understanding of a shared historicity and experiences of repression and human rights violations. Again, these political issues were perceived to be intrinsically related with a traditional relationship to land and resources. Thus,

> in our situation, we have the moral legitimacy – dominance has really oppressed and marginalized indigenous peoples for a long time ... state has acquired ownership over forests, indigenous peoples have been kicked out because of protected areas ... The facts are there.
>
> (Interview with indigenous peoples' representative to the UNFCCC, 25 May 2012, Bonn)

On the other hand, indigenous peoples' spacing practices raised awareness among party delegates and triggered learning processes. Thereby they contributed to a shift in synthesizing processes on the side of negotiators who (at least in part) came to acknowledge the terminological interests of indigenous peoples like including the plural-s of the term 'peoples', even though questions of who is indigenous were not really debated as interviewees have indicated.

> I think, to be honest, we were not aware about the sensitivity of having an s or an e ... I think it was just out of ignorance or because these are issues which are typical CBD things, you know? There, they have been discussed extensively and here you are talking with climate change negotiators ... I mean, that was the first time they were talking about the role of indigenous people, indigenous peoples and so on. I think only during the negotiations they realized, actually, that there is some sensibility behind that ... And you cannot expect him [a climate scientist] from one day to another day to be an expert on social safeguards. So I think it's also a matter of creating understanding what it actually means.
>
> (Interview with former EU delegate to the CBD and UNFCCC, 24 May 2012, Bonn)

Thus, the professional background of many negotiators within the UNFCCC had just given way to omitting any strong rights-based language like referencing UNDRIP. In part, this was also due to weak coordination mechanisms between the different national ministries:

> They [national government] recently had a policy on indigenous peoples. And some delegates do not know that. These are technicians of the ministries. Frankly speaking ... [they] did not know that there is something like that. And we tell them. Part of it is linking national policies and that as much as possible ... There is usually no coherence between what national policies are ... My delegate came and asked me: 'Did we sign this?'
>
> (Interview with indigenous peoples' representative to the UNFCCC, 25 May 2012, Bonn)

Finally, indigenous peoples were increasingly able to frame their demands as policy-relevant forms of expertise, authority and means to achieve credibility (interview with indigenous peoples' representative to the UNFCCC, 25 May 2012, Bonn; for more detail see Wallbott, 2014). Thus, it became easier to link the issue of indigenous peoples' rights with a broader win-win narrative (targeted at the mechanism's effective implementation and sustainability), and with positioning indigenous peoples in a rather technocratic administrative way as the local managers of REDD+. Thereby, indigenous peoples were argumentatively positioned in the centre of an anthropogenic setting of natural resource stewardship. From this, it can be deduced that the rights debate gained momentum when it became clear that REDD+ negotiations were actually about material, geographical spaces on the ground, and that indigenous peoples' concerns were not only related to indigenous historicity of marginalization and domination but also adhered to climate-related functionality, which could be translated into standardized technocratic language. This was a more easily accessible framework for negotiators:

> They [national governments] also recognized that the topics they are talking about are really territories of indigenous peoples, and that is a fact and that is proven. They know very well the situation related to the forests in their countries, they know that indigenous peoples have customary claims to these territories … It [the collaboration of indigenous peoples] is also one thing to ensure that it [REDD+] succeeds.
>
> (Interview with indigenous peoples' representative to the UNFCCC, 25 May 2012, Bonn)

Thus, the aforementioned environmentalization of indigeneity – and with it the group-specific reframing of the negative imprint of the Anthropocene concept – seems to have played out in the REDD+ negotiations as well. Here, however, a specific ambivalence exists. On the other hand, indigenous peoples would often come to the negotiations in their traditional clothing. Like that they were easily distinguishable from Western negotiators inside the venues. This is often perceived as indicating a special authenticity and expertise as it would reflect relation to the community level (interviews June 2014, Bonn). As such, the conscious decision to dress in that way can be interpreted as another instance of intertwined cultural invocation/political strategy. On the other hand, though, a 'professionalization' of indigenous peoples' negotiation practices, or, in other words, their adaptation to the dominant technocratic institutional logic of the UNFCCC – whose language and style are still prone to the rationalizations of Western educational and knowledge systems – has been reported as crucial for getting their message across. Thus, it can be argued that the reframing of indigenous peoples' submissions in line with the dominant technical language and substance of UNFCCC negotiations, which are heavily based on standardization of information, influenced their standing and credibility from the perspective of the interpretative framework of negotiators:

> I think they became more concrete … What they wanted to get out of the process or what they wanted to get into the text …. I think it started off with a lot of side events, and of course that's good to get an understanding of what's going on out there. But it doesn't really – it's not a concrete proposal for the negotiation text. And I think over time they became more and more active and organized, like environmental NGOs, for instance, coming with concrete text proposals, explaining very clearly what they actually wanted in the text or what they did not like.
>
> (Interview with former EU delegate to the CBD and UNFCCC, 24 May 2012, Bonn)

This led to higher levels of including indigenous peoples' arguments. However, in another reading this could be interpreted as the soaking up (or even co-optation) of alternative normative frames that will further justify the exclusion of those indigenous voices who do not want to engage with the UNFCCC (including the refusal to lend credibility and legitimacy to this process). This is one way in which the construction of spaces has produced new exclusionary mechanisms. This development is captured nicely in the experiences of one interviewee (observer to the UNFCCC since 1998) who has shared the impression that the lobby for indigenous peoples (from within their community and from non-indigenous supporters) had been very weak around the turn of the millennium. In this context he recollected his first encounters with indigenous peoples' groups at international meetings:

> They performed something like a rain-dance – a different world. And I think over the years they have managed … they have people being right in the centre, as chairs. And by now they have people who have studied this, lawyers, who know the Western system and can work with it. Back then there were events when I thought 'Guys, with this you won't have any chance'. I support them but it is just a clash of two different worlds. I think they saw that eventually, that you have to work differently, that you have to – I put it casually now – work towards the enemy from the inside. Then you can counteract. It seems to happen now. Back then I was a bit shocked – I was thinking 'Guys, when you want to achieve something, you have to play the game better, even when it's hard'.
>
> (Interview with observer to the UNFCCC,
> 14 June 2014, Bonn; own translation)

This quote illustrates how the actual space of international climate meetings can be perceived as a 'situated spatial order/ing' in which indigenous peoples express their particular relationship with the environment through particular intangible performances. At the same time, this atmosphere and space is constantly reshaped through the altering of attributed instances of authority and credibility. Thus, indigenous peoples have achieved recognition as relevant subjects and knowledge-holders in the climate realm. Yet, they contribute to the stabilization of the UNFCCC order by aligning with its dominant governance arguments.

Conclusion

In this chapter, I have developed an analytical framework that applies a sociology of space approach to the study of the objectives and prospects of international negotiations and of the Anthropocene. I have illustrated this approach with the example of indigenous peoples' lobbying practices in UN climate negotiations on forests that have depended to a large extent on putting forward environmenalized images of indigenous agency that could be contrasted with dualistic framings of industrial society–nature relations. Thus, the emphasis of this chapter has been on the arguments to consider the indigenous in global policymaking vis-à-vis the environment.

In terms of the overall urgency to act, the chapter highlighted the relevance of preserving the world's forests to the benefit of global public goods like a stable climate and broad biodiversity. Given the dependence of indigenous peoples on forests and the spatial proximity of their livelihoods and natural resource governance, any effective and legitimate policy needs to take their substantial and procedural rights into account. Ultimately, this calls for global responsibility to safeguard indigenous rights and to ensure their participation in shaping international mechanisms for environmental regulation. However, at the same time, it could be argued that a meaningful engagement with indigenous peoples hinges on the recognition of traditional knowledge patterns and authorities, and thereby eventually challenges dominant Western paradigms of environmental governance arrangements. Finally, with view to the increasing complexity of natural resource governance across different levels and spaces, it can be concluded that the struggle of indigenous peoples' representatives for recognition of their rights in international climate negotiations can be interpreted to not only be concerned with influencing the development of politics beyond the nation state. Rather, it is at least equally, if not more so, motivated by the prospect of an additional tool or argument to boost indigenous voices in nation states. Expanding the scope of application of indigenous rights norms to more issue areas internationally thus has a concrete material but also ideational significance, as the contestatory practices of previously excluded collectivities, their critique and active protest, spread. On the other hand, positioning indigenous peoples as objects of political regulation before REDD+ is operational on the ground may be perceived as a risk management tool for forest finance investors and governments. Accordingly, determining the political conditions that shape the governance of locale spaces in the Anthropocene will continue to be a matter of distributing recognition and material assets – and ultimately of challenging dominant power constellations.

References

Aggarwal, A., Varghese, P. and Soumitri, D. (2009) Forest resources: Degradation, livelihoods, and climate change. In The Energy and Resources Institute (ed.), *Green India 2047: Looking Back To Change Track*. New Delhi: The Energy and Resources Institute, pp. 91–108.

Anaya, S. J. (2004) *Indigenous Peoples in International Law*, 2nd ed. Oxford: Oxford University Press.

Banerjee, S. B. (2004) Comments to Shane Greene: Indigenous people incorporated? Culture as politics, culture as property in pharmaceutical bioprospecting. *Current Anthropology* 45(2): 224–225.

Brown, M. F. (1998) Can culture be copyrighted? *Current Anthropology* 39(2): 193–222.

Cadena, M. and Starn, O. (2007) Introduction. In Cadena, M. and Starn, O. (eds), *Indigenous Experience Today*. Oxford, New York: Berg, pp. 1–31.

Comaroff, J. L. and Comaroff, J. (2009) *Ethnicity, Inc.* Chicago: Chicago University Press.

Coombe, R. J. (1998) *The Cultural Life of Intellectual Properties*. Durham: Duke University Press.

Greene, S. (2004) Indigenous people incorporated? Culture as politics, culture as property in pharmaceutical bioprospecting. *Current Anthropology* 45(2): 211–224.

Gulbrandsen, L. J. (2012) International forest politics: Intergovernmental failure, non-governmental success? In Andresen, S., Boasson, E. L. and Hønneland, G. (eds), *International Environmental Agreements: An Introduction*. London/New York: Routledge, pp. 24–58.

Harvey, D. (1990) *The Condition of Postmodernity*. Cambridge and Oxford: Blackwell.

Hathaway, M. (2010) The emergence of indigeneity. *Cultural Anthropology* 25(2): 301–333.

Hayden, C. (2003) From market to market: Bioprospecting's idioms of inclusion. *American Ethnologist* 30(3): 359–371.

Hodgson, D. L. (2011) *Being Maasai. Becoming Indigenous. Postcolonial Politics in a Neoliberal World*. Indiana: Indiana University Press.

Lefèbvre, H. (2006) [1974] Die Produktion des Raums. In Dünne, J. and Günzel, S. (eds), *Raumtheorie. Grundlagentexte aus Philosophie und Kulturwissenschaften*. Frankfurt am Main: Suhrkamp, pp. 330–342.

Levin, K., McDermott, C. and Cashore, B. (2008) The climate regime as global forest governance: Can reduced emissions from Deforestation and Forest Degradation (REDD) initiatives pass a 'dual effectiveness' test? *International Forestry Review* 10(3): 538–549.

Löw, M. (2008) The constitution of space. The structuration of spaces through the simultaneity of effect and perception. *European Journal of Social Theory* 11(1): 25–49.

Mende, J. (2015) The imperative of indigeneity: Indigenous human rights and their limits. *Human Rights Review* 16(3): 221–238.

Muehlebach, A. (2001) 'Making place' at the United Nations: Indigenous cultural politics at the U.N. Working Group on Indigenous Populations. *Cultural Anthropology* 16(3): 415–448.

Oberthür, S. and Stokke, O. S. (eds) (2011) *Managing Institutional Complexity. Regime Interplay and Global Environmental Change*. Cambridge, MA: MIT Press.

Okereke, C. and Dooley, K. (2010) Principles of justice in proposals and policy approaches to avoided deforestation: Towards a post-Kyoto climate agreement. *Global Environmental Change* 20(1): 82–95.

Pache, A.-C. and Santos, F. (2013) Embedded in hybrid contexts: How individuals in organizations respond to competing institutional logics. In Lounsbury, M. and Boxenbaum, E. (eds), *Institutional Logics in Action, Part B*. Bingley: Emerald, pp. 3–35.

Silva, C. L. (2012) *Environmentalizing Indigeneity: A Comparative Ethnography on Multiculturalism, Ethnic Hierarchies, and Political Ecology in the Colombian Amazon*. Dissertation, University of Arizona [Online]. Available from: http://s3.amazonaws.com/academia.edu.documents/30229175/azu_etd_11999_sip1_m.pdf [accessed 25 June 2015].

Sud, R., Vir Sharma, J. and Kumar Bansal, A. (n.d.) *International REDD+ Architecture and Its Relevance for India*. New Delhi: Ministry of Environment and Forests/The Government of India and The Energy and Resources Institute.

UN ECOSOC (1983) *Study of the Problem of Discrimination against Indigenous Populations*. E/CN.4/Sub.2/1983/21/Add.8. New York: United Nations Economic and Social Council [Online]. Available from: http://www.un.org/esa/socdev/unpfii/documents/MCS_xxi_xxii_e.pdf [accessed 25 June 2015].

UNFCCC (2010) *Report of the Conference of the Parties on its Sixteenth Session*. Cancun: United Nations Framework Convention on Climate Change [Online]. Available from: http://unfccc.int/resource/docs/2010/cop16/eng/07a01.pdf#page=2 [accessed 25 June 2015].

Veber, H. (2004) Comments to Shane Greene: Indigenous people incorporated? Culture as politics, culture as property in pharmaceutical bioprospecting. *Current Anthropology* 45(2): 232.

Wallbott, L. (2014) Indigenous peoples in UN REDD+ negotiations: 'Importing power' and lobbying for rights through discursive interplay management. *Ecology and Society* 19(1): 21.

14 Conclusions

Complexity, responsibility and urgency in the Anthropocene

Fariborz Zelli and Philipp Pattberg

Back to the beginning

In our introduction (Pattberg and Zelli, this volume) we established the Anthropocene as a contested concept – welcomed by some, critically discussed by others – that assumes an emerging epoch in planetary history with an unprecedented and ubiquitous human imprint. We also stressed that social sciences are still lagging behind when it comes to capturing the reasons, processes and implications of this new epoch in greater detail.

As a result of this imbalance, crucial and ardent political and social questions have not been put under sufficient scrutiny. The question that we asked in our introduction is whether the Anthropocene can help (re-)invigorate respective research or whether it is just one more buzzword. Political scientists, sociologists, psychologists, human geographers and scholars of other social science disciplines need to give us more insights into the changes that the Anthropocene hypothesis implies for key issues of their fields of research, such as the fit and effectiveness of governance institutions, the participatory and distributive justice of political and social processes, and shifts in the relation between humans and their environment.

These implications are not trivial, since the Anthropocene hypothesis goes beyond all possible boundaries, both spatial and temporal. Our actions affect nature with everything and everyone that is part of it, here and somewhere else, now and tomorrow. This blurring of boundaries presents a growing and novel challenge to governance, which represents a major intentional and collective aspect of human action. What could we have done better? How quickly and how adequately can and should we act and react in our governance efforts? Where can we induce meaningful change?

Against the backdrop of this changing context of human action, and of governance in particular, we unpacked the Anthropocene into three key challenges. First, *urgency*, asking how quickly we need to act and how we can make a difference by deriving meaningful recommendations from our analyses; second, *responsibility*, addressing, for instance, variations of responsibility across different groups of actors and respective changes over time; and third, *complexity*, looking inter alia at different forms of intricacy and diversity – material, ethical, institutional, spatial – and the relations between them.

None of these three aspects is new to the scholarly debate on governance, but in their combination and intensity they mirror the unprecedented challenge that the Anthropocene implies for political processes. All contributors to this volume addressed these three challenges in their analyses. They had no other choice: understanding and examining governance in the Anthropocene necessarily leads us to questions of urgency, responsibility and complexity.

Apart from these three cross-cutting key challenges, this volume was structured around different scholarly approaches towards the Anthropocene: understanding, analysing and addressing. Contributions to the first part informed the reader about different understandings of the Anthropocene, their limits and their conflicts about the adequacy of the concept. This part followed up on the contested nature of the Anthropocene to which we referred at the very beginning of our introductory chapter. In the second part, authors analysed the challenges to and changes of governance processes in the emerging Anthropocene, with a particular focus on the role of political institutions. And thirdly, contributors looked at the implications of the Anthropocene for questions of legitimacy and accountability, discussing options to address emerging shortcomings.

In the next section, we present key findings of these contributions along the book's three parts, i.e. in terms of crucial conceptual, institutional and accountability-related arguments. Following this, we will highlight some of the major results through the lenses of urgency, responsibility and complexity. We conclude with an outlook on requirements for further research.

Key findings of the volume

In *Part I* experts tried to make sense of the Anthropocene, engaging in a virtual critical discussion across their chapters. They stressed advantages and disadvantages of the term, and they came forward with suggestions for making the concept more useful as normative guidance towards a just society and meaningful political change.

For Arias-Maldonado (Chapter 3) the concept reminds us that a separation between humanity and nature is ontologically no longer tenable. While the Anthropocene marks the end of nature as a sphere unaffected by humans, there is also the chance for a new beginning. We can now develop a hybridized understanding of our natural environment, by accepting intricate overlaps between society and nature.

Wissenburg (Chapter 2), by contrast, started from a fundamental critique of what he calls the narrative of the Anthropocene, stressing three main weaknesses. First, he pointed to the lack of a certain natural scientific basis. Second, the social implications of the Anthropocene need much more attention. Third, and most importantly for Wissenburg, the narrative is not normatively loaded, leaving it open as to which type of society and society–nature relationship we should ultimately aspire to (cf. Beck 1986).

Hailwood, in Chapter 4, shared Wissenburg's scepticism and went even further by rejecting the concept altogether. Unlike Arias-Maldonado, he interpreted the end-of-nature argument as inherently flawed. For Hailwood, it repeats the very same motivations for human intervention that caused environmental deterioration in the first place. Even humble perspectives and ethics of anti-domination may fall into this trap. Ultimately, he sees no a real chance for a fundamental change if human action remains at the centre of our causal and ethical reasoning.

Where do these different interpretations leave us? Or, rather, how can we alter the concept, or narrative, of the Anthropocene to address some of the critical observations? Arias-Maldonado, following his relatively positive assessment, refrained from radical suggestions of de-growth and instead advocated what he sees as a more realistic endeavour: an enlightened rearrangement of socionatural relations that allows for the protection of remaining natural forms and processes.

Wissenburg and also Meisch (Chapter 5), on the other hand, called for more fundamental ethical changes. Following medieval political philosophy, Wissenburg suggested the ideal of the body ecologic, a theory of good planetary citizenship that guides humans in dealing with alternative and contradictory futures. Such theory not only needs to define a good society, but also a good nature for that society. For Wissenburg, this is a revolutionary theoretical step, since so far, only a few ecological political thinkers (e.g. Eckersley 2004, 2007; Dobson 2007) have challenged the social compatibility of green ideas in their writings on deep ecology or the green state.

In a similar vein, Meisch argued that a normative theory is more important than creating grand political designs. He identified sustainable development as the conceptual core of the Anthropocene, requesting justice for present and future humans in the face of a deteriorating natural environment. But this abstract conceptual core needs further theoretical justification. To develop a suitable theory that further specifies rights and duties, Meisch built on Martha Nussbaum's Capability Approach (Nussbaum 2006) and Alan Gewirth's Principle of Generic Consistency (Gewirth 1978, 1996). Both approaches conceptualize justice in terms of human dignity and related rights that allow for determining claims of access and allocation. For Meisch, respect for people's freedoms and rights finds its institutional equivalent in a diversified governance landscape that reflects ethical and legal pluralism, rather than a unitarian governance structure.

This suggestion leads us to *Part II* on the role of institutions in the Anthropocene. For global climate governance Widerberg (Chapter 6) found a highly diversified governance architecture. This assessment is in line with earlier observations that institutional complexity and fragmentation have become structural characteristics of global environmental governance today (Biermann et al. 2009; Zelli 2011; Zelli and van Asselt 2013). But while previous assessments characterized global climate governance as only loosely coupled (Keohane and Victor 2011), Widerberg's social network analysis yielded different results: institutions at different levels are linked through hybrid institutions, thus creating a relatively dense network. Moreover, a few actors, such as country or

234 Fariborz Zelli and Philipp Pattberg

city governments, play the role of 'orchestrators' (Abbott et al. 2015) in the emerging regime complex on climate change. They provide coherence and consistency through frequent activities in a series of institutions, thereby intensifying the network as a whole.

Also the institutional landscape on sustainable biofuels has gained in complexity over the last years, as Moser and Bailis found in their analysis in Chapter 7. Biofuels governance has significantly changed due to a massive ramp-up of production. The EU seeks to orchestrate a complex of diverse sustainability standards and certification criteria, by taking a hybrid transnational governance approach with its Renewable Energy Directive (EU-RED). However, in contrast to climate governance, Moser and Bailis found that the EU approach does not live up to this orchestrating goal, since it does not conform to existing institutional scripts on standards and certification. The result is a conflictive institutional architecture, with tensions between different standards and understandings that go back to conflicts between knowledge and value systems.

While Widerberg as well as Moser and Bailis focused on the implications of institutional complexity in the Anthropocene, van Leeuwen and Prokopf looked into the potential causes of institutional change in two other fields of environmental governance. For Arctic shipping governance, van Leeuwen found in Chapter 8 that ship owners lack significant regulatory and economic motivations to participate in non-state market-driven initiatives. As a result, the institutional landscape in this issue area remains rather state-led in nature, with the International Maritime Organization (IMO) at its centre. Arctic shipping governance thus shows a very different type of institutional design than climate governance, with the latter characterized by a boom of transnational institutions in recent years.

Prokopf (Chapter 9) equally argued that institutional change needs motivational and attitudinal change as a prerequisite. In fact, for the case of Rhine river governance such a shift of motivations has eventually taken place. This, however, came at a price. It took a sequence of accidents and floods to redefine relationships among states and between riparians and the river. These discursive and ideational changes ultimately induced institutional change, providing the International Commission for the Protection of the Rhine (ICPR) with an extended mandate.

Contributors to *Part III* geared their chapters towards the implications of the Anthropocene for questions of legitimacy and accountability. Baber and Bartlett (Chapter 10) heeded Meisch's and Wissenburg's calls for an ethical foundation of the Anthropocene, translating them into concrete suggestions for democratically legitimate institutions. They cautioned however that, at the international level, such institutions should not take the shape of an overarching, unitarian structure. Instead, and similar to Meisch, Baber and Bartlett embraced institutional diversity as an appropriate and flexible governance landscape for a legally pluralist society. They further recommended new democratic principles and deliberative techniques for norm-building, policymaking and implementation processes across levels.

In Chapter 11, Kühner's analysis of the compliance system of the United Nations climate regime showed how such a flexible mix of principles, procedures and institutions can work in practice. She found that soft instruments, like the processes for measurement, reporting and verification play a crucial role. The structure of the exercises and the facilitation by experts helped most regime members to comply with their commitments. In other words, incentives through soft instruments prevented hard actions from the enforcement side of the climate regime's compliance mechanism. Kühner concluded that there is much more potential of soft instruments that needs to be exploited further.

In another study on global climate governance, Isailovic (Chapter 12) discussed how changing patterns of authority in the Anthropocene entail changing legitimacy concerns for the global South. More concretely, the arrival of new private and hybrid governance arrangements has altered two traditional divides: North–South and private–public. The transformation of world politics in the Anthropocene hence draws new fault lines and blurs old ones, creating new winners and losers when it comes to participation, distributive justice and exposure to environmental change.

Finally, and similar to Meisch or Hailwood, Wallbott (Chapter 13) advocated a broadened understanding of the Anthropocene that goes beyond Western, anthropocentric knowledge forms and practices. She developed a relational sociology of space approach to analyse political processes in the Anthropocene. She illustrated her approach for the case of strategic practices of indigenous peoples in international climate negotiations on forests. Wallbott was able to show that these practices take place in more than one space. On the one hand, they are defined by the physical boundaries of indigenous actors, but at the same time these strategies are also shaped by institutional mandates, social asymmetries and normative imprints. In other words, when we analyse the political implications of the Anthropocene we should not only look at the complexity of political institutions and processes, but also at the co-existence and interrelation of different spaces for political action.

Complexity, responsibility and urgency

As the above summary suggests, *complexity* plays a major role in the concepts, analyses and recommendations of our contributors. All of them agree that there are several types of growing complexities in the Anthropocene that cannot be reduced. Wissenburg distinguished three of them: the natural complexity of the planet's ecology; the psycho-social complexity of humans and their institutions; and the political or moral complexity of bringing both together in a meaningful way. Wallbott added further dimensions by referring to the increasing complexity of both actors and spaces. Previously excluded collectivities like indigenous communities are brought into the politics of the Anthropocene. By going beyond their original life-world and space of social action, these actors blur certain boundaries across societal levels while, at the same time, creating new fault lines.

But how much do we know and can we know about these different complexities in the Anthropocene? On this question our authors clearly disagree. Arias-Maldonado optimistically argued that, eventually, we might gain proper insights into the intended and non-intended causal impacts of human behaviour. Likewise, Widerberg predicted that new tools like network analysis will enable us to visualize or even untangle complex relations between global governance institutions.

By contrast, Hailwood claimed that the very concept of the Anthropocene deprives us of this possibility, as it is too simplistic and does not do justice to the normative complexity of our environmental situation. Baber and Bartlett turned this argument on its head, holding that the Anthropocene is not a narrowing, but a flexible concept: it helps us to make sense of the immense complexity of the physical and cultural worlds, including the limited human understanding of them.

The contributors also differ in their approval of institutional complexity. Some, like Kühner, Meisch, and Baber and Bartlett, welcomed a diversity of institutions and instruments from an ontological point of view, inasmuch as it reflects ethical and legal pluralism and the need for flexible responses in the Anthropocene. However, as Meisch and Wissenburg cautioned, this diversity needs to be grounded in certain overarching principles like human dignity or ideas of the good society and the good environment.

Others, like Moser and Bailis, voiced concerns from an empirical perspective. To a certain extent, institutional complexity may mirror the material complexity of an issue area, e.g. in the case of sustainable biofuels (Bailis and Baka 2011). This, however, does not mean that the emerging institutional landscape provides the best fit for addressing this material complexity. As shown in their case study on EU-RED, the current governance architecture, with the new EU directive at its centre, left several urgent environmental and socioeconomic issues unaddressed. In a similar vein, Prokopf argued that, although the complexity of a policy issue may eventually be mirrored in the respective governance landscape, this evolution does not proceed in a continuous manner. The institutional development of Rhine river governance, for example, was a rather bumpy, two-step realization that was further shaped by longstanding value systems.

Another insight is that institutional complexity differs considerably across levels and issue areas. While, as Widerberg and Isailovic showed, climate governance is marked by an ever increasing number of public and transnational institutions, van Leeuwen qualified the general impression of increasing institutional complexity in global environmental governance. For Arctic shipping she does not expect a stronger institutionalization of private governance in the coming years, due to both strategic interests and public perceptions of the shipping industry.

With regard to *responsibility*, all authors share a certain degree of scepticism. Arias-Maldonado summarized this consensus: while the Anthropocene clearly attributes responsibility to all of us, this has so far not translated into major changes of behaviour. More fundamentally even, Baber and Bartlett, echoing similar concerns by Meisch, Hailwood and Wissenburg, cautioned that the Anthropocene concept might perpetuate a flawed understanding, namely one of human responsibility for controlling the environment and our ill-understood relationship with it.

In addition, Meisch criticized the vague and ambiguous moral basis of the Anthropocene concept that makes it difficult to specify responsibilities of and for certain actors. To address this vagueness, Meisch's theory of justice seeks to determine the responsibility of collective and state actors in the Anthropocene: these actors have a duty to protect the generic rights of other humans and to enhance their capabilities respectively.

Other authors greeted the increasing set of analytical tools and policy instruments to establish, exercise or evaluate responsibility. Kühner examined a flexible compliance system that combines soft and hard instruments for actors to take on responsibility and to be held accountable for their environmental actions. And for Widerberg, network analysis can help us to identify central players and fora within an increasingly complex governance network. These players gain responsibility through their position in the network and can be important addressees for policy recommendations.

This brings us to another argument, namely that the Anthropocene redefines subjects and objects of responsibility. Isailovic emphasized that shifts of authority in global climate governance also imply changes of responsibility within the global South and between North and South. On the other hand, Wallbott reminded us that the new quality of responsibility in the Anthropocene also brings about new types of addressees like indigenous peoples. This shift in responsibility, she further argued, leaves us with a discursive challenge: a meaningful engagement with indigenous actors depends on the recognition of traditional knowledge patterns and authorities. In this sense, and in contrast to Hailwood's expectations, the Anthropocene might eventually see the erosion of dominant Western paradigms of anthropogenic governance arrangements.

Finally, contributors highlighted that ultimately all of us have responsibility in the Anthropocene, for instance, to hold both state and non-state actors accountable. As Kühner suggested, we can serve as external triggers for the behaviour change of these actors. For Prokopf, awareness is key for a general sense of responsibility to evolve. The open question is where this awareness will come from: through social learning or, as so often with environmental issues in the past, through external shocks like natural disasters (cf. Sabatier 1993, 1998). Prokopf concluded that the slow realization of responsibility in the public might render the role of the state even more important as an orchestrator or even initiator of learning processes.

Coming to *urgency*, all our authors confirmed, not surprisingly, the growing need to act through flexible governance solutions – and to do so differently for different contexts, across regions and spaces (Isailovic, Wallbott) as well as across issue areas such as climate change (Widerberg, Isailovic), forestry (Wallbott), rivers (Prokopf), high seas and shipping (van Leeuwen), biodiversity or biofuels (Moser and Bailis).

238 Fariborz Zelli and Philipp Pattberg

However, our contributors disagreed to what extent the notion or narrative of the Anthropocene can help to alert us. For Arias-Maldonado the concept stresses the urgency of various transformations that humans have to induce to ensure equitable prosperity for future generations. Baber and Bartlett named a series of challenges that transformations, and emerging governance architectures in particular, need to address: knowledge generation and dissemination, ubiquity of action, effectiveness of implementation, and openness to learning and adaptation. Meisch added that urgency is not a topic of the future, but about here and now, e.g. regarding sea level rise, loss of biodiversity, or a growing environmental refugee crisis.

Hailwood was more sceptical on this issue. He conceded that the Anthropocene expresses urgency in a dramatic and eye-catching way, but he did not read the dimensions into the concept that other authors derived from it. He maintained that the Anthropocene in its current framing leads to a simplified and homogenizing view of the problem, thereby repeating earlier mistakes. Prokopf shared this scepticism in her analysis of Rhine river governance. She found that, more often than not, we only sense the urgency to act in light of repeated disasters and accidents, not due to new concepts or buzzwords. The challenge then remains how humanity can be convinced to take action before experiencing disasters and reaching critical tipping points.

Given the openness or contestation of the Anthropocene concept, what should we actually do? And what should we do first? Building on his ethical theory, Meisch provided a straightforward criterion: we should provide every human being with the means to live a life in dignity. He held that such an altruistic approach might lead the Anthropocene concept away from technological fatalism and a focus on Western lifestyle. Coping with urgency then means to concentrate first on those who cannot exercise their generic rights. Hailwood, on the other hand, cautioned against an ethical foundation that reiterates the anthropocentric focus of the past. Instead, acting urgently should mean to move, as quickly as possible, towards a more humble human approach with nature and for nature.

Besides conceptual and ethical foundations, the urgency to act also depends on practical matters, such as the appropriateness of governance institutions, i.e. the question of institutional fit (cf. Young 2002). Isailovic stressed that in our future analyses we have to observe whether the shifting patterns of authority and responsibility in the Anthropocene will ultimately deliver. Does the involvement of new actors and institutions help us to address new challenges and complexities? And is the evolving institutional landscape more adequate and fit to address social and ecological questions than previous governance arrangements?

Notwithstanding these critical views and words of caution, our authors also saw reasons for optimism, i.e. for a timely reaction to some of the challenges that the Anthropocene implies. Arias-Maldonado referred to the general capacity of humans to adapt to new circumstances relatively well. But he also cautioned against any technological fatalism. We cannot rely on systemic adaptation, but have to actively deal with the growing complexities that will set lasting challenges to our governance efforts for decades to come.

Some of the case studies showed what such intentional and successful adaptation of governance mechanisms can look like – namely by providing flexible mixes of processes and institutions. Moser and Bailis welcomed EU-RED as a timely approach to deal with urgent sustainability challenges of global biofuel foodstock production. In spite of some shortcomings, the directive with its hybrid governance approach has helped embed trans-territorial biofuel production in a relatively fast way. Similarly, Kühner praised the mix of hard and soft instruments in the compliance system of the United Nations climate regime. This pragmatic approach has proved more acceptable to a larger group of actors and helped trigger quick and important behavioural changes.

Where do we go from here?

One purpose of this book was to explore to what extent the emerging Anthropocene poses new challenges to the development, processes, fairness and effectiveness of environmental governance today. In the same vein, our authors discussed how these challenges alter the questions we should ask as governance researchers.

While our edited volume, with its selection of case studies and themes, could not provide an exhaustive overview, the above summary documents an impressive amount of insights that the distinct contributors to this book gathered on environmental governance in the Anthropocene. These insights make clear that many of the specific questions we need to ask as researchers – about complexity, responsibility and urgency as well as other dimensions – may not be new as such. What is new though are the combinations and interlinkages of such questions. By tying society and nature more closely together than ever before, the Anthropocene confronts us with an unprecedented intensity and contingency of our actions and their consequences – and of how we should do research about them.

Against this backdrop, our authors identified key research gaps that merit further investigation by scholars from different backgrounds. We can only list a few of these in the following. One key challenge will be a further conceptualization of the Anthropocene. While a conceptual consensus is neither feasible nor desirable the normative openness of the term leaves considerable space for a fruitful ethical debate. The controversial interpretations in this volume and the different ideas for fleshing out the concept normatively reflect this potential. How can we derive guidance for social and political action from the Anthropocene and its redefinition of the human–nature nexus? To put it shortly: what makes us take action? Can we get a stronger moral motivation from principles of human dignity, a good society and a good nature – as Arias-Maldonado, Baber and Bartlett, Meisch and Wissenburg suggested? Or do we need to be more radical and can we leave anthropocentrism behind as Hailwood insinuated? Can we move away from fatalist attitudes that often make us wait too long, as Prokopf found?

A related research challenge is the further identification and mapping of different complexities. Our authors pointed to a series of them: natural, psychosocial, spatial, moral and institutional ones. Which methods can help us assess these complexities, the relations between them and their implications for political action in the Anthropocene? To this question, authors like Kühner, van Leeuwen, Moser and Bailis, Prokopf, Wallbott and Widerberg gave seminal answers, showing the potential of approaches such as social network analysis, discourse analysis and a polycentric perspective.

A whole comparative research programme could evolve around such questions, as Widerberg insinuated. Such a programme may uncover crucial commonalities across different issue areas, e.g. about the relationship between complex actor networks, institutional settings, political effectiveness and fairness. As Widerberg further suggested, such insights could help build theories on how complexity and responsibility in the Anthropocene emerge and change over time.

Furthermore, and following Isailovic's suggestion, such a research agenda can help us to assess the suitability of our institutional architectures for dealing with the new challenges of an intensified society–nature nexus. Will the emerging patterns of authority deliver, or do we need further or different types of institutional change? Is a concentrated or fragmented institutional architecture better equipped to deal with specific problems in the Anthropocene? Which mixes of institutions and instruments are the best fit for which issue area, level, process and human context?

Finally, Kühner's study reminds us of the importance of policy evaluation in an era marked by growing complexity and uncertainty. The intricacy of environmental governance today puts an unprecedented burden on on-the-ground processes of complying, measuring, verifying and reporting. We need flexible tools for practitioners to adapt governance processes to these realities – but also for researchers to provide an adequate assessment of these processes, which can ultimately help to further enhance them.

Coming to a final outlook, we would like to point out an aspect that surprised us. When making their policy recommendations, almost all contributors to this volume stressed the notion of agency: they firmly believe that we as humans can still make intentional changes for the better. These recommendations, however, contrast with insights the very same authors give us into systemic dynamics, unintended consequences and growing complexities.

Their carefully optimistic and agent-based perspectives may have been unavoidable since the book's key concept, the Anthropocene, highlights the ubiquity of human action and consequences thereof. Their perspectives may also go back to the other theme of the book, governance, and to some of the governance challenges we identified: urgency and responsibility relate directly to the needs and conditions for human action.

But is optimism a good advisor for the suggestions we derive from political analyses? Whatever makes our authors, and us humans in general, believe in the potential of our actions, the question remains to what extent meaningful interventions can be crafted in an ever more complex world. This brings us back to one of the key meta-theoretical debates in social sciences: the relationship between agency and structure (cf. Archer 1995; Bourdieu 1977, 1990; Giddens 1984). If we want to leave our readers with some optimism at the end of this book, we have to assume a mutual constitution of the two. There are options for agency to shape structures, but there are also structural limits and contexts to our actions.

Thirty years ago, asking 'how do we want to live?' seemed a suitable question when Ulrich Beck (1986) announced the beginning of the second modernity. But today, well into the Anthropocene, we should also ask 'how *can* we live?' What are our options, but also our limits for governance in an ever more intricate connection of our social and natural worlds?

One key realization that many still need to come to is that certain consequences cannot be prevented. We are beyond the point of avoiding dangerous climate change altogether, as we are incapable of stopping species loss and irreversible damage to ecosystems today or tomorrow. The Anthropocene also reminds us that things have happened already that no governance effort can turn around. It took time to get the level of human imprint on nature that we are witnessing today. And the steps that brought us here have already taken their toll.

To be clear, this is not a call for complacency, but for a socioecological realism of acting within limits and complex contexts. The systems theorist Niklas Luhmann (1986a, 1986b) once recommended that, in the face of natural disasters, mankind should carry on its lifestyle in a normal and unimpressed manner, since we can never save our natural environment in a targeted and intentional way. This book and its contributors could not be further away from this message. Our social and political behaviour matters more than ever. Knowing our limits can guide our behavioural change and help us make informed decisions about how to make the most of that change. And it can prepare us better for some unintended and unavoidable consequences.

Thus, notwithstanding its shortcomings discussed in this book, the Anthropocene concept reminds us that both outright optimism and outright pessimism are misplaced. We have entered an epoch where there are no optimal solutions, quick fixes or silver bullets. In this sense – and coming back to one of the questions in our introductory chapter – the Anthropocene can indeed be a constructive, reinvigorating challenge for our research and actions, not just a buzzword. We have to do our best, in continuous, smart, flexible and embedded steps, to make society, nature and their nexus as equitable and sustainable as possible. We hope that the conceptual, theoretical and empirical insights of this volume could inform our readers about a few such steps – and give them inspiration to explore their own options and limits of acting and governing in the Anthropocene.

References

Abbott, K. W., Genschel, P., Snidal, D. and Zangl, B. (eds) (2015) *International Organizations as Orchestrators.* Cambridge: Cambridge University Press.

Archer, M. (1995) *Realist Social Theory: The Morphogenetic Approach.* Cambridge: Cambridge University Press.

Bailis, R. and Baka, J. (2011) Constructing sustainable biofuels: Governance of the emerging biofuel economy. *Annals of the Association of American Geographers*, 101(4): 827–838.

Beck, Ulrich (1986) *Risikogesellschaft. Auf dem Weg in eine andere Moderne*. Frankfurt: Suhrkamp.

Biermann, F., Pattberg, P., Van Asselt, H. and Zelli, F. (2009) The fragmentation of global governance architectures: A framework for analysis. *Global Environmental Politics* 9(4): 14–40.

Bourdieu, P. (1977) *Outline of a Theory of Practice*. Cambridge: Cambridge University Press.

Bourdieu, P. (1990) *The Logic of Practice*. Redwood City, CA: Stanford University Press.

Dobson, A. (2007) *Green Political Thought*, 4th ed. London: Routledge.

Eckersley, R. (2004) *The Green State: Rethinking Democracy and Sovereignty*. Cambridge: MIT Press.

Eckersley, R. (2007) Ecological intervention: Prospects and limits. *Ethics & International Affairs* 21(3): 293–316.

Gewirth, A. (1978) *Reason and Morality*. Chicago: University of Chicago Press.

Gewirth, A. (1996) *The Community of Rights*. Chicago, London: University of Chicago Press.

Giddens, A. (1984) *The Constitution of Society*. Cambridge: Polity Press.

Keohane, R. O. and Victor, D. G. (2011) The regime complex for climate change. *Perspectives on Politics* 9(1): 7–23.

Luhmann, N. (1986a) Die Welt als Wille ohne Vorstellung. Sicherheit und Risiko aus der Sicht der Sozialwissenschaften. *Die Politische Meinung* 31: 18–21.

Luhmann, N. (1986b) *Ökologische Kommunikation. Kann die moderne Gesellschaft sich auf ökologische Gefährdungen einstellen?* Opladen: Westdeutscher Verlag.

Nussbaum, M. (2006) *Frontiers of Justice. Disability, Nationality, Species Membership*. Cambridge, MA, London: Belknap.

Sabatier, Paul A. (1993) *Policy Change and Learning: An Advocacy Coalition Approach*. Boulder, CO: Westview Press.

Sabatier, Paul A. (1998) The advocacy coalition framework: Revisions and relevance for Europe. *Journal of European Public Policy* 5(1): 98–130.

Young, O. (2002) *The Institutional Dimensions of Environmental Change: Fit, Interplay and Scale*. Cambridge, MA: MIT Press.

Zelli, F. (2011) The fragmentation of the global climate governance architecture. *Wiley Interdisciplinary Reviews: Climate Change* 2(2): 255–270.

Zelli, F. and van Asselt, H. (2013) Introduction: The institutional fragmentation of global environmental governance. *Global Environmental Politics* 13(3): 1–13.

Index

For Product Safety Concerns and Information please contact our
EU representative GPSR@taylorandfrancis.com Taylor & Francis
Verlag GmbH, Kaufingerstraße 24, 80331 München, Germany